The First Woman President of India
Reinventing Leadership
Smt. Pratibha Devisingh Patil

The First Woman President of India
Reinventing Leadership
Smt. Pratibha Devisingh Patil

Sunaina Singh

ALLIED PUBLISHERS PVT. LTD.
New Delhi • Mumbai • Kolkata • Lucknow • Chennai
Nagpur • Bangalore • Hyderabad • Ahmedabad

ALLIED PUBLISHERS PRIVATE LIMITED

1/13-14 Asaf Ali Road, **New Delhi**–110002
Ph.: 011-23239001 • E-mail: delhi.books@alliedpublishers.com

47/9 Prag Narain Road, Near Kalyan Bhawan, **Lucknow**–226001
Ph.: 0522-2209942 • E-mail: lko.books@alliedpublishers.com

17 Chittaranjan Avenue, **Kolkata**–700072
Ph.: 033-22129618 • E-mail: cal.books@alliedpublishers.com

15 J.N. Heredia Marg, Ballard Estate, **Mumbai**–400001
Ph.: 022-42126969 • E-mail: mumbai.books@alliedpublishers.com

60 Shiv Sunder Apartments (Ground Floor), Central Bazar Road,
Bajaj Nagar, **Nagpur**–440010
Ph.: 0712-2234210 • E-mail: ngp.books@alliedpublishers.com

F-1 Sun House (First Floor), C.G. Road, Navrangpura,
Ellisbridge P.O., **Ahmedabad**–380006
Ph.: 079-26465916 • E-mail: ahmbd.books@alliedpublishers.com

751 Anna Salai, **Chennai**–600002
Ph.: 044-28523938 • E-mail: chennai.books@alliedpublishers.com

5th Main Road, Gandhinagar, **Bangalore**–560009
Ph.: 080-22262081 • E-mail: bngl.books@alliedpublishers.com

3-2-844/6 & 7 Kachiguda Station Road, **Hyderabad**–500027
Ph.: 040-24619079 • E-mail: hyd.books@alliedpublishers.com

Website: www.alliedpublishers.com

© 2013, Dr. Sunaina Singh

No part of the material protected by this copyright notice may be reproduced or utilized in any form or by any means, electronic or mechanical including photocopying, recording or by any information storage and retrieval system, without prior written permission from the copyright owner.

ISBN: 978-81-8424-816-6

Published by Sunil Sachdev and printed by Ravi Sachdev at Allied Publishers Pvt. Ltd. (Printing Division), A-104 Mayapuri Phase II, New Delhi-110064

Smt. Pratibha Devisingh Patil

Mapping the Sojourn

2007–2012 President of India

2004–2007	Governor Rajasthan
1991–1996	MP & Chairperson, House Committee, Lok Sabha
1988–1990	President, Maharashtra Pradesh Congress Committee
1986–1988	Deputy Chairperson, Rajya Sabha
1986–1988	Chairperson, Committee of Privileges, Rajya Sabha
1985–1990	MP, Rajya Sabha
1983–1985	Cabinet Minister, GoM—Social Welfare and Civil Supplies
1982–1983	Cabinet Minister, GoM—Urban Development and Housing
1979–1980	Leader of Opposition, Maharashtra Legislative Assembly
1977–1978	Cabinet Minister, GoM—Education
1975–1976	Cabinet Minister, GoM—Prohibition, Rehabilitation and Cultural Affairs
1974–1975	Cabinet Minister, GoM—Social Welfare & Public Health
1972–1974	Cabinet Minister, GoM—Social Welfare
1968	Birth of Daughter Jyoti
1967	Birth of Son Rajendra
1967–1972	Deputy Minister, Govt. of Maharashtra (GoM)—Housing, Public Health, Prohibition, Tourism and Parliamentary Affairs
1965	Law Graduation Married Dr. Devisingh Shekhawat
1962–1967	Youngest Maharashtra Legislative Assembly Member at 27
19 Dec 1934	Birth

Preface

Reinventing Leadership: The first Woman President of India—Smt. Pratibha Devisingh Patil, writing this book has been a personal journey of rediscovery for me. While I was cognizant of what can be achieved if determined and resolute, it is the kind of leadership one sets out for oneself that determines the indomitable spirit and will to move ahead. This book came to me at a vital time in my life, as I was set to get my daughter married and then before I could read through the empirical data, so painstakingly provided to me by the President's Secretariat, I found myself in the chair of the Vice-Chancellor of one of the most challenging universities. I was torn between my commitment to deliver the book, and the proactive role of leading an institution with potential. There was no turning away from my responsibilities, they define me, and so I embarked on the dual role of maintaining flexible and dynamic balance.

I decided that the book cannot be a biographical journey of Madam Pratibha Patil, the first woman President, nor should it deal with the emotional trajectory of the woman behind the President, I decided to look at the woman as President, as I realized that less has been said about her achievements and attainments. I also recognized that her grace and quiet demeanour, very often seen as her major assets has ironically kept her engagement with the national progress low profile and unsung. She has indeed brought about a transformation in the landscape of Rashtrapati Bhavan with her developmental strategy. She pioneered many initiatives as the second section of the book will unravel, thereby reinventing leadership from a woman's perspective in the social fabric of the country. Has she been successful in shattering the glass ceiling? The answer would be in the affirmative, a sustainable society, she has shown us, is one that aligns its goals, processes and politics in ways that are life-affirming and regenerative. Her leadership role in the sustainability movement in India has brought practices to the fore that is often associated with the woman bastion: increased cooperation, intuition, collaboration, reaching across differences, and enhancing the cultural values. But this helped in evolving leadership polemics for herself; to me this was a significant trail to assess the very often dubbed the 'silent' President and reading the empirical data on her development initiatives has led me to believe that she is not just a 'working' President but a leader reinventing the leadership domain, contouring and shaping a new direction for the nation's growth and progress. The book therefore endeavoured to do justice in explicating her commitment to the nation through her work. The book does not draw attention to the woman intentionally lest her work is only assessed from a gendered lens; I personally thought that her work is beyond binaries of man-woman polemics. I modestly admit that I may not have done complete justice to the work of Smt. Pratibha Patil. But she has revealed an exceptional leader in her reinventing herself in every new role that life has sprung on her.

Smt. Pratibha Patil's splendid legacy in Indian politics is not simply an accident in Indian history but an unrelenting determination at her personal front as well as India's call of destiny for this diminutive but resolute woman. Her selfless service to the people of India in her more than fifty years in public life is an inspiration. And with an ideal blend of private and public sphere, she is a motivation for the women of India and beyond. Her initiatives, ideas and insights and policy briefings have stimulated me to write this book. In a meeting with her during the process of writing this book I was fascinated by her dedication and commitment for the common cause of progress of the country, even, at the end of her tenure.

I must place on record my gratitude to Smt. Pratibha Patil, an inspiring leader for giving me the platform to be a small part of her life through this book. I am indeed humbled and honoured to have been able to record and write on her work. I must acknowledge Dr. Devisingh Shekhawat, Smt. Jyoti Rathore and Shri Rajendra Shekhawat for giving me the space to shape the book as per my vision. The credit must be given to Ms. Rasika Chaube and Dr. Chhaya Mahajan whose book 'An Inspirational Journey' has been of immense help in providing source material on Madam Pratibha Patil's early life. I would like to thank the entire President's Secretariat for their unvarying support in providing complete empirical data on the Honourable President's work. I must acknowledge and particularly mention the names of Ms. Rasika Chaube, Joint Secretary and Financial Advisor to the President; Ms. Vijay Thakur Singh, Joint Secretary and Social Secretary to the President and Smt. Archana Dutta, Officer on Special Duty (Public Relations). I am particularly thankful to Shri R.J. Jadhav (IAS), Private Secretary to the President of India, for his constant help in the course of writing the book.

I would also like to express my appreciation to Shri G.K. Das, Private Secretary to Smt. Pratibha Patilji and Manjiri Joshi, Personal Assistant in the President's Secretariat for providing relevant data and information. I also express my appreciation to Mr. Sharad Gupta of Allied Publishers for his general guidance on the structure of the book. My gratitude to Mr. N. Ram, former Editor-in-Chief of 'The Hindu', for allowing me to publish the interview of Smt. Pratibha Patil with him and Mr. Parveen Swami. I am also thankful to the Raj Bhavan of Orissa (Odisha) for providing permission to use their website which has been of immense help in providing the source materials. I also acknowledge the website of ROSHNI—A Green Innovation for Sustainable Habitats (A Rashtrapati Bhavan Initiative) (URL: http://roshni-rb.gov.in/roshni.html), the official website of President of India during the period of Smt. Pratibha Patil (URL: http://presidentofindia.nic.in) and the Roshni Prachodaya Society (URL: http://roshni-prachodaya.org) for the source material.

I affectionately acknowledge Dr. Siba Sankar Mohanty's help in research and editing, without whose committed support this book would not have been possible. I am grateful for excellent help extended by my junior colleague Dr. Angela Moorjani and Aparna for their assistance. I must also mention the help extended by my secretary, Mr. Srikant. The final word is for my family and friends without their support and resolute faith in me, this book would indeed not have been a reality. In the journey of life, my children Shraddha and Pranay have been my impetus and inspiration, thank you for being there.

Sunaina Singh

Contents

Mapping the Sojourn .... *vii*
Preface .... *ix*

Section I: The Beginning

1. Introduction 3
2. The Journey Begins 16

Section II: Initiatives

3. It Took a Woman… to Empower Other Women................ 39
4. Roshni: Lighting up Lives 74
5. India and Overseas Business Collaboration 95
6. Agrarian Advancement 132
7. Social Milieu: Issues and Concerns 157

Section III: Reflections

8. On Education 179
9. Engaging the Pravasi Indian 191

Section IV: Conclusion

Conclusion 203
Postscript—Interview with Praveen Swami 207
    'The Quiet Legacy…'

Section–I
The Beginning

Introduction

*For I dipt into the future, far as human
eye could see,
Saw the Vision of the world, and all the
wonder that would be.*

—*Alfred Tennyson*

On the 15 August 1947, the renaissance of India began with Pandit Jawaharlal Nehru heralding the birth of the nation. He gave the grand vision of the independent India effectively emerging out of the shackles of the empire. He envisioned an India free from the stratification of class, caste, creed, religion and gender inequality. The battle continues, as the process of reinventing the social and political ethos in the globalized context keeps evolving and the nation continues its journey of self-discovery.

The day of 19 December 1934 was a memorable day for Gangaba (mother), Nanasaheb (father) and the family members as they were blessed with a girl child, who none realized would write her own destiny. She is the harbinger of a new era in the quiet Rajput family by taking the family legacy to the pinnacle with her distinctions. On 25 July 2007, India ascended into another milestone, adorning its splendid edifice of democracy, by electing the first woman President of the Republic of India, after sixty years of independence. History was created. Treading into this landmark position would not have been a simple passage for Smt. Pratibha Patil. It is her positive mindset, relentless pursuit of goals, diligence and determination that drew her closer to her resolute plan of addressing the deeper concerns of India.

India is a federal state with unitary spirit, the configuration of Indian democracy is erected on the structure of its numerous diversities—linguistic, socio-cultural, religious, geographical etc. To value India, one must be part of the palpable vibrancy of its diversity. The head of this largest democratic republic of the world, the President of India, is to be both objective and impartial, keeping with the secular fabric of the nation. The office of the President also demands she uphold the Constitution and take care of the integrity and dignity of the spirit and ethos of democracy. Smt. Pratibha Patil with her modest background and education, diversified experience at the grass root level, as well as state and national echelon and an exceptionally gentle and unpretentious persona of supreme integrity was best suited for this premier position. It certainly is not easy to step into the proverbial shoes of Dr. Abdul Kalam, an acclaimed scholar-scientist-intellect. Smt. Pratibha Patil's grace, dignity, her quiet poise and unassuming gentleness made her stride into the Rashtrapati Bhavan with a calm confidence. Amidst the palpable patriarchal doubt and distrust, the intellectual scepticism and the political cynicism, Smt. Pratibha Patil managed to capture the imagination of India with her steadfast resolve to purge and address varied social issues.

Smt. Pratibha Patil's entrance into the Rashtrapati Bhavan was marked by the newly established coalition political set up. When Dr. Abdul Kalam's tenure as the President of India was coming to a close there were many speculations and discussions on the suitable successor to head the Country. The United Progressive Alliance (UPA) headed by Smt. Sonia Gandhi found this in the personal traits and the wealth of experience of Smt. Pratibha Patil. There was scepticism and tittle-tattle from different quarters, can this lady steer the largest democracy in such a critical phase of its history? She silenced all her critics by winning the election with a thumping majority over her opponent Bhairon Singh Shekhawat, a political veteran, and firmly reinforcing the faith of Smt. Sonia Gandhi. After five years, in July 2012, she left a legacy of 'working President' and tenacity for progress and advancement for her successors to emulate.

II

In spite of Christine de Pizan's *The Book of the City of Ladies* (1405), which raised issues pertaining to the rights of women, and Mary Wollstonecraft's *A Vindication of the Rights of Woman* (1792), which was written in the backdrop of the French Revolution considered to be the first in human history to champion the ideals of liberalism, and which also raised issues for female suffrage and rights, in the so called progressive Europe and America, it was not until 1918 in UK, and 1920 in USA that franchise was extended to women in the men's world. The US is yet to have a lady at the White House. In India, the framers of our Constitution made no distinction in the name of gender and though India had the merit of having the service of a woman Prime Minister, it was not until 2007 that it could find a lady occupying the Rashtrapati Bhavan.

Participation of women, both in intellectual and political arena in India is well-known. Both at regional and at national level there are political parties where leadership is provided by women. Indeed, the first elected woman president of the Indian National Congress was Sarojini Naidu in 1925 is "fifty years earlier than the election of the first woman leader of a major political party Margaret Thatcher in 1975 in Britain."[1] Whether it is the well known women intellects of our Upanishad era, Gargi or Maitreyi or the valour of Jhansi ki Rani, women have been in the forefront at the call of destiny and yet the Indian scepticism of a woman's potential is a mystery. The life span of this incredulity is indeed inscrutable. Smt. Pratibha Patil's sojourn into this highest office is predated by many political and personal trajectories. She was fortunate to be born in a family with modern outlook in those days when distinction between boys and girls did exist, which encouraged her to pursue higher education. At that time, the orthodoxy of the Indian society demanded that women should be confined to the candid walls of the household, men to the public world. Education was mostly the men's bastion. For the women, education and the public space were perceived as the forbidden fruit which will bring to the family utter damnation. Both her parental and marital family were exceptionally supportive of her spirit of service for the nation. In Dr. Devisingh Shekhawat she found an unconventional, enlightened and extraordinary husband and friend. Her two well brought up children understood the tacit dedication of their mother to the nation.

Her education and entrance into the public domain became an encouraging and optimistic force for the women of her region. In 1962, she astounded everybody by winning the election of Maharashtra State Assembly and becoming the youngest Member of the Legislative

Assembly (MLA). Her journey since then has become consummate; she cruised from one pinnacle to another. Beginning with the MLA of Maharashtra State Assembly to serving as the Minister with numerous portfolios of Maharashtra Government; Leader of Opposition, President Maharashtra Pradesh Congress Committee; Deputy Chairman of Rajya Sabha; Member of Parliament, Lok Sabha and Governorship. This eventful and demanding journey culminated into the peak of its grandeur when Smt. Pratibha Patil stepped into the highest office of the country. W.B. Yeats, the famous English poet once stated that—one is young actually when one is old. For this determined and industrious lady of 73 (years of age) with youthful vigour, the expedition had just begun.

The modus operandi of Smt. Pratibha Patil has been simple: go to the people, understand their problems and requirements, feel their angst and work for them. Right from the inception of her political career in Maharashtra to its culmination in the Rashtrapati Bhavan as the President of India, she has constantly raised concerns for the exploited and oppressed with particular focus on the marginalised groups in the society. Gandhian principle of truthfulness and non-violence, Nehruvian modern outlook with scientific temper and Ambedkar's constitutional methods has been the guiding principles of her life and political career. A firm believer and an expert on the Constitution of India, she sometimes has been labelled by many as a walking constitution. Perfectly balancing her political career and family life she stands as a luminous example of modern Indian womanhood. Imbibing the ethos of the secular tradition of India, she has drawn her inspiration and moral strength from various religions and religious scriptures like Hinduism, Buddhism, Islam, Christianity, Sikhism, Jainism etc. and the Bhagvat Gita, the Koran, the Bible etc. Her grounding on the religious scriptures has added to her compassionate and humane deportment and has helped her fight for the oppressed and demoralized of the society.

On the first day of her assuming the highest office of the country she made evident her concern for the deprived and marginalized sections of the country. In her speech of assumption of office as the President of India she stated her vision of continuing her work and battle for the advancement of society. She quoted Marathi poet-saint, Sant

Tukaram, who said: "One who befriends the poor and the oppressed, recognise him to be a Saint, for God is with him". Smt. Pratibha Patil's commitment to serve the best interests of the people of India has found fruition in many fronts. Loyal to the roadmap she set for herself, all her endeavours were to fulfil the promise she made to herself. Assuming office at a significant moment when the country is marred by internal problems on the domestic side; and India's rising stature as a global player internationally, Smt. Pratibha Patil has maintained a fine balance and shown lots of courage and commitment in steering India's image as the President. She has upheld the dignity of the post. Being a great believer in Gandhian and Nehruvian ideals she has been a promoter of truth, non-violence and simple living, and at the same time she has appealed the people to develop scientific temper which will help in the progress of our country as well as the human civilization. She constantly counselled the Government that fruits of India's development must reach the marginalized sections of the society first.

During the five years of her tenure she has strived to honour the promises she made to the people of the country. The most significant of this has been the empowerment of women. When her nomination for the highest post of the democratic republic was filed, the entire world was keeping an eye on these developments as the largest democracy of the world was preparing the red carpet to welcome, probably, its first woman Head of the State. India achieved this distinction by electing Smt. Pratibha Patil as the President of India whereas many old and developed democracies of the world labelled as the champions of liberalism and gender equality are waiting for a woman to adorn the highest position in their country. Soon after assuming the responsibility as the President, Smt. Pratibha Patil initiated a number of programmes for the upliftment of the women. Her past experience of working at the grass root level has immensely helped her in this regard, as she had the knowledge and understanding of the ground realities at the base. Women must be equal partners in India's growth story. Her election as the first woman President of the country was indisputably a step forward for India maturing as a democracy. She stepped into the highest office with composed and unspoken munificence and five years later, redefining leadership through her commitment to the cause of progress of the country, she relinquished the office with the same grace and dignity. In this quietness, a history has been written and a legacy has been carved to emulate. In one of her interviews to NDTV, answering the question pertaining to her plans after she relinquishes this highest post, Smt. Pratibha Patil recalled her days in Maharashtra politics when she was asked by the Chief Minister to choose a portfolio. She expressed her preference for social welfare Ministry to the surprise of the Chief Minister, as this was the portfolio generally given to the junior ministers and since Smt. Pratibha Patil was a senior leader, she was entitled to a better portfolio. But Smt. Pratibha Patil consciously opted for this as this Ministry covered within its ambit "the women, scheduled caste, scheduled tribes, physically handicapped, orphan children, all these neglected sections of the society and I wanted to work for them, so please give this portfolio. So this has been my passion and I think, after sometime, after retirement, I will again do the same work so that I can go along with my brothers and sisters who are in need."[2] Studies reveal that when women are entrusted with a leadership role, the nation's ecological sustainability, economic development, gender equity, public health, social stability and education get better. Smt. Pratibha Patil indeed redefines leadership.

III

From women empowerment to ecological issues, agrarian advancement, India's foreign relations, Indian overseas communities, and the higher education system, Smt. Pratibha Patil in her term of five years has through her insights, initiated these pertinent concerns by evolving the ground reforms and policy initiatives. The general perception about the President of India is that of rubber stamp President. But a clear analysis of the initiatives and programmes and their successful execution and undertakings of Smt. Pratibha Patil proves this position wrong. In one of her interviews to 'The Hindu',[3] she agrees with her esteemed predecessor President K.R. Narayanan that (her) image of a President (of India) is of a working President, not a mere rubber stamp President.

In the brief period of five years she made the Rashtrapati Bhavan effervescent with her diligence and dynamism. She stepped in at a key period in India's political tradition when the coalition government was going to be the future of Indian politics and the economic growth required that it carried all the sections of the society with it. It does become imperative to record and study the initiatives and programmes pioneered by Smt. Pratibha Patil as President of India. And this is where the idea of this book came in. I realized that she has effectively reinvented leadership through her work. Society per se has long undervalued human qualities and characteristics allied primarily with the feminine as compassion, relational intelligence, empathy, progress, cooperation, collaboration, embodied experiential learning, intuition, and self-awareness. Yet these qualities are essential for creating a life-affirming, more inclusive, healthy and just development of a nation and its culture. Smt. Pratibha Patil through these very attributes has tried to steer the country through her ingenuous plans and proposals for the country's development. The mandate of the book on Smt. Pratibha Patil 'An Inspirational Journey' is a biographical sketch of her life. None exists on her work and accomplishments; this book therefore, confines itself to the five year period of Smt. Pratibha Patil's leadership at Rashtrapati Bhavan. Her work, I believe merits a study, the road map she set for herself is indicative of her commitment to the nation. The book is therefore based on her initiatives; case studies on the implementation of some of her vision for an equitable and just India and her numerous programmes. The book limits itself to the empirical work undertaken by her; the source material made available for the book is from the President's Secretariat. Also her speeches at various forums and interviews to various television channels and newspapers have provided valuable source material in understanding her policy insights and methodologies. Under the rubrics of four sections: 'The Beginning', 'Initiatives', 'Reflections', and 'Conclusion', the book sojourns by touching upon the passage of Smt. Pratibha Patil from 1962 Maharashtra State Assembly to her tryst with the highest office of the President of India.

The first chapter of the book entitled **'The Journey Begins'*** provides a brief biographical sketch of Smt. Pratibha Patil from her birth in Jalgaon in 1934 to becoming the President of India in 2007. Born in a

---

* This chapter is centred on the book, Chaube, Rasika and Chhaya Mahajan. An Inspirational Journey—Pratibha Devisingh Patil, the First Woman President of India. New Delhi: S. Chand Group, 2011.

family which is a fine blend of tradition and modernity she is grounded in the Indian value system. Well educated and schooled in the cultural paradigm, the year 1962 marks the turning point in her life. She wins the Maharashtra Legislative Assembly election becoming the youngest member of the Assembly. This provided her the valid and bona fide opportunity to carry out her work for the downtrodden and marginalised sections of the society. The other big thing that happened to her during this time is her marriage and her children. In Dr. Devisingh Shekhawat, she found the perfect partner who encouraged her to pursue her political ambition. Her diligence and determination took her from one achievement to another. There was no looking back for her. Her goal has been to serve the common man and the marginalised sections of the society. This commitment to the people took her from a small village in Jalgaon to the Raisina Hills, Rashtrapati Bhavan. Some people say that this long journey of fifty years concluded in the Rashtrapati Bhavan, but I believe that for Smt. Pratibha Patil a new journey has just begun.

The second section reinvents the quintessence of leadership, the section, in effect is the body of her diverse attainments ranging from women empowerment to agrarian advancement to ecological sustainability in the form of 'Roshni' to overseas collaborations to social concerns. Smt. Pratibha Patil's education and subsequently her political career which led her to the grass root level provided her a better understanding on the conditioning of the women in the society. One question that always grappled her imagination was the inequality between men and women. The remedy to this malady she found in the empowerment of women. From the very beginning of her political career in Maharashtra politics to the Centre, she initiated policies and programmes for the empowerment of women. The prejudice against women should end and the potential of women should be harnessed for the growth of India. Though many programmes and policies have been drafted and enacted, yet many more need to be done for the upliftment of women. After stepping into the highest office of the country, it became the foremost objective of Smt. Pratibha Patil to empower women. She initiated many programmes and provided many policy insights for women empowerment. This forms the core of the second chapter, **'It Took a Woman... to Empower Other Women....'** Apart from critically analysing Smt. Pratibha Patil's various initiatives, programmes and policy insights for women empowerment as the President of India, this chapter also provides life story narratives of some women being empowered by the initiatives of Smt. Pratibha Patil.

The hasty pace of urbanisation supplemented by the apathetic destruction of forests has driven us to serious environmental hazards and ecological imbalances and devastations. Any further heedless attempts towards the nature will certainly lead the whole of the world to ultimate doom. For a better and healthier living matrix and to leave a better world for our future generation where they can have a fresh lease of unpolluted air, we have to love and nurture the nature, then only nature can nurture us. Herein germinates the ingenious brain child of Smt. Pratibha Patil's ground-breaking conception 'Roshni' which with its very simple method strives "to equip us better to brave the challenges of living in harmony with nature." The vision of 'Roshni' is to create an eco-friendly and sustainable urban habitat. This very simple way of perseverance of nature started with her concerted effort in modulating and transforming the Rashtrapati Bhavan as a paradigm of eco-friendly urban habitat. The success of 'Roshni' percolates to many levels in India. And 'Roshni' carries all the promise of becoming a global concept. The third chapter, **"Roshni': Lighting up Lives'** which has been named after Smt. Pratibha Patil's concept of 'Roshni' makes critical analysis of ideas and insights on environment and ecology in view of 'Roshni', implementation and realization of the programme 'Roshni' and percolation of 'Roshni' at many levels with the case study of Raj Bhavans of Bhopal and Odisha (Orissa).

The fourth chapter, **'India and Overseas Business Collaboration'** is an analysis of her vision vis-a-vis the foreign trips and their outcomes for India's growth prospects. Interdependence and engagement of different nation states at international level is the key to the multi-lateral world order. No individual country can perceive to grow by itself without planning and carrying out its global engagements. Smt. Pratibha Patil's scheme of a world order is based on mutual respect, trust and benefits, and where the rich and developed countries help the less rich and less developed countries to grow. Love your neighbour is the essence of this order. And in this interconnected globe and

Smt. Pratibha Patil's vision of the whole world is a family, 'Vasudhaiva Kutumbakam' (वसुधैव कुटुम्बकम्), is the civilizational canvass upon which all the countries of the world stand as neighbours to each other. To take the emergent India to the world, promote trade and business relations and create educational, socio-cultural etc. collaborations and linkages Smt. Pratibha Patil undertook trips to twenty four countries. Her first visit to the distant country Brazil speaks volume of India's realisation and growing engagement with Latin America. Her visits to these countries as head of the state has yielded many dividends in the signing of MoUs in many sectors, germination of goodwill and growing interest on India and promotion of bi-lateral and multi-lateral engagements and linkages in many fields.

The fifth chapter, **'Agrarian Advancement'** evinces how agriculture occupies a pivotal place in the physiological, social and psychological space of the Indian people not only because of providing food to its more than a billion population but also providing livelihood to 70% people of this country and contributing a very significant chunk to the GDP. The recent global economic meltdown exposed the weak and pretentious foundations of many of the labelled developed economies of the world. It is believed that India could manage to overcome this economic debacle because of its firm agrarian foundation. This economic unrest has made it clear that no country can sustain without the development of its agrarian sector. Though India keeps a vigilant look on its agricultural sector, yet much needs to be done for the optimal development of this sector. This chapter attempts to delineate Smt. Pratibha Patil's initiatives and policy insights for the agrarian advancement in the country. Smt. Pratibha Patil argues that about 60 percent of the cultivated land in India comes under rain-fed farming. And rain-fed farming yields 44 percent of the food production, supports 40 percent of the population, mostly belonging to the poorer sections of society and affords living to 60 percent of the livestock population. But the potentialities of the production of rain-fed farming have not been harnessed fully, and there is no hesitation to say that this has been a neglected sector of our agriculture. Smt. Pratibha Patil seriously advocates for the development of rain-fed farming in India which will not only enhance immensely the living standards of the poor farmers but also contribute significantly for India's growth. Also the corporate or industrial sector can play a very prominent role for the development of rain-fed farming. The information, knowledge and use of the modern technological innovations in agriculture should be disseminated at the grass root level. More significantly the common perceptions and prejudices against the farmers must change. Smt. Pratibha Patil also advocates for the second Green Revolution which should be environmentally sustainable, broad based and directed towards underdeveloped areas.

Smt. Pratibha Patil from the very beginning of her political career has been a champion against the evils that have deeply shaken the milieu of the Indian society. She has always fervently expressed the concern that India cannot fully grow, its democratic ethos cannot find full realisation as a peaceful, happy and progressive nation and its stature as a key global player cannot be established unless India fully drives out the social evils from its domain. After taking charge as the President of the country Smt. Pratibha Patil intensified her lifelong battle against the social evils like ragging, female foeticide, female infanticide, child marriages, dowry, alcoholism, etc. The sixth chapter, **Social Milieu: Issues and Concerns** makes a critical enquiry into Smt. Pratibha Patil's measures and initiatives of deracinating this social menace from Indian society.

The seventh chapter, **'Reflections'** provides Smt. Pratibha Patil's critical insights and reflections on some of the prominent issues of the country, particularly education and Pravasi. From the captivating mountains of Kashmir to the grandiose oceanic enchantress of Kanyakumari, India stretches its canvass in which more than one billion of its people add spectacle to its diversity with their splendor of plurality in culture, religion, language, ethnicity, dress, food habits and so on. This natural specter of diversity holds the true spirit of our democracy. Education is the real emancipator of people. In a democracy like India which is committed to the people, education is a right to every citizen of the country and it is the responsibility of the state to provide education. Only by educating all the sections of the population, the true growth of India can be achieved. In this present day coordinated world order which is based on mutual aid, no single country can exist standing isolated and detached especially a country like India which is emerging as a key global player. India's engagement with the world order has been based on its principle of non-interference, mutual respect and trust, and non-violence. The other very significant group that has not been accorded representation until recently are the 'Pravasi', our overseas Indians who could be equal partners in the growth story of India. They are a strategic asset and a soft power who contribute very significantly to the economic development, are helping us in generating social and intellectual capital and most significantly they are facilitating diplomatic relationship of India with their host countries.

It is very difficult to provide a final statement on the initiatives and achievements of Smt. Pratibha Patil as some of her programmes are still underway. But, considering the packed five years and the limitations of the real power of execution of the President of India, it has to be accepted that she has reached the zenith of her parameters and achieved what is possible. Most of her initiatives have yielded successful accomplishments and others are in the right direction of progress. She says in her interview to 'The Hindu', "Things move slowly ... but I think you can see they are moving in the right direction. People are realising what the issues are, and coming to understand the need for us to act. You will see the result – perhaps not as fast as we would all like, but surely."[4] There is no doubt that the dedication, assiduousness and down-to-earth approach of Smt. Pratibha Patil as the President of this country has yielded and will certainly yield more dividends for India. I close the book with the concluding observation and a post script in the form of one of her last significant interviews as the President of India, opening up a new chapter of perseverance in her life.

Positioning myself as a woman writing on the redefining leadership position has accorded me with a great personal satisfaction of critically analysing the success story of a remarkable personage, the first woman President of India. She not only stands as an inspiration to the women and the common masses of India, but also a dignified ambassador to the world representing India's maturing as a democracy and the country's commitment to gender equality. This book is a modest academic endeavour at blending diverse initiatives, programmes, insights and the vision of Smt. Pratibha Patil's legacy to the Rashtrapati Bhavan as reinventing a quiet leadership.

References

Note: If a reference number occurs twice or more in the chapter, it is another reference to the same source.

[1] Sen, Amartya, *The Argumentative Indian*. New Delhi: Penguin, 2005, p. 7.
[2] "Full transcript: President Pratibha Patil's interview to NDTV," Updated: May 07, 2012. URL: http://www.ndtv.com/article/india/full-transcript-president-pratibha-patils-interview-to-ndtv-207063NDTV.com.
[3] Swami, Praveen, "The quiet legacy of President Pratibha Patil", *The Hindu*, May 25, 2012.
URL: http://www.thehindu.com/opinion/interview/article3453077.ece.
[4] Swami, Praveen, "The quiet legacy of President Pratibha Patil", *The Hindu,* May 25, 2012. URL: http://www.thehindu.com/opinion/interview/article3453077.ece.

The Journey Begins

'Work out your own salvation. Do not depend on others'.
*—**Gautam Buddha***

'Change does not roll in on the wheels of inevitability, but comes through continuous struggle.'
*—**Martin Luther King Jr.***

Tai has great potential. I must fortify and strengthen her wings so that she can soar high. Smt. Pratibha Patil, known popularly as 'Tai' had an incredible support system in her father Narayanrao. His aim was to make his daughter strong and did not hesitate in putting the sails in her wings. He was himself a man of great vision who believed that women can soar high if given the education and freedom to choose their life's goals. It also goes to his credit that he valued his very progressive wife Gangaba's wish to allow and encourage Tai to study. One must remember that at a time when girls in the community were denied education, Narayanrao encouraged Tai to study law after her double Masters in political science and economics. Narayanrao's father had encouraged his four sons to study law; Narayanrao went a step ahead in equipping Tai with the requisite knowledge that she craved for.

Sonusingh Anna Patil was a Member of Parliament and Minister of State for Home Affairs in the cabinet of Morarji Desai. A well respected statesman in Maharashtra political circles, Anna, as he was popularly known, was of the view that, 'if contemporary educated women come forth and accomplish something exemplary it will be easy for other Indian women to identify and emulate'. Anna had plans for the young Tai when he heard her deliver her maiden speech in Chalisgaon at Akhil

---

Note: This chapter is a biographical sketch of Smt. Pratibha Patil, the effort is to sum up the book, 'An Inspirational Journey: Pratibha Devisingh Patil—The first Woman President of India,' coauthors—Rasika Chaube and Dr. Chhaya Mahajan 2010, India. S. Chand and Company on behalf of Shram Sadhana Delhi.

Bharatiya Kshatriya Sabha and thought she should be part of public life. This was also the time when the Chief Minister Yashwantrao Chavan Saheb had put forth a policy to bring young educated women into politics. Anna spoke to Tai's father Narayanrao and the elder brother Abasaheb about her initiation into politics. Young Tai was reluctant to join politics as she did not like the idea of soliciting votes. She was however convinced by her father and Annasaheb when they said she could make a difference especially in empowering women if she was inside the system. This appealed to her as affecting changes in the society was close to her heart and her consent came spontaneously.

The Legacy

Tai's belief that, 'Family roots provide the required strength and stability; but this needs to be supplemented with one's own diligence and perseverance', is reflected even today through her work. Tai belongs to the Solanki clan, originally the denizens of the Tonk district in Rajasthan. In the eighteenth century they migrated to Maharashtra due to the war situation prevailing then. They made Maharashtra their 'Karmabhoomi' though they continued to maintain the cultural trait of Rajasthan and ate the Rajasthani foods like, 'Dalbaati.' Ramji Solanki, Tai's grandfather had seven children and Narayanrao was the youngest. Ramji Solanki also known as Buwasaheb, was a money lender and slowly grew to be the commander of 52 villages through his compassion and providing effective leadership; in no time he became the 'chief' and was called 'Patil,' the administrative head of the region.

In 1967 when Tai won the election from Edlabad, she gave the entire credit to her grandfather's goodwill. Buwasaheb discharged his responsibilities from a two storied 'Haveli'. He was blessed with wealth but he always beseeched for 'Saraswati'. His sons became lawyers. Tai acknowledges the creative thinking of her grandfather, "it is education that gives culture, transforms one's outlook towards life and helps one climb social ladder". But Buwasaheb did not encourage his daughters to study due to the prevailing social bias. But Pratibha Tai has rewritten the fortune of the women belonging to the Patil family.

Childhood Memories

Tai was born on 19 December 1934, in Jalgaon, in Maharashtra to Gangaba and Narayanrao. Third amongst the six siblings, Tai was brought up in an atmosphere where family values were paramount. Her childhood memories are replete with the memories of her grandfather. Gangaba was broadminded with a very modern outlook. She got a private tutor to teach Tai to play harmonium, because she liked to play it.

When Tai was seven and a half years old her mother was diagnosed with Tuberculosis. She was taken to a sanitarium in Miraj (near Sangli) and the children were looked after by Gangaba's widowed sister Baasaheb, and Maushi, who was a distant cousin. After her mother's demise Nanasaheb became both mother and father for the children. Nanasaheb educated his daughter but expected her to follow a strict code of conduct. She had to be home by evening even if it was at the cost of her music which she loved. To watch movies or theatrical performances or any shows she was allowed to go for matinee shows, with an escort. Though she did not like the restrictions but never had the courage to question her father. Baasaheb and Maushi's religious values had an impact on her, which made her God fearing without being ritualistic.

Early Schooling and Friends

When she was 7 years old, Tai's father was transferred to Chalisgaon from Jalgaon. She started her elementary school at 'Bal Varga' and her mother showed a lot of interest in her education. She soon realized the value of education. Her father again got transferred to Jalgaon and her mother was worried about Tai's education as there was no decent school nearby. She wanted to admit Tai in the municipal school. On the first floor of the building where they were staying, resided a police officer named Chakranarayan whose daughter Kakku was two years older to Tai and went to the same school. When Nanasaheb (Narayanrao) heard that Tai would go to school with Kakku he agreed to send his daughter to school.

After the first year she got tutored at home and she cleared second and fourth the same year and joined 'New English School' which was later renamed 'RR Vidyalya'. She soon picked up English. But Mathematics was a subject she was weak in and it was because of the teacher who was very strict and would often beat up the children, that Kakku made a plan of evading the Math teacher by not attending school. They did not go for five days but soon they were caught and were admonished. From that day they decided never to skip school.

Years later, as the Governor of Rajasthan when Tai was to inaugurate a 'Conference on Mathematics', she was hesitant, while inaugurating the conference she said, "I was poor in Mathematics. That was the reason I was in two minds before coming to address you. While in Mathematics two plus two is four, it is not always so in politics... thus, I preferred to be a politician. Now with politics getting tougher day by day, I prefer to stand before you as a Governor, no more Mathematics, and no more politics".

Tai also had a problem with Sanskrit. The teacher was strict and expected the students to do their work on time; Tai was once punished for not completing her work. But she turned every incident into learning something new. She had other friends Shashi Sathe, Kala Kalvit, Leela Choudhari, Kunda Chitre and Kamla Patil. They all spent wonderful time together. Kakku was however closer; both of them saved money and bought a 'Bible'as Kakku was a Christian; Tai often went to the church and participated in the activities. When Kakku had to leave Jalgaon Tai was distraught, but the vacuum was soon filled by Sophia Khan, whose father was a Deputy Inspector General of police, who replaced Kakku's father and was allotted the same house. Both the girls became very close friends and Tai even kept Roza in the holy month of Ramadan. Tai's family never opposed her from going to church or keeping Roza, they had a secular approach and this was imbibed by Tai from the early days of her childhood.

Growing up—Those Who made a Difference

Though Nanasaheb was a conformist, yet at the same time he defied regressive social norms. He was a healthy blend of modernity and traditional values. While he extended every possible support to Tai in enhancing her caliber, he also ensured that she stayed within the parameters of the prevailing value system. Anna Patil wanted Tai to address the 'Akhil Bhartiya Kshatriya Mahasabha' at Chalisgaon for people to realize that their region had gone beyond the traditional conception of not educating the girl child and also that society had educated young minds who could make a difference. It turned out to be the most powerful speech in the 'Mahasabha'.

Nanasaheb did not hinder Tai from public speaking, in fact, he encouraged her to raise certain social concerns affecting the common man. The public exposure transformed a hesitant Tai into a composed and confident orator and taught her a major lesson—"Nothing is impossible if one is resolute and tenacious".

Nanasaheb was austere about the social etiquette of Tai, an incident worth mentioning—Once when she accompanied him to a wedding ceremony she applied 'kajal' and he asked her to remove it. As a young girl she was distressed. After returning home he took her to her mother's photograph and told her to observe the simplicity of her mother's face, he reminded her that their society was neither progressive nor has it evolved, therefore it becomes necessary that she should set personal limits within the parameters of the social norms. This advice set her thinking, and it ingrained in her mind to learn to maintain a fine balance between modern thinking and traditional values. Her tenure as the President of India has been an exemplary blend of tradition and modernity.

After matriculation Tai applied for science in Moolji Jaitha College, Jalgaon hoping to become a doctor along with her brother Abasaheb and cousin Inder, but Nanasaheb discouraged her as there was no medical school in Jalgaon and asked her to opt for Humanities. College was a great experience for Tai; she made many friends and also learnt to play table tennis. She was very good at it, she and her friend Indu played regularly in the ladies room. With her superb skills and practice she became the college champion in table tennis. There was an inter-college table tennis championship at Nashik, her principal Mr. Y.S. Mahajan convinced her father, and she be allowed to participate with her brother as her chaperon. Tai brought laurels to her college, later she also won a championship at Nagar.

For her post-graduation, Tai took up political science and economics as they were the only subjects available at M.J. College. In those days students were allowed to take two masters' degrees. The selection of the subjects helped her later in her political career. She had to go to Pune to write her exams and was accompanied by Maushi. She passed with superior scores and her teacher for economics was none other than Y.S. Mahajan, her principal.

Later in 1978, she helped him to contest an election from Jalgaon when she was a Congress MLA. Sureshdada Jain, who was an affluent and powerful resident at Jalgaon also wanted to contest the election and asked Tai to recommend his name. But since Tai had promised Y.S. Mahajan she stood by him, even the Congress President Indira Gandhi gave him the candidature and Sureshdada Jain had to contest from another political party. With the help and support of Tai Y.S. Mahajan got elected with a thumping majority. He said to her, "I was your guru in college but in politics you proved to be my guru". Thus, with encouragement of Nanasaheb, Annasaheb and Yashwantrao Chavan, Tai catapulted into politics.

Meeting Yashwantrao Chavan—A New Beginning

Yashwantrao Chavan, the Chief Minister of Maharashtra was one of the most perceptive and futuristic leaders of his time. He encouraged educated women of the region to enter politics. His bungalow was colossal and sprawling, yet it was always full of people, and getting to meet him was difficult. Nanasaheb, Abasaheb and Tai went to meet him, and after a long wait Tai and Abasaheb were able to talk to him. Tai, in all her simplicity and candidness expressed her wish to join the Congress, she also articulated that at college she was not too enamored with politics but his appeal to educated women to contribute to the success of our nation ignited her imagination. She said she was always inspired by the lives of leaders like Mahatma Gandhi and Jawaharlal Nehru. She believed that she could uphold the work in the interest of the party and being a woman she would have an edge over the others and be able to reach out to the women of the nation.

Yashwantrao Chavan was impressed with her honesty and candidness and saw a huge potential in her. Tai was given the ticket for contesting the Legislative Assembly elections from Jalgaon. The sitting Member of

Assembly was Bhalerao, a veteran communist leader. It was a herculean task to contest with such a veteran politician but, Tai won the election. Her approach was sincere, warm and committed; she struck an instant chord with the people. Since this first election, Tai is one of the few politicians in the country who have never lost an election.

Yashwantrao Chavan was indeed a man of vision, he has brought into public life one of the most respected discoveries—the future President of India.

The First Election—1962

The Assembly election of 1962 was a major turning point in Tai's life. Back then, elections were different. There was no concept of individual campaign; canvassing for nominated candidates was the party's responsibility. Tai's nomination was neither the outcome of charity nor an offshoot of her family links. Yashwantrao Chavan wanted to encourage young educated girls and true to his word he gave her a ticket from Jalgaon. The contest was a tough one; she had to compete with veterans like, S.N. Bhalerao, who had defeated Y.S. Mahajan in the earlier legislative assembly elections. Unfortunately, the support from the local Congress camp was not very encouraging, when the sitting Member of the Parliament Raghunathrao came to Jalgaon, Nanasaheb apprised him of the situation. He counseled the party members saying that they were working for Congress and not an individual. The advice was effective and every party leader joined the election drive. Tai went from home to home and campaigned, the women were impressed so were men and in no time she became a household name. In her address, the problems of social, political and economic arena were analyzed at length. The solutions offered were realistic, pragmatic and achievable. The promises were practical and therefore, could be fulfilled. She realized that "people are not gullible. They have a mind of their own".

"Beginning of a new leadership" read the headlines of 'Gavkari'. Tai was elected with thumping majority and she handled her success with magnanimity, she was victorious at the young age of twenty seven.

Member of the Legislative Assembly and a Lawyer

Tai was too grounded to be effected by the new found success; she was the youngest Member of Legislative Assembly. She interacted with everyone patiently and heard them personally. Meeting people, resolving problems and touring the constituency became an inseparable part of her life. As an MLA, she worked overtime, she said "within Government, giving directions is the easiest thing, and following it up and ensuring that it reaches its culmination is what is difficult".

Chinese aggression shook the nation the year Tai joined politics, efforts were made by each and everyone to contribute in their own way to this cause; Tai started collecting funds in her constituency and she received tremendous response. As days went by her responsibilities grew, she attended Assembly sessions at Mumbai and Nanasaheb always sent Baasaheb or Maushi as chaperons. Nanasaheb's expectation from Tai was always high, he believed that being in politics should not be a hindrance to pursue higher education, and he motivated her to study law. Although he realized that she had no time to study, he wished to see her possess a degree in law, one of the acclaimed disciplines of study, and respecting his aspiration she got enrolled for law in Law College, Mumbai. T.K. Tope, the Principal was very proud of his student; she finally got her degree in the year 1965. She was now a politician with a legal insight and this was an enviable combination. Nanasaheb asked her to handle a case of a dispute between a husband and wife, under his guidance. She not only won her first case but also realized her father's dream. In the year 1967 when Rajendra, her first child was about six months old she fought for the Legislative Assembly for the second time and won it. She was made the deputy health minister by the Chief Minister, Vasantrao Naik.

Marriage

"Finding a groom befitting Tai's qualifications was going to be arduous," Baasaheb had proclaimed. Tai on the other hand had her own conditions, "I prefer a partner, who permits me to continue my efforts in the social and political field. He should be mature, thoughtful and should not insist on dowry".

Nanasaheb laid the responsibility of finding a groom for Tai on Abasaheb's shoulders. With the help of K.K. Rajput, Abasaheb found a match for Tai in Devisingh, the youngest son of Ramsingh Shekhawat of Amaravati. Devisingh had a master degree in Chemistry and was working as a teacher in Ner Pinglai, and later in 1962 joined as a Chemistry lecturer in Shivaji Science College, Amaravati. He also started his own activity "Paramount Scientific Syndicate" and looked after it in the evening.

The Shekawats originally hailed from district Sikar from Rajasthan but Devisingh's great grandfather had migrated and settled in Chandrapur, Maharashtra. He was born on 19 April 1934, in Chandrapur. He was selected for studying medicine in Nagpur Medical College, the letter came to him at Khallar which was delivered to his uncle, and his uncle could not deliver it to him as the letter fell into the water while he was crossing the inundated river Chandrabhaga. So, he pursued his study in Chemistry, and became a teacher and then lecturer. His other interests were music and listening to great orators. The family believed that he was the most eligible match for Pratibha.

Devisingh's close friend Dr. Suresh Padhye helped him in catching his first glimpse of young Pratibha Patil in her MLA hostel room. He saw a young woman sitting on a reclining chair, clad in a white saree with the 'pallu' on her head and a vermillion mark on her forehead. She looked serene, gentle and full of dignity. Devisingh however, first saw her in the government guest house and within four months in the same guest house, the engagement was solemnized. They got married in Jalgaon, Khandesh on 7 July 1965.

The In-Laws House

Immediately after her marriage, Tai went to her in-laws house at Chandrapur in Amaravati district. She was the youngest of the daughters-in-law and everyone was curious how a daughter-in-law of political background would behave. But she surprised everyone by her devotion to the family and household works. One day she surprised the entire family by cooking a delicious meal, and gathered a lot of praise for her culinary skills.

She made all efforts to strike a balance between her personal and professional life. Despite the paucity of time, both Tai and Devisingh liked being with each other. She had great regard for him and he respected her simplicity and the potential for growth. In 1965, when Tai got her law degree, Devisingh was very happy and celebrated the occasion.

Soon after the birth of their first child Rajendra, Tai had to face Assembly elections once more. She was in a dilemma whether to contest or not as she felt she could not devote much time to the family. Senior leader Abasaheb Khedkar encouraged her to continue her good work in politics. After meeting him, Tai had more clarity on her future goals and could make her decision easily; she contested the elections and won yet again. The couple has always acknowledged their indebtedness to the Almighty for the good people they were surrounded by and the genuine advice they got from them.

The Second Election—1967

Tai was chosen to contest from Edlabad, now known as Muktainagar. She received the unstinted support of Sonusingh Anna, Keshavrao Patil, Abasaheb, and her husband Devisingh stood behind her as solid as the rock of Gibraltar. She won the election and the Chief Minister Vasantrao Naik offered her the post of Deputy Minister in his Government and gave her the portfolios of Public Health, Prohibition and Tourism. She was also given independent charge of 'Repair, Maintenance and Reconstruction' for the Housing Department. During her assignment as the minister, the young Tai had to stay in Mumbai for long durations and she missed her family. After some time, she was made the guardian minister of Amaravati District, and this aided her to visit her hometown more frequently.

Abasaheb Khedkar convinced Devisingh to shift to Mumbai. Devisingh decided to do research in Chemistry and he joined the Haffkine Institute in Mumbai and commenced study under the guidance of Dr. Delhiwala. After three years he submitted his paper in the 'Pharmaceutical Congress' held in Chandigarh. It was received with tremendous appreciation. Soon there was another happy addition to their family, Jyoti their daughter was born on 17 April 1968. Tai's idea of a happy family was fulfilled. The happiness doubled when in the year 1972 Devisingh got his doctorate from the University of Mumbai. Tai grew both as a politician and a family person.

Dr. Devisingh—Partner through Thick and Thin

After presenting his thesis in Mumbai, Dr. Devisingh started his own college in Amaravati in the year 1972 called 'Vidya Bharati Science College'. By the year 1985 the college grew and faculties of Commerce, Pharmacy, Library and Information Science, Arts and a few Post-graduate courses were added and established.

Both Tai and Dr. Devisingh were drawn to community service, he made palpable difference in the lives of the people of Vidarbha and was eventually made the Mayor. He also won the Assembly seat from Amaravati and in the year 1988–90, when the water problem in Amaravati became acute he remonstrated against the inaction of the civic authorities till the issue was resolved. He also advocated for the cause of 'affordable education for all'. Years later on the occasion of his 75 birthday, his scholarly achievements were summarized. Dr. Ved Prakash Mishra, the Vice Chancellor of Datta Meghe Institute of Medical Sciences said, "The contribution of Dr. Shekhawat in the field of education has been in line with our Constitution: education for all; to the weakest of the weak; poorest of the poor and remotest of the remote".

Clash of Titans is inevitable when there are two towering personalities in the family. On one hand, Tai was tactful, subtle and yielding and on the other, Dr. Devisingh was unequivocal, adamant and short tempered. On one occasion, Dr. Devisingh was angry with Tai as she was busy with some visitors when he had returned from an outstation visit and admonished her. She quickly sent a resignation letter to the Chief Minister Vasantrao Naik stating ill health as the reason. Dr. Devisingh was not aware of the resignation. Vasantrao Naik immediately called Tai and realized that it was a minor dispute in the family; he contacted Dr. Devisingh and told him that Tai was an asset to the party and she should not take such a step. With every confrontation the couple grew closer and learnt to respect each other and with every elevation in her career, Dr. Devisingh stood by her.

When either one had to go abroad for an assignment the other looked after the family. Despite their hectic lives both could still spend some precious time together. Their partnership is one of the finest illustrations of a successful relationship. When they went to England to be with their daughter for two months they did all the household chores together and enjoyed the unique togetherness that came in with sharing. Even today for every birthday Dr. Devisingh buys Tai a saree. Their relationship of mutual respect and love could be guiding post for many youths.

Rajendra and Jyoti

Although the eagle soars high, it remains vigilant of its offspring. Despite hectic schedules both Tai and Dr. Devisingh have never found wanting in fulfilling their responsibility as parents. The children were looked after by Maushi who attended their school functions when the parents could not make it. The children missed the parents but rapidly realized the relevance of their mother's work and the importance of their father's contribution to education. Despite their busy schedule, Tai and Devisinghji were quite vigilant about their children's progress at school. Any laxity in studies and untoward behavior was contained well in time. When Rajendra was in fifth standard he was impertinent towards elders, Tai suitably punished him and later drew him close to explain the importance of culture and respect, while boosting his morale, that he was a wonderful child and must always continue to be good to others. This little personal talk was entrenched in his mind. The children had all the facilities they wanted but, Tai was always anxious that they should never become complacent. Tai would always be vigilant of the company they kept as she wanted them to be completely grounded and levelheaded. The children frequently visited Chandrapur and Jalgaon to be with their families and both acknowledged that the rustic-rural life was always better than the hub of city life. Their family vacations are the most cherished moments of their life together.

Tai and Dr. Singh never thrust their views on their children. Both the children are well educated and independent. Rajendra pursued his Bachelor of Commerce from Osmania University, Bachelor of Law from Mumbai University and Jyoti is an Electronics Engineer from Mumbai University. Both the children are happy in their arranged marriages.

Rajendra got married to Manjari in the year 1992. Jyoti got married to Jayesh, an engineering alumni from IIT. They have two children each. They currently look after the various trusts run by their family.

Tai has created such a harmonious and amicable family that neither the children nor the grand children really felt the need to form their own social circles. Dr. Devisingh's 75 birthday was indeed an occasion to witness the flood of near and dear ones who joined to be a part of the celebration.

Commitment to Congress—Equation with Indira Gandhi

Like her commitment to her family, Tai's dedication to the Congress Party never wavered. In the world of politics even stalwarts are susceptible to allurement; but Tai prominently emerged as one without avarice. After Indira Gandhi declared a state of emergency in the year 1975, there was an inimical reaction in the country. Consequently, Congress lost the elections and Janata Party came into power. Morarji Desai became the Prime Minister and Sonusingh Anna Patil got the opportunity to become a senior minister in his cabinet. He asked Tai to join the Janata Party. But Tai answered, "Does anyone leave one's near and dear ones just because they are going through a bad phase? And again I am in Congress because of my conviction, and its policies and principles. I would neither leave Indiraji nor Congress. This would be against my principles."

When Indira Gandhi was canvassing from Chickmagalur which was her constituency for the sixth Lok Sabha elections, she encountered a lot of antagonism, the youth, influenced by the torrid canvassing from the opposition tried to disrupt her address, Indira Gandhi angrily advanced towards the boys breaking the security arrangements when Tai intervened and averted a major pandemonium.

In 1979, when Indiraji visited Jalgaon, Tai was the leader of the opposition. She wanted to invite Indiraji for lunch and after the meeting as the convoy was moving towards the helipad, Tai redirected the vehicles to her house, Indiraji relented saying, coming all the way to Jalgaon and not visiting Tai's house was unthinkable. She had lunch there, before proceeding to the next place.

After the assassination of Indiraji, Rajiv Gandhi was conscious of Tai's unswerving faith in his mother and the commitment to the ideology of the Congress Party. He was always ready to acknowledge Tai's selfless contribution to the Party; so when she became the Deputy Chairman of Rajya Sabha on November 1986, Rajiv Gandhi voiced his faith in her dedication in his speech, "Sir, her experience in the political field..., will no doubt help her in discharging her duties and in carrying the whole House with her when she is in chair. I have no doubt that she will be impartial and fair and will have the support of the Government benches and of the Opposition as well. My congratulations to her".

Vidhan Sabha—the Fertile Ground that Shaped Tai

Within the family, she was referred as 'Tai on wheels' for she was always on the move, though she entered politics by default, it turned out to be the perfect profession for her. Her political career has been an upward moving graph, from the legislative assembly, to Rajya Sabha, Lok Sabha, then a short stint as a Governor and finally the President of India. She attributes her success to the love of the people and the blessings of the Almighty.

She always had a straight forward approach, honesty in functioning and near total compliance to party thinking. At the same time she never hesitated to put forth her opinions fearlessly. She is a voracious reader and a great orator; she could draw analogies and could quote from mythologies and scriptures. Once when Vasantrao Naik was to unveil the statue of B.R. Ambedkar, he could not attend the function, Tai was the Deputy Minister and she gave an impromptu speech where she said that just as Lord Krishna had to fight the cruel 'Kansa', the same way Ambedkarji had to fight hundreds and thousands 'Kansas'.

During the Chinese aggression of India she started 'Jalgaon Mahila Gruha Rakshak Dal' to supplement the stretched out security services. At about the same time, Tai took up the cause of the workers of 'Gendalal Textile Mill'; it was a sick unit and many workers had lost their jobs, she urged the Government to take up the Mill. Though the Mill did close down finally, but the workers remembered Tai for the concern she demonstrated.

During her second stint as MLA from 1967 to 1972 Tai was made the Deputy Minister and was accorded the portfolios of Health, Prohibition, Tourism, Housing, Parliamentary Affairs and Social Welfare. Her keen sense of justice was apparent when she spoke about the 'atrocities and social boycott of the Harijans'. She said that 'instead of showing sympathy we should actually try to reduce their woes...... We all have to help the Government to give these classes an opportunity to represent their community at social and political level.'

In the early seventies, she was convinced that there was an adverse repercussion of the play 'Sakharam Binder'. She ensured that the Police Second Forum Bill was introduced so that government could exercise required control. She said about the play, "vulgarity is very subjective, what is perceived as vulgar by one may not be so in the eyes of the other, but we have to think of the society at large...."

After the famines of 1976, under Indira Gandhi's 'Poverty Alleviation Programme', temporary jobs were created and wages were increased to compensate the calamity. But the situation did not improve much because the money earned was mostly spent on drinking liquor. Addiction had become a menace particularly among the labour class. She felt that if the family needs to be economically empowered, the women have to be brought into the loop; they would use the money for education, health and nutrition of the children.

She established a 'Mahila Arthik Vikas Mandal' (Women's Financial Development Corporation) and also a Women's Bank. She wanted women to be financially independent, and for economic independence women must be efficient in their work. 'Technical schools' should be established to train them, laws should be efficiently implemented, and the sale of home-made products should be organized and exhibited. At her behest, the 'Mission for Socio-Economic Empowerment of Women' was announced in the year 2009 by Government of India, wherein providing micro-finance at low rates of interest to the women below poverty line was one of the primary charters. She felt that along with economic empowerment, education is also a must for women to help them come out of the superstitions and backward thinking. She stated 'Femininity is a great gift of nature. Women must respect it at all times and display sobriety and serenity. Modernity and liberation is more a mental attitude and is no way linked to one's physical appearance only.' She was consistently dedicated to the society and the populace of Maharashtra. In 1984, she set up an engineering college at Bambhori near Jalgaon for the benefit of the rural students.

Tai never neglected the requirements of her State or Constituency. When, in May 1970, communal riots broke out in Jalgaon she rushed to the area and stayed in the area till the situation had improved. On communal or caste issues her disposition was very progressive. Once when Mandal Commision recommendations were being debated she gave a gripping speech, she said that if backwardness prevailing in some castes had to be removed then all must work together. She also stated that Hindu religion never preaches that one caste is superior to the other; according to Bhagwad Gita all are children of God therefore, Mandal Commission report must be given a serious thought.

Tai has done monumental work in the field of education. In 1977, when she was the Minister of Education she found that most of the colleges in Maharashtra were in financial distress; she released the salaries from the Government treasury for the employees. On another occasion, at the Convocation ceremony of Swami Ramanand Teerth Marathwada University, she spoke about need based practical teaching using modern techniques and also about the improvement of the standard of the teachers.

In 1972, she established a charitable trust 'Shram Sadhana' and laid the foundation for low cost hostels for working women. During 1977 Maharashtra State elections, when the Congress was contesting after the 'Emergency' imposed in 1975, Tai still won the election by a margin of seven hundred votes. But since no party got an absolute majority in the election, a coalition government was formed and Congress sat in the opposition and Tai was made the opposition leader. Tai stood with Congress through thick and thin.

Leader of the Opposition

In an attempt to give the electorate an opportunity to vindicate her stand regarding 'Emergency' the then Prime Minister called for state elections in 1977. Dr. Fakhruddin Ali Ahmed, the then President of India, dissolved the fifth Lok Sabha and called for elections. Janata Party came to power with Morarji Desai as the Prime Minister. The coalition party demanded action against Indira Gandhi for her actions during 'Emergency'. On 19 December 1977 Indira Gandhi was finally put behind bars. Tai, in Jalgaon, took a procession on the streets as a protest and she was arrested and detained for ten days.

During the 1978 State Assembly elections, despite the dynamic leadership of Vasantdada Patil, Congress witnessed a major setback in Maharashtra. Congress sat in the opposition and Prabhu Rau was the leader of the opposition. Due to internal conflict, Tai was later made the leader of the opposition. She participated actively in Call Motions, Question Hours, Budget Debates and No Confidence Motions keeping the Government accountable and on track. Under her charismatic leadership the grounds of victory for Congress in Maharashtra were consolidated.

Consequent to the collapse of the Progressive Democratic Front, the Assembly was dissolved and Tai recommended fresh elections. The Congress won and Tai emerged as a winner from Edlabad despite the impediments created by the opposition. She was, however, not made the Chief Minister, as a member of a minority community was given a chance and was assigned the portfolio of Minister for Urban Development, Civil Supplies and Social Welfare. Tai was thereafter drawn to national politics – she moved in as a Rajya Sabha member and subsequently was elevated to the position of Deputy Chairman.

Tryst with Rajya Sabha

After her first victory in 1962, Tai scaled many peaks. She entered Rajya Sabha and within a short span she was elected as the Deputy Chairman. She participated actively in the Rajya Sabha proceedings. To many it was remarkable to see her in-depth knowledge on issues ranging from family planning, banking, and co-operative societies to Babri Masjid. She was concerned about the growing population and its impact on the economic growth. She not only propagated methods for controlling population but also voiced her concern about the sensitive issues on many occasions. She also spoke in support of the deprived sections of the society.

She was elected as the Deputy Chairman of Rajya Sabha and during the felicitations most of the leaders, cutting across party lines praised her. Dipen Ghosh remarked, "Rajya Sabha is known to get stormy and rowdy but Pratibha Tai with her quiet, soft nature will be able to render peace here whenever the need arises". Tai accepted the felicitations and said, "We have always tried to preserve the dignity and decorum during the discussions in the House. Therefore my task is not going to be difficult...." Once in chair, Tai conducted the proceedings effectively and impartially. Tai's mature handling was the outcome of her inherent strength which is a quality of a seasoned politician. Tai's tenure as Deputy Chairman was indeed remarkable. S. Gurupadaswamy said, "She was not only astute but also charming. There were occasions when the opposition entered into confrontation with her, but all these parliamentary skirmishes ended in good humor". P. Shiv Shankar said, "Though a diminutive figure, the exterior being soft, her interior had been very strong, she had handled the house in the most tempestuous of times and her handling was so adept that it undoubtedly infused a great confidence in one and all".

Tai—the Member of Parliament

Tai was given a ticket for contesting the sixth Lok Sabha elections from Amaravati and she won with a huge margin of 55,481 votes and was sworn in as the Member of Parliament on 9 July 1991. The Congress came to power and formed the Government, Dr. Manmohan Singh was the Finance Minister and Narasimha Rao was the Prime Minister. When Dr. Manmohan Singh presented the Budget, Tai complimented but also added that, "this Budget does not recommend any solution or provision to counter the dangers of increasing population". She was never the one to accept things as they were and was always trying to look proactively at the growth graph of the nation. When the demand for grants for Agriculture, Food and Rural Development Ministry was being debated she said, "I think we can propose this change and ask the Reserve Bank to allow the Urban Cooperative Banks to provide finance for agriculture as well".

Consequent to the Babri Masjid demolition, a No Confidence Motion was introduced in the Parliament in 1992. Tai said, "If we are all sincere and honest to our oath of allegiance, we should not demolish any temple or any mosque. We should rather try to bring peace and harmony in the country".

Tai was deeply stirred by the large scale disaster caused by the earthquake in Latur on 30 September 1993. She was concerned about institutionalisation of measures which could mitigate the loss of life and property in future.

In 1995, Tai was invited to the 'World Conference for Women'. While speaking on the occasion, Tai voiced her sentiments about women's empowerment. She had always been vociferous about issues which concern women. During a debate on agriculture it was Tai who highlighted the silent contribution of women in 'Green Revolution', she asked for concessions for women farmers as they too were a part of the weaker section, and her demand was immediately accepted. It was at Tai's instance that a committee of governors was set up in 2008 to make recommendations for the socio-economic empowerment of women.

Flight to Governorship

In 1996, after having savored a high profile political career for several decades, Tai decided to stay away from limelight, but the Congress leadership was firm not to let Tai's experience dissipate. Consequently, she was offered the Governorship of Rajasthan. On the insistence of Congress Party, Tai accepted the offer. The state was governed by Vasundhara Raje of Bharatiya Janata Party. Tai discharged her duties meticulously, impartially and in the best interest of the State.

She was the head of the State of Rajasthan, Chancellor of all State Universities and Chairperson of the West Zone Cultural Center. She encouraged diverse activities and addressed also the 'International Conference on Exploration and Utilization of Moon', inaugurated the 'National Conference of Association of Plastic Surgeons of India', encouraged 'Aao Gaon Chale,' a rural health project and a rally against 'Bhroon Hatya' (foeticide).

She interacted with people below poverty line, addicts, deprived and destitute women, war widows etc. Due to her efforts, War Widows' Hostel and Rehabilitation Centre in Jaipur again became operational. In order to give thrust to primary healthcare in the backward locales of Rajasthan namely, Barmer, Banswara, Bharatpur, Jhalawar and Sikar, Tai initiated a proposal based on the 'Parinche Valley' project of Pune District wherein a female 'Community Health Volunteer' is trained and equipped to provide health services and education at the village level, especially to rural women. She evolved a scheme named 'Mahila Swayam Siddha Kendra' to provide temporary housing, education and vocational training to widows and also established two schools for tribal girls and boys in the tribal belt of Udaipur. In pursuance with her commitment to 'eradication of social evils', she organized a colloquium on 'De-addiction, eradication of social evils, illiteracy and poverty'. In Raj Bhavan, she went through the program for next day every night to ensure that the needs and tastes of the guests were well taken care of.

In June 2007, she resigned from the post of Governor to head towards the highest office.

And then—The President of India

Dr. Kalam's tenure as the President of India was coming to an end. Speculations, as to who would be the next Head of the State were rampant. While the Congress was engrossed in identifying a candidate who would be acceptable to the left, BJP was contemplating on the candidature of Bhairon Singh Shekhawat; the third front was appealing for the continuation of Dr. Abdul Kalam. Bhairon Singh Shekhawat announced his decision to contest as an independent candidate. Dr. Abdul Kalam made it clear that he was not keen to recontest. Congress President Sonia Gandhi announced the name of Smt. Pratibha Devisingh Patil. Tai filed her nomination on 30 June 2007. As expected she won the election with 6,38,116 votes as against 3,31,306 votes of Bhairon Singh Shekhawat. She was indeed going to be the First Woman President of India and the First Woman Commander-in-Chief of the Indian Armed Forces. Tai took oath at 14:30 hrs in the Central Hall of the Parliament on 25 July 2007.

In her address, shortly after taking oath as President, Smt. Pratibha Patil described herself as the republic's "first servant" and said her sincere endeavour would be to live up to the high expectations of the people who elected her to the top post. She was given "national salute" by the President's bodyguards.

Earlier, setting in motion a series of ceremonial drills before the swearing-in ceremony, the Military Secretary to the President, Maj. Gen. Vinod Chopra, went to Smt. Pratibha Patil's 9 South Avenue residence and invited her and her husband to the Rashtrapati Bhavan. After the President's Bodyguards gave a national salute to Dr. Kalam, the outgoing President accompanied Smt. Pratibha Patil to Parliament House, led by the horse-mounted bodyguards. They were received at the gate by Rajya Sabha Deputy Chairman K. Rahman Khan, Lok Sabha Speaker Somnath Chatterjee and Chief Justice K.G. Balakrishnan.

The Twelfth President of India and the first Woman President Smt. Pratibha Devisingh Patil was now the new incumbent of the magnificent Rashtrapati Bhavan. The journey which started in 1962 in Jalgaon as a young political aspirant attained its zenith in 2007 in New Delhi. But for Tai, "The journey has just begun".

Notes: *All references are from:*

'An Inspirational Journey: Pratibha Devisingh Patil—The first Woman President of India, coauthors—Rasika Chaube and Dr. Chhaya Mahajan 2010, India. S. Chand and Company on behalf of Shram Sadhana Delhi.

Section–II
Initiatives

It Took a Woman…
to Empower Other Women…

> "We never know how high we are
> Till we are called to rise;
> And then, if we are true to plan,
> Our statures touch the skies."
> —*Emily Dickinson*

> "In India, we have had success stories of women moving out of poverty as a result of literacy movements.… Imparting education to women and girls is important for bringing about social change and for the full development of societies."
> —*Smt. Pratibha Patil*

In a time of great social prejudice against women, Smt. Pratibha Patil joined politics as a Congress Party worker and made a remarkable place for herself in an age of male dominance. She established a firm foundation for herself by excelling in academics and her background in political science and law was the shaping force behind her interest in women and the weaker sections of society. Politics seemed the obvious course for her to transform her avocations into constructive policy. However, once politics gave her a position of pre-eminence and power, she chose to use the platform to address certain areas that were fundamentally problematic in the Indian social fabric. In particular, the situation of women loomed large above all others. It occurred to Smt. Pratibha Patil that it would, indeed, be well nigh impossible for India to achieve true progress if the position of women in our nation remained at a status quo. If women were suppressed, exploited and down-trodden, then half of India's population was in a backward and pitiful condition. Therefore, if India were to be put on the road to true progress that must be initiated from path-breaking change being brought to the women of our nation. Starting from this premise, Smt. Pratibha Patil has evolved a strategy to affect long-term and holistic change, change from a grass-root level, change that can be measured and monitored, change that will bring in its wake the real progress that every worthwhile citizen of our nation has yearned to see.

The Catalysts

In a predominantly male world, if a woman could find a place of pre-eminence, there had to be a person or more than one person responsible for empowering her. It is not surprising that the credit for the first step towards empowering young Pratibha came from her own mother. With a foresight rare for the day and time in which she lived, she took an assurance from her husband before she passed away, that he would educate their only daughter, Pratibha. Once she proved her academic excellence, there were several avenues that opened up before her.

Smt. Pratibha Patil joined politics in response to Chief Minister Yashwantrao Chavan's rousing invitation to all educated women to serve the nation. Thus at the tender age of 27, Smt. Pratibha Patil began her career as an MLA (Member of Legislative Assembly). The year was 1962. A Marathi daily "Gavkari" declared prophetically that "it was the beginning of a new leadership".[1] After actively participating in state politics for two and a half decades, Smt. Pratibha Patil entered the Rajya Sabha first and then Lok Sabha in 1991. It is to her credit that she never lost an election. This one fact alone is sufficient to be a source of inspiration to the women of our nation: it is possible for a woman to survive even in the turbulent world of politics. Having been selected to serve as Governor of Rajasthan in 2004, she held that post until elected to be the First Woman President of India. The role was almost iconic as she became a "symbol of a changing India of the 21st century".[2]

Active social and political campaigner of the times, Sonusingh Anna Patil felt that by joining politics young Pratibha Patil could do something constructive for women. With her inclination towards community work, there was a consensus among the elders that young Pratibha Patil would make an inspiring woman-leader for the feminine half of the Indian population. Encouraged by her brother Abba Saheb—who felt that only a woman could understand and sincerely support the cause of women—she was confident that their trust in her was not misplaced and she, in response, took up the call. Straining against the restrictions and unfair boundaries placed on young girls growing up at the time, yet simultaneously conscious of her own good fortune in being permitted a proper education, it birthed in her deep inner being, a resolve to work for the emancipation and granting of greater liberties to women.

The Beginning

Sonusingh Anna Patil proposed that young Pratibha address the 'Mahasabha' at Chalisgaon—a forum through which the value of education for women could be made known. The year was 1960. The theme was 'The Importance of Education for Women'. Her father, Nanasaheb, instilled in her a deep regard for the education that she had been privileged to receive and encouraged her to hold out the baton to other women in India. He believed that if anyone could, Pratibha could. In contemplating permitting his only daughter to enter the dubious realm of politics, he had remarked rather thoughtfully, "I must fortify and strengthen her wings so that she too can soar high."[3] He had every intention of keeping his word to his dying wife: he would not differentiate between his sons and his daughter in the matter of education!

Although her foray into public space had a tentative beginning, it built into her the confidence necessary to take one's spot in the glare of politics. This was a defining moment in her life as she discovered her place in the sun. Her speech was powerfully delivered and had a profound impact on all those who were present. In fact, it did more than that: it set the stage for her public debut into politics. As Anna (Sonusingh) had anticipated, she would lead by example. If the women of the nation were to progress, it would take a woman of fearless courage to show the way. This woman that destiny had picked for the job was Smt. Pratibha Patil.

Nanasaheb continued to encourage her, especially when the then Chief Minister of Maharashtra, Yashwantrao Chavan appealed to women to enter into the political arena. He felt that among the most deserving of women candidates was Smt. Pratibha Patil. Her genuine interest in developing as a leader would propel her to the very forefront of leadership. It was a stroke of good fortune that at the same time as Smt. Pratibha Patil stood at the threshold of her life, Yashwantrao Chavan was at the helm of political affairs in Maharashtra. A man of incisive political acumen, he was able to see that the time was then ripe to draw women into the mainstream of India, particularly, educated women. He was able to envisage the immense potential that lay untapped by leaving women out, and he desired to turn this situation around. It was his expressed commitment that "educated and committed women will be given preference" in the forthcoming Assembly elections.[4]

She stood for elections first from the constituency of Jalgaon and won almost effortlessly. This is the first of a long series of elections that Smt. Pratibha Patil won, having the rare distinction of never losing an election that she contested. After she made her electoral speech, the local newspaper 'Gavkari' declared that this was the "beginning of a new leadership."[5] Of course no one knew it, but this was her first tryst with destiny that was to lead her all the way to the highest position of our nation, as its premier citizen, taking her to the path-breaking role of becoming the first woman President of India.

During her tenure as MLA, Smt. Pratibha Patil had ample opportunities to observe first-hand the huge gender divide in the very fabric of Indian social life. Although women bear almost all responsibility for meeting the basic needs of the family, they are systematically denied the resources, information and freedom of action they need to fulfill this responsibility.

The vast majority of India's poor are women. In many instances, the men spend the major part of their income on themselves, and that often on alcohol. Most of these poor women are illiterate. The combination of being a woman and that compounded with being illiterate puts them in a doubly vulnerable position. Of the millions of school-age children not in school, the majority are girls. Where resources are scant, they are spent on necessities. If stretched further, they are utilized on the male child.

It disturbed her deeply that society made use of tradition and age-old customs to suppress women and keep every privilege from them. Dowry was still rampant and it distressed her to see the anxiety of families desirous to get their daughters married, but troubled by their inability to meet the groom's financial demands. Young Pratibha Patil made it a point to insist that no dowry would be given in her own wedding.

In addition, the circumstances of poverty impinge on women even more harshly than they do on men. The world food price crisis continues to have a severe impact on women. While it is customary around the world for most people to eat two or three times a day, distressingly a significant percentage of women eat only once, and this is for the obvious reason of scarcity. When poverty is intense, many women deny themselves even that one meal to ensure that their children are fed. These women are already suffering the effects of even more severe malnutrition, which inevitably will be their children's fate as well. The impact of this crisis could be felt by a developing nation for many years. The realization that came to Smt. Pratibha Patil from her interactions with women across the country during her career is that it is possible to stop this vicious cycle of poverty and oppression from continuing through the generations. But it would take a huge effort and her resolve to move with this herculean task made her ponder that she would have to carry it out simultaneously at several levels. It would necessitate actions being carried out at the most individualistic levels and checked at the highest levels of governance. The leader in her asserted that for real transformation to take place, change would have to be initiated through the entire fabric of the Indian social and political scenario. Fundamentally, this change would centre on empowering women. Studies show that when women are supported and empowered, all of society benefits. Their families are healthier, more children go to school, agricultural productivity improves and incomes increase. In short, communities are strengthened. For Smt. Pratibha Patil, this was a dream that needed a destination.

And for her, the road map to stem the discrepancy women have to be empowered through financial independence. In turn, financial independence could be more easily achieved through education, although she also saw that economic sufficiency can be additionally augmented by financing women in small scale cottage and industrial projects.

With these basic core principles established firmly, it was now left for Smt. Pratibha Patil to work out a viable strategy to bring her vision to the drawing board in order to make the plans that would effect change. Deeply conscious that a set of circumstances had conspired to empower her, from her late mother's insistence on her getting a good education, to the trust of Sonusingh Patil, the support of her family, and the faith reposed in her by her father, her aunt under whose tender care all siblings grew up and her brother, Smt. Pratibha Patil felt this was something that she must pay forward by doing whatever lay within her capacity, to empower the women of India. It became the guiding principle of her career. In every post she held, she made sure to do what she could, to ameliorate the suffering of people, in particular, the women. Being woman, the task was both easy and daunting. Easy, because she could empathise with her fellow-women in their helplessness, bound as they were, by the multiple shackles of womanhood, poverty, illiteracy, suppression and meaningless tradition. Daunting, because the task was onerous and time-consuming, deep-rooted and far-reaching. But not one to shy away from a challenge, Smt. Pratibha Patil boldly advanced to take it on.

Among her many enterprise that were begun towards this end, the following are the most significant initiatives that heralded a gradual transformation in the social fabric for women in general and brought a change in thinking in the national ethos towards woman centric development in particular.

Shram Sadhana

In 1972, Smt. Pratibha Patil started a trust called 'Shram Sadhna' which was dedicated to providing low cost hostels exclusively for working women. This, a pioneering effort as she was moved by empathy on noting the difficulties faced by young women coming from small towns to work in India's huge metropolitan cities. The idea could only germinate from concern and the commitment towards woman's progress. Perhaps, a small step but a worthy one for women who brave the world by leaving the secure confines of their homes in quest of a livelihood and identity. Her daughter, Jyoti, now manages the hostels for working women in Pune and Delhi. Both her children are now involved in providing safe environments for women in urban cities.

Zila Mahila Gruharakshak Dal

During the Chinese invasion, Smt. Pratibha Patil took the initiative to start up the 'Zila Mahila Gruharakshak Dal' to augment the security services, and set an example by passing all the requisite tests and being appointed as the commander. She delivered a stirring address to the women to inspire them to serve the nation in its hours of need. All members were trained in the use of rifles and participated in a daily morning drill. Smt. Pratibha Patil herself was conversant with handling a rifle. She motivated women not only to be strong in self-defense and protect oneself but also to be their own masters. From Smt. Pratibha Patil, this was a significant message for the meek and submissive women.

Mahila Arthik Vikas Mahamandal

The plight of poor and illiterate women of Maharashtra saddled with alcoholic husbands, moved her to create opportunities for them to earn their own livelihood. This culminated in the establishment of the 'Mahila Arthik Vikas Mahamandal' (Women's Financial Development Corporation). The idea met with opposition from a few cabinet colleagues, but Smt. Pratibha Patil was determined to go ahead with her plans to aid the helpless women of her state. Once she had the Cabinet approval, she went ahead in her attempts to create job opportunities for women, particularly those below the poverty line. Smt. Pratibha Patil was convinced that if she could not use her position for the upliftment of women, then her entire career would have been fruitless. The models she established were highly successful. It wasn't long before other state governments began to follow suit.[6]

Smt. Pratibha Patil also argued fervently for setting up an all Women's Bank that would be "operated by women, for women."[7] It was not an easy task getting the government and the Reserve Bank of India to initiate the enterprise, but eventually, after much persuasion, the banks were established, making resources and finance available to small business enterprises run by women.

She also established a cooperative sugar factory, she wanted Mahila (Women) Shareholders to boost she economic condition of women farmers.

Five-Point Formula for Women Empowerment

Smt. Pratibha Patil was constantly thinking of ways and means to improve the position of women in our country. It seemed clear to her that the most infallible method for women to be truly liberated was through financial independence. Towards this end, she came up with a five-point formula for women:

- For economic well-being, it is not only important for women to be busy in work, but also to be self-confident and efficient in their work.
- 'Technical Schools' for women should be established in rural areas.
- There should be efficient implementation of laws relating to women.
- Organization of exhibition and sale of homemade products by women.
- Participation of women in different processes.[8]

The issue of empowering women through financial means has always been close to her heart. Hence, when her proposal to start the 'Mission for Socio-Economic Empowerment of Women' was approved by the UPA Government, it brought the greatest satisfaction to Smt. Pratibha Patil. One of the primary charters of this mission is to make available microfinance at exceedingly low interest rates to women who exist below the poverty line. The basic premise underlying this provision is that women are born expert managers of finance. They exhibit all the skills of financial management in running their homes economically and with expert attention to detail. If their resource base is expanded, they are bound to show great expertise in the management of increased revenues as well.

Smt. Pratibha Patil also lamented that blind faith in religion and superstition were holding women back from truly breaking forth into real progress. She firmly believed that the key for them to be truly liberated was in improving their financial condition. However, Smt. Pratibha Patil also understood that before financial independence could become a reality, women had to be put out of their ignorance and blind adherence to tradition that was programmed to keep them in bondage. It was clear to her that the only means to achieve this was through education. Education had done it for her. And education would do it again, for other women. To lift women out of their drudgery and pitiful conditions she planned a two-fold approach: financial aid and education.

In 1989, Smt. Pratibha Patil led a delegation to Australia to participate in the 'World Women Parliamentarians Meet'. In 1995, she attended the 'World Women's Conference' in Beijing, where she was asked to address the gathering on behalf of India. Smt. Pratibha Patil spoke on the power that could be harnessed if only women would unite. Recalling a poem from her childhood, she went on to recite it: "If all the rivers in the world were one river, what a great river it would be, if all the trees in the world were one tree, what a great tree it would be". Stretching the metaphor to women, she went on to add "If all the women in the world would speak in one voice against terrorism and war and in favour of peace, what a great voice it would be."[9] Needless to say, her comments met with resounding approval as the audience broke into a thunderous applause. In favour of the health of the family Smt. Pratibha Patil has famously been quoted as saying that she believes that "Men and women are two wheels of a chariot. If one wheel is weak then the chariot finds it difficult to progress; so will the family, society and the nation. If the chariot has to move smoothly and progress in the right direction both the wheels have to be equal and should move together in perfect harmony."[10]

Smt. Pratibha Patil always seized any opportunity to champion the cause of women. She effectively used her position to leverage any concessions or subsidies that may have been available to serve the cause of improving the position of women. She vouched for the contribution of women to the Green Revolution and vociferously spoke for the seventy-five percent subsidy on drip and sprinkler irrigation systems that were being given to the weaker sections of society to be extended to women as well. She contended that women were arguably a 'weaker section' of society as per our constitution. Her earnest presentation of the case for women as deserving candidates for such a subsidy won the hearts of all those present, including the then Minister for Agriculture, Balram Jhakar, who accepted her suggestion.

Smt. Pratibha Patil took her efforts to ameliorate the condition of women a step further when she assumed the office of Governor of Rajasthan, and eventually, of President of India. In 2008, she initiated the setting up of a Committee of Governors to study and make recommendations for the "socio-economic empowerment of women."[11] The findings and suggestions of this committee finally led to the Government of India's decision to establish a Mission for the Socio-Economic Empowerment of Women. The higher the position that Smt. Pratibha Patil achieved, the greater the momentum of her efforts directed towards the issue closest to her heart—the upliftment of women of her nation.

Smt. Pratibha Patil delighted in interacting with the '*aam aadmi*'—the ordinary people of India. She'd take the time to tell them of the great big world out there, and how they could be a part of it, if only they would rise up to the occasion, and face the challenges along the way. She used these opportunities that brought her in touch with the far and distant, neglected and forgotten folk of India, to bring them a glimpse of another reality, so far, yet so close.

Outreach to Widows

Smt. Pratibha Patil reached out to the war widows of Rajasthan, in a truly effective manner during her tenure as Governor of that state. She made a genuine effort to solve the problems that some of them faced with various government departments. She wrote around twelve hundred letters to the widows listed in Rajasthan, resolving pending issues of almost four hundred of them. She revitalized the defunct War Widows' Hostel and Rehabilitation Centre in Jaipur, meant to be a safe haven for widows.

Mahila Swayam Siddha Kendra

Another effort made with women at the forefront of the thrust was a scheme called 'Mahila Swayam Siddha Kendra' a proposal for the growth and progress of the impoverished women. This project was directed at offering housing, education and skill-based training for destitute women, and widows in particular, so that they could earn a livelihood and thereby dignity could be restored to them. Smt. Pratibha Patil made sure that a sizeable piece of land of around fifty acres was set aside for this noble purpose in Rajasthan.

Healthcare Ingenuity

An extremely worthy cause that got Smt. Pratibha Patil's total support was the initiation of an ingenious idea for healthcare at the village level, a project started and successfully run by the 'Foundation for Research in Community Health'. It involved a unique woman-based approach to rural health, whereby a lady 'Community Health Volunteer' gets trained and equipped to serve other rural women in the area of healthcare. Smt. Pratibha Patil was of the opinion that seventy percent of the healthcare issues in rural India can be handled quite easily and successfully by women trained in basic medical procedures. The trained women could go a step further by increasing awareness of simple hygiene among their fellow-villagers and also expose false ideas and widely practiced social evils. The Government of Rajasthan saw the potential of such an idea to provide inexpensive solutions to rural health problems while simultaneously educating the village populace through utilization of the woman-power. It approved the implementation of this project in five very backward areas of the state.

Another example of her pragmatic approach to the long-standing issues that plague Indian society was demonstrated when Smt. Pratibha Patil was Deputy Minister of Health in Maharashtra. She arranged for lady doctors to head the Primary Health Centres in rural areas in order to increase the comfort level of women-patients. This was generally found to be a very sensible move on her part. Rural women who tended to shy away from male doctors lost out on some great government sponsored programmes. They could now benefit from these to the complete extent of the original intent of such schemes.

First Citizen

In 2007, Smt. Pratibha Patil was elected as the First Woman President of India and, consequently, became the First Woman Commander-in-Chief of the Indian Armed Forces.

The Chief Minister of NCT Delhi, Smt. Sheila Dikshit commented that "Shrimati Pratibha Patil's election as the Head of State of the world's largest democracy symbolizes the empowerment of every woman."[12] Laying the foundation for her role as India's first woman President by remembering the brave women of the past who had led the struggle against foreign rule shoulder to shoulder with our men—women like Rani Lakshmibai, Begum Hazrat Mahal and Rani Chennamma—she made plain her agenda to make a definitive contribution towards the betterment of the condition of the women of our country. She made it clear that education was close to her heart as was also the cause of the thousands of disadvantaged women of our nation. "Empowerment of women is particularly important to me as I believe this leads to the empowerment of the nation."[13] The new President of India had spoken once again from her heart, revealing those issues that were plainly at the centre of her concerns.

Smt. Pratibha Patil openly admitted that she always preferred to take up the portfolio of Social Welfare Ministry because it gave her an opportunity to do something constructive for the disadvantaged strata of society. In her own words, this ministry gave her access to the "marginalized, the physically challenged, the deprived, which includes fifty percent of the population, that is women."[14] It was through this channel that she felt she could best serve the most deprived and suppressed in our society.

Microfinance

From her knowledge of women as being excellent managers of finance, Smt. Pratibha Patil pushed the cause of microfinance for women at every level possible. She truly believed that the key to alleviating the poverty of families lay in providing financial assistance to the women. Her emphasis on this aspect of growth was reported in the press: "The President, Ms. Pratibha Devisingh Patil, today stressed the need for "growth with equity" which can be enabled by encouraging Micro, Small and Medium Enterprises (MSMEs)—the second largest employer after agriculture."[15]

The potential for the involvement of women in these sectors is huge and hence Smt. Pratibha Patil constantly emphasized on the role that MSMEs could play in improving the lifestyle of the population, the rural population in particular. Needless to say, the scope to employ women in such industry is also great and this in turn will impact financial independence of women, prosperity of the family leading to economic growth in society as a whole.

"To meet the objective of growth with equity, it is essential that there is an enabling eco-system for such enterprises (MSMEs) to grow and prosper," President Pratibha Patil said, after giving away national awards for excellence to the medium, small and tiny units.[15] Smt. Pratibha Patil never missed a chance to make known the programs closest to her heart. At every opportunity, she emphasized the cause of women, believing with all her heart that the key to India's development lies in the progress of our women.

"Finance should be made available for (self-help groups of) women for starting their own businesses so that they can become economically independent. Dalit women should also go ahead on the path of social progress without any sense of inferiority."[16] Every encounter with distressed women had a profound impact on Smt. Pratibha Patil—she never forgot it. It played upon her mind until she could formulate a solution and then she relentlessly worked towards making it a reality.

On one occasion she met a group of women from Manmad. These women related to her the severity of their financial crisis, as Maharashtra was reeling under a fierce drought. Various circumstances conspired to deprive them of government aid and opportunities for work. Their circumstances were such that they could not work even if they so desired. Smt. Pratibha Patil could not rest until she came up with an idea: she envisaged a government sponsored corporation that would extend financial aid to the under-privileged women so that they could set up their own little businesses and sustain their families. As individual families prospered, so in turn would the nation. It was this concept that eventually evolved into the 'Mahila Arthik Vikas Mahamandal'. It began rather tentatively after much debate and discussion in the cabinet and the remarkable persuasive skills of Smt. Pratibha Patil. She persevered in pushing her idea with the then Chief Minister of Maharashtra, Vasantrao Naik, who did not relent easily but agreed only after the proposal was discussed thoroughly. The 'Mahila Arthik Vikas Mahamandal' was a resounding success in Maharashtra and other states began to look upon it as a successful developmental model for the upliftment of women. The success of the program ratified the high esteem that Smt. Pratibha Patil held women in. It proved the women worthy of the trust that she had reposed in their abilities. "A woman is blessed with inborn management skills," she had once remarked, "which help her in managing her home. If given an opportunity she can get recognition as an able and expert manager."[17]

On Reversing the Erroneous Representations of Women

Smt. Pratibha Patil has increasingly reported being deeply agitated by the derogatory representation of women by the media in India. The lowering of standards in advertising troubled her mind. As with everything that left its lingering mark on her, she could not help but do something about it. She galvanized the support of all the women MPs regardless of their political affiliation, and prepared a memorandum voicing her displeasure and commenting on the impact such imaging of women could have on future generation of Indians. She had the complete support of all the women, and even some of the leaders, like Shri L.K. Advani, declared on the floor of the House that they agreed with her protests wholeheartedly. This memorandum was presented to the then President, Shri Shankar Dayal Sharma, who forwarded it to the Minister of Information and Broadcasting.

Smt. Pratibha Patil has always been a "silent crusader",[18] one who believes in action without any of the usual dramatic overtures that typically accompany efforts of amelioration of any kind, in public circles. As public attention was not what she was after, she remained unaffected, by its presence or absence. The only thing that mattered was if she was able to use her offices to help those in such dire need.

Spreading Awareness

As President of India, Smt. Pratibha Patil approached the problem of the suppression of the Indian woman with a multi-pronged strategy, maximizing the power potential of the office that she occupied for the betterment of the women of our country. She made use of her tenure as President to draw attention to the multitude of women's issues plaguing the female—half of the populace, with a passion and a sensitivity that only a woman could have mustered.

Writing in 'The Hindu' on the 15th of Jan., 2012, Rajesh Ahuja reported on the emphasis that President Smt. Pratibha Patil put on bringing women into the mainstream at every level of society, political and economic, as "equal partners".[19] She spoke of making young girls aware of their rights even from childhood and highlighted the need to change the paradigm by teaching girls judo and karate in schools as this would make them capable of defending themselves, while increasing their self-confidence. She further stressed the need to take every measure to make women feel "strong and self-reliant".[19]

Smt. Pratibha Patil continues to emphasise that empowerment of women is of prime importance to provide a solid base for the country's integral development. Addressing an international Symposium on 'Empowerment of Women and the Girl Child' to commemorate the 175th birth anniversary of noted Urdu poet and social reformer Maulana Khawaja Altaf Hussain 'Hali Panipati' who lived here, she said that a peaceful society could be created if the energy of women was properly utilized. "We have to create an environment where women are brought to the mainstream whether, it be the family, society, and at the national level as 'equal partners,'" she asserted.[19]

On this occasion Smt. Pratibha Patil also took the opportunity to voice her concern over the latest census figures that reveal an imbalanced sex ratio, with the number of girl babies born being fewer than male children. She said that the government would be notified that measures had to be initiated to check this anomaly before it had serious repercussions.

She also made a point of congratulating Haryana Chief Minister, noting in public that he had started several schemes for the empowerment of women and of the girl child, and the results were already being demonstrated in some areas such as a correction of the sex ratio, although, she acknowledged that there was yet much to accomplish.

Smt. Pratibha Patil was so convinced that the education of women was key to the progress of our nation that she said on one occasion: "If we make women literate, they will be self-reliant and the beneficial impact on society will be manifold; the rate of infant mortality comes down and the quality of life improves. Also, when women are taught how to read and write, they in turn begin to send their girl child to school, breaking the pattern of social gender discrimination, which is a strong barrier to girls' education. It is important that in schools, girls must get equal opportunity to study and acquire necessary skills and knowledge. Specific education programmes with targets should be launched for education of girls."[20]

Governor's Conference

In 2008, she convened a Governor's Conference at Rashtrapati Bhavan to discuss and debate the modalities of state level empowerment of women. The purpose of this conference was to enlist the involvement of people across government, financial and educational institutions and the women themselves to study the needs, examine the problems, brainstorm solutions and then finally, to engage responsible bodies to make sure that the resolutions become a reality. To Smt. Pratibha Patil goes the credit for initiating actions that would redress a multitude of serious problems being faced by women from across the length and breadth of the country. Caught in the frustrating red tape of our system, but for her initiatives and determination, many of them might have languished in their difficult situations and never had their issues resolved.

The Conference held in 2008 had for its study and perusal the broad focus of:

- Identifying and prioritizing areas for speedy socio-economic development of women.
- Identifying gaps in existing current socio-economic programmes.
- Recommending faster implementation of schemes and programmes, both State-sponsored and Centrally sponsored ones.
- Suggesting methods for effective coordination between central and state governments in implementation and monitoring of women's developmental schemes.
- Recommending means for the eradication of social evils that preempt women's development.
- Considering the establishment of a national level institutionalized mechanism to monitor the implementation of gender-equality programs.
- Setting up of mechanism for performance appraisal and audits of programs related to women.

- Considering the possibility of establishing an apex body to strengthen existing agencies that provide financial support to women's Self-Help Groups (SHGs).
- Utilization of media to increase awareness of gender-related social evils.
- Reviewing of text-book content from school level upwards, to eliminate gender-biased material.
- Educational institutions urged to introduce more vocational courses for women to train them for employment in emerging employment sectors.
- Examine the potential of Governors in promoting women's socio-economic development and empowerment.

Through its agenda, the Conference conveyed Smt. Pratibha Patil's urgent desire to effectively transform the lives of the oppressed women of the nation, and to use every mechanism available in her power to do so. The President's office sent out a strong message that recommendations were to be turned into actions at the earliest. Change was the need of the hour. No more time was to be wasted.

"In India," she said, "women play an important role in agricultural operations. Sixty percent are engaged in the farm work and contribute in a big way to food production and economic growth. Women have also increased their participation in high-end vocations." So with this high level of economic participation, the President held that economic planning must change to where it "promotes gender equality."[21]

The intensity of Smt. Pratibha Patil's approach towards this issue was so forceful that the deliberations of the Committee of Governors led to the establishment of a National Empowerment Mission that would focus on the implementation of every possible means to empower women. The Conference also spelled out its vision which is summed up in the following:

- Holistic empowerment of women.
- Eradication of exploitation, discrimination and social evils.
- Creation of an enabling environment for achieving full potential.

- Ensuring rightful share in allocation of resources and decision making.
- Making women equal partners in family, society and the nation building process.

It is plain to see that the vision of the Conference is highly utopian and will take a total transformation of ideology at the grass-root level before it can become a reality. However, it is also highly commendable that the First Woman President decided to make a meaningful beginning in the direction of giving women their rightful place as equal stake-holders and beneficiaries in every aspect of life. The Mission was officially launched by Smt. Pratibha Patil, the President of India, on the 8th of March, 2010, the Centenary Year of International Women's Day.

It was probably a highlight of her career, desirous as she had always been, to see the plight of women improved. In her inaugural address she stated what she firmly believed that the "empowerment of women is crucial for the empowerment of our nation."[22] With the launch of the mission Smt. Pratibha Patil felt confident that the pro-active stance of the government could make the timely delivery of "women-centric and women-related programs" a reality in the foreseeable future.[23]

Smt. Pratibha Patil emphasized the truth that the amelioration of women's problems would take a concerted effort of all those involved—the state and central governments, NGOs, civil society and every citizen of this great country. The transformation would have to take place at several levels of thought and real-time changes. "If social justice and social equality has to establish then there is a need to bring about ideological revolution accompanied by economic programme."[24]

Present Status

As a result of the efforts of Smt. Pratibha Patil, the National Mission Authority was constituted with the PM at the helm as Chairman. Missions were set up in 18 states and a State Resource Centre for Women was established in 6 states.

A 3-year plan of action was drawn up with two major areas of focus:
1. A high level committee was set up by Government of India under the chairmanship of Smt. Rupa Paul, former justice of the Supreme

Court of India to study the status of women and suggest policy interventions based on assessment of women's needs.
2. The provisions of the Rashtriya Mahila Kosh, established in 1993 as a Credit Fund for Women, was to expand its services by:
    (a) Extending collateral-free micro-finance and livelihood support to women.
    (b) Enhancement of its corpus from ₹ 100 crores to ₹ 500 crores.
    (c) Restructuring in order to serve the women more effectively.

Initiatives

The list of initiatives begun by Smt. Pratibha Patil that were directly related to the advancement of women are many. To list a few path-breaking ones:

- The most significant one was the convening of the Conference of Governors at which a consensus was arrived at to set up the National Commission for Empowerment of Women. This move gave a major thrust to investigations of the condition of women at various levels and also to provision of solutions through different governmental and non-governmental avenues.
- As Smt. Pratibha Patil felt moved to do something to assist the wives of staff working on President's Estate to make them feel empowered. She set up small Self-Help Groups (SHGs) to mobilize the women to take up an occupation that suited their skill set. As a result, many women started earning a livelihood through the making of spices, vermin-compost, organic manure, running beauty parlours, manufacture of environment-friendly paper bags, etc.
- Smt. Pratibha Patil gave her strong support to the initiative of the Ministry of Health and Family Welfare in its Signature Campaign to 'Save the Girl Child'. Support coming from such a high level lends immense strength to a cause and helps it gain tremendous momentum.
- She decided to mark International Women's Day in 2009 with yet another pro-active measure—she opened up the Rashtrapati Bhavan to women from disadvantaged sections of society, making

it possible for women to approach her, interact with her, and receive her pragmatic counsel. Smt. Pratibha Patil apprised the ladies of various schemes like Self-Help Groups and advised them to seek employment as empowerment is the direct result of sound finances. She encouraged women to create the right atmosphere in their homes and to seize every opportunity to prove themselves.

Speaking at Indapur, she repeated this thought saying that women empowerment is the most necessary need of the hour. She said that the establishment of Self-Help Groups is one of the effective tools that has been established towards this end. The Self-Help Groups in various parts of the country have successfully undertaken projects like electricity distribution, milk business, among, others. Economic parity is important aspect in women empowerment, she said.[25]

- Smt. Pratibha Patil called for a meeting with the Chairpersons and Member Secretaries of the State Women's Commission in 2010. She motivated the ladies to work towards combating prevalent social evils, and keep up the fight against common plagues like domestic violence, female foeticide and child marriage. She encouraged the women workers by declaring her faith in them and her firm belief that the Women's Commissions should indeed act as "agents of social change".

- On one occasion, Smt. Pratibha Patil spotted a group of children belonging to construction workers engaged in work at Rashtrapati Bhavan. Moved by their obvious plight, she jumped right into action, setting up a crèche called 'Sopan' for the children of labourers working on the premises. 'Sopan' at any given time, has ten to fifteen children on its rolls. Children enrolled here are looked after well: they are given new clothes, wholesome food and medical attention (if required). They are also provided with pre-school education and well-equipped areas for recreation.

- The Tata Steel Company was among the first to galvanize their women into creating a group for women's empowerment. Named 'Tejaswini' the group of ten women ably led by Smt. Urmila Ekka comprises of women above the age of fifty from among the socioeconomically disadvantaged strata of society. The group's agenda includes the recognition of the skills and talents of the women, the development of these abilities and the provision of a platform for the demonstration of their strengths. Smt. Pratibha Patil met with the group and congratulated them on their pioneering service to the cause of women engaged in industry, so far a male-dominated domain. She also encouraged them to keep up the levels of determination, declaring that through sheer dint of hard work they could change the position of women in our country.

- It has always been possible in India to send one's complaints to the President of India as a last resort. Smt. Pratibha Patil saw the manual procedure to be slow and the cause of inordinate delay in redressal, making the system inefficacious. In 2009, after completing two years in office, she arranged for the system to be digitized and launched 'Helpline', the official online portal through which ordinary citizens can make known their grievances and requests to the highest office in the country. The system has been seen as a welcome extension of the democracy that we enjoy in India. Many denizens have made their problems known to the President's office and the President's Secretariat has duly resolved several of them.

  Cases of delays or non-payment of pension or arrears are frequently received and promptly dealt with. Among them: Mrs. Pramanik of West Bengal, Mrs. Tejam of Maharashtra, and Mrs. Dhanam. All of these women were facing issues with regard to the disbursement of their pensions. The matter was swiftly dealt with and the problem redressed once they contacted President Smt. Pratibha Patil through the portal.

  Even a matter of seemingly little significance was not ignored by Smt. Pratibha Patil a complaint regarding a blocked sewer that the civic authorities in Delhi were ignoring, was taken up and quickly resolved.

The clear message of Smt. Pratibha Patil seems to be that no matter is too large to handle nor any too insignificant to deserve the attention of the office. As the First Citizen, the President is committed to addressing any and all issues related to the citizens of the nation.

Smt. Pratibha Patil has set many a precedent to underscore the value of women operating in different arenas of life and to underscore their contribution to the nation as being of priceless value.

In a recent interview with Smriti Ramachandran that took place on the 15th of April, 2012, Smt. Pratibha Patil expressed her views on the need for the next generation to focus on nation-building in order to overcome many difficult challenges that confront us as a people. "She said it was imperative to usher in electoral reforms to maintain the country's healthy secular and democratic characteristics. Education, women's empowerment and focus on moral values should be at the core of the reforms. My message to youth is to strike a balance between consumerism and values", she remarked.[26]

Creating a Safe Environment for Our Women

Smt. Pratibha Patil was also concerned about the safety of women in Indian metropolitan cities as there has been a surge in the number of crimes committed against women. Speaking at a function in an educational institution at Lucknow, she remarked that the law enforcement agencies need to focus on the safety of women. While women were making strides towards financial independence, they had opened themselves up to other risks. Along with the importance of empowerment, these issues need to be addressed simultaneously, she said. Commenting further on the issue, Smt. Pratibha Patil said, "Families worry about the lack of security for women members of the family in India of the 21st Century. This deserves the fullest attention of law and order authorities. To create stable societies women need to be empowered. Societies which understand this are not only able to deal with the changes needed for it, but can mould change itself".[27]

Smt. Pratibha Patil was referring to the increase in crime against women in several metro cities. Women, especially those working until late hours, had become the victims of sexual crimes, like molestation and rape. In addition, the age-old problem of women battered by their husbands continues. While Women's Organizations can provide some help, the most important agent who can bring change in the lives of women, is women themselves. Only empowered women can save women from the ignominy of the harassment they have traditionally been the victims of. Growing urbanization must address the concomitant needs of working women, encouraging them to be independent while at the same time, looking after their safety-needs.

As one is aware, with growing urbanization, the security of women needs to be focused upon by all those concerned. In several metro cities, many women, especially working women, have been facing serious crimes against them, such as rape or molestation. Also several housewives are being battered in their homes by their husbands and they need to be helped out by women organizations. This would mean that women empowerment is very essential for women to assert themselves.[27]

Real People... Real Lives... Real Changes...

Madhu Kumari

Madhu Kumari, a national football player from Patna, was living a life of abject poverty, having struggled unsuccessfully to get a job. But for the timely intervention of Smt. Pratibha Patil, this saga of untold misery might have continued indefinitely. Smt. Pratibha Patil responded to a report in an English daily that depicted the pitiful condition of an individual who had once made the nation proud in the field of sport. Smt. Pratibha Patil ensured that the State Government created posts with reservations for sports persons and Madhu Kumari was one among the beneficiaries of the new provision.

"I have finally seen the light after wading through a tunnel for 15 long years. This has been possible only because of the President's interest in my case...only she could understand what a woman truly feels," a jubilant Madhu told 'The Hindu'.[28]

The footballer had lost her father when a child, and was being taken care of by her brother, a tea-vendor. But for Smt. Pratibha Patil's timely assistance, her life might have been crushed by despair, in spite of her contribution to the nation through her sporting talent. Such incidents go a long way in instilling hope in other struggling, yet aspiring stars.

Aparna Ghosh

Aparna Ghosh lost her husband in a freak shooting accident in West Bengal. Adding to the tragedy of her loss were her dire financial circumstances. Seeking justice from the authorities for thirteen long years and finding no help forthcoming, she sought redressal by writing to the President through her 'Helpline'. "I had written to the President on earlier occasions as well, but this time I received a response immediately," she said.[29] She was promptly given a job on compassionate grounds by the Govt. of West Bengal and she was relieved because of the immediate response of Smt. Pratibha Patil, the President of India.

Anita Munda

Anita Munda, a poor tribal woman from Jalpaiguri district of West Bengal had a unique predicament. Having secured 65% of marks in her Higher Secondary Examination, intelligent and desiring to study further, but crippled by the unfortunate circumstances of her family, she had been married to a poor struggling farm labourer. Her poverty-stricken parents were in no position to help her either. Hopeless of ever pursuing her dream of higher education, she threw in her lot with her labourer husband. Her story was featured in a newspaper and caught the attention of Smt. Pratibha Patil. She immediately got her office to spring into action. Anita was admitted to a college in her district and all fees were paid by the Govt. of West Bengal. Another dream was turned into a reality. Another life was spared the drudgery and frustration of an ambition unfulfilled.

Pinki Gupta

Enterprising Pinki Gupta from Chhattisgarh wrote to President Smt. Pratibha Patil sending along samples of her handmade products, crafted out of waste products like plastic bags and 'paan masala' pouches. She was highly impressed by the ingenuity displayed by the young lady. She considered the many levels of potential in the girl's creative enterprise: firstly, she had produced a useful product from waste; secondly, she had accomplished this without any training; and lastly, Smt. Pratibha Patil saw the immense possibilities in this, if only Pinki could train other women from small towns and villages. Here was the possibility for finance generation with little or no investment. Here was one solution to the problem that had been turning around in the mind of Smt. Pratibha Patil for a long time—how to empower the women of our country. The key to empowerment definitely lays in financial independence and in Pinki's creativity, she could see one possible means to helping women to achieve it, without much education, training or capital. She was invited to Rashtrapati Bhavan.

Commenting on the reason for inviting Pinki on this occasion, an official remarked, "The President is very particular about making women self-reliant and empowered. She has been persistently instructing government agencies and non-government organisations to ensure that women are given the necessary exposure, opportunities and skills that will help them come at par with men."[30]

The occasion was International Women's Day and there would be a plethora of Women's Organizations present. It would be an ideal opportunity to showcase Pinki's ingenuity. Smt. Pratibha Patil also introduced her to Secretaries of several ministries like the Women and Children's Ministry, Micro, Small and Medium Enterprises, Chemicals and Fertilizers and also a few representatives from industry to look into the economic potential of this unique idea. Pinki's work impressed many who were present and several came forward to partner with her in the area of entrepreneurship and job creation. A local NGO called TRIWE, dedicated to the development and education of tribes and rural women, conducted a series of training workshops for a number of villages under the banner of the Khadi and Village Industries Commission. The organizers introduced several other handicrafts to the women, like bag-weaving, candle-making, wood-carving and agarbatti making. In addition to other trainers, Pinki Gupta also demonstrated the crafts that she had been developing. Subsequent to this exposure, she applied for a loan to start up a small-scale industry of her own. The recognition that she received from President Smt. Pratibha Patil turned her life around completely. She now runs her own business and also trains other women to become independent through the creative use of ordinary materials around us.

Sangita Bauri, Sunita Mahato and Afsana Khatun

Today, Sangita Bauri, Sunita Mahato and Afsana Khatun are students sponsored by the National Child Labour Project and proud recipients of the National Bravery Award for 2010. Their story is a perfect example of how education can empower the lives of people, and as it did in this case, the lives of young girls. These girls were being coerced into early marriage by their parents, but resisted because of their love for studies. "I am very happy to see what these three girls have done to oppose a social evil like child marriage. These young school-going girls will be a source of inspiration for many others like them in and around their village," Smt. Pratibha Patil said, as she invited and met the three girls and their parents at Rashtrapati Bhavan.[31]

It was the National Child Labour Project who intervened and offered to help them continue their education. When Smt. Pratibha Patil found out about these brave and committed girls, it warmed her heart. Always one to encourage women to fight for education and independence, she publicly acclaimed their stand. The resultant attention they received from the local Panchayat and the Chief Minister's office took care of their financial needs. The national bravery award and the concomitant publicity has done much to spread the word against early marriage and the importance of taking a stand, regardless of one's age or gender, in favour of the enlightening power of education.

Padma Ruidas

Similar to this story is that of Padma Ruidas, a young girl from West Bengal. Enjoying her education, Padma was dismayed when her poor parents, daily wage earners, chose to get her married as they could no longer afford to send her to school. She appealed to President Smt. Pratibha Patil who immediately sent forth the help that was needed, timely and fortuitous. 'Prayas', a local NGO offered to sponsor her education in school and the district authorities helped her parents get employment. This was another story with a happy ending—a situation turned around because of Smt. Pratibha Patil's interest and action.

Roshni Devi

In a quite remarkable manner, life took a dramatic turn for Roshni Devi, a village Sarpanch from Haryana, when Smt. Pratiba Patil appreciated her for strong action against alcoholism, as she is also of the opinion that it is one of the social evils that is destroying the institution of the family in our nation. When Smt. Pratibha Patil heard that Roshni Devi had garnered massive support for her campaign to shut down the liquor shops in her village, even bringing pressure from the Excise Department, she was deeply impressed and invited Roshni Devi to the Rashtrapati Bhavan to commend her efforts. She was felicitated in 2009 and a film was made on her campaign by the Ministry of Social Justice and Empowerment, to showcase what one woman can do to put brakes on social malaises like alcoholism.

And the story of Roshni Devi does not end there... Encouraged by the President's support and the media blitz, she has since taken up several other measures to empower the women of her village. She was encouraged to take part in a national workshop organized under PRIA's (Society for Participatory Research in Asia), Women's Political Empowerment and Leadership (WPEL) programme. She launched a series of powerful developmental initiatives for clean environment, community toilets, preventing female foeticide, etc. Delivering on her election promise of banning alcohol consumption in the village, she got passed a resolution seeking the closure of all liquor shops within a kilometre of the village in the Panchayat.[32] Her original initiative and the acclamation of India's highest office worked together to help Roshni Devi learn valuable lessons on building leadership skills and ways to influence people to achieve development objectives. She acknowledges that the training organised by PRIA have played a major role in helping her find and develop her strength as a woman and as a leader of her community. Smt. Pratibha Patil, quick to spot a woman who has made a difference and a powerful leader who has the potential to continue to impact her community in the future, invited her, along with a delegation of women to the Rashtrapati Bhavan at the end of June 2012, to felicitate her for showing such remarkable leadership skills. The presidential invite will surely go a long way in further strengthening the hands of this extraordinary woman leader of Haryana. Certainly, the President is desirous to showcase what Roshni Devi has accomplished in order to inspire thousands of women across India to take up the cudgels against areas of male domination and succeed in making a secure place for themselves.

Sarjana

Smt. Pratibha Patil has also been known to be profoundly moved by humanitarian motives and has on more than one occasion, done all in her power to promote such aspirations whenever they have been displayed. When six-year old Sarjana felt compelled to do her bit for the relief of those struck by the cyclone 'Aila', all she had to offer was her voice and her efforts. So she boarded trains running between Basirhat and Hridayapur and sang and danced to entertain the captive audience of passengers, in exchange for a few rupees. The grand total she accumulated for all her trouble was ₹ 205, which she donated for the relief of the cyclone affected villagers, to the Governor. When Smt. Pratibha Patil heard about little Sarjana, she was touched by her selfless gesture and invited her to Rashtrapati Bhavan. "The imposing halls of Rashtrapati Bhavan on Wednesday seemed too small to match the noble deeds of six-year old Sarjana who presented a cheque of ₹ 205, earned all by herself by singing in trains, to President Smt. Pratibha Patil for the country's relief fund."[33]

While Smt. Pratibha Patil was amazed at a demonstration of such a will to do something for those in dire circumstances coming from a six-year old, she also hoped that many other citizens would be motivated to become involved on hearing Sarjana's story.

Sultana Begum

The range of circumstances that have moved Smt. Pratibha Patil into acts of compassion is demonstrated by this story. Middle aged Sultana Begum runs a tea stall near Howrah from which she also sells bangles to support her penury-stricken family. But when millions of such women share this fate in our country, why should this particular story move our President? The reason, she is the widow of Mirza Bedar Bakht, the great grandson of the last Mughal Emperor, Bahadur Shah Zafar, who had died penniless. When Smt. Pratibha Patil found out about the deplorable condition of Sultana Begum, she was moved deeply and arranged for her pension to be raised from a meagre ₹ 400 a month, to ₹ 6000.

Lotika Sarkar

Young or old, the help of the President's office was available to all during the tenure of Smt. Pratibha Patil. Prof. Lotika Sarkar, an elderly lady, once Dean of Delhi Univeristy's Law Faculty, was restored to her life of dignity and peace by Smt. Pratibha Patil. Her home had been illegally occupied and having no one to help her, she might have lost her residence, but for the President's providential intervention.

Shruti and Gore Bhatla

Shruti and Gore Bhatla are twins who suffer from a rare condition called 'ontogenesis imprecate' which in simple terms means that they will never grow beyond the two feet of height they have already achieved. The disease required that the nineteen year old twins get expensive treatment that the family could ill-afford. They made a representation to President Smt. Pratibha Patil who was taken aback by the cheerful dispositions of the girls in spite of their medical predicament. Through the President's good office, financial aid was made available to them through the CM's relief fund that enabled their parents to get the appropriate treatment they required. Encouraged by the President's support they went on to compose an album of songs that they readied for release. President Smt. Pratibha Patil was impressed by their never-say-die spirit and awarded them the Bal Shri Award and they have also won the Shaurya Award. The 16-year-olds suffer from a physical disability but it doesn't stop them. The duo recently sung for their first music album. "We are thrilled that it is almost ready for release," they remarked.[34]

Manjuma Iqbal

When a newspaper reported that Manjuma Iqbal, winner of the Uttam Jeevan Raksha Padak for saving her son's friends from drowning, while unable to rescue her own son, wanted to return her award, it got Smt. Pratibha Patil's attention. The note said that Manjuma had been unceremoniously handed over an amount of cash and this act had humiliated her rather than honour her sacrifice and bravery.

Smt. Pratibha Patil decided to set this affront right by arranging for her to receive the award from the Govt. of Uttar Pradesh in an honourable manner.

Bulti Bagdi

Smt. Pratibha Patil never missed an opportunity to recognize a woman who had taken a stand against any kind of oppression or injustice. It quickened a sensitive spot in her to see women awaken to take their rightful place in the scheme of things. Hence, when she heard Bulti Bagdi's story, she was encouraged that indeed, there was hope for the women of India. Bulti was indignant to find her bridegroom drunk at the wedding ceremony, and worse, demanding more dowry before the ceremony could begin. She raised a strong protest at which the bridegroom's party beat a hasty retreat. The entire community supported Bulti as word got around of her stance against alcoholism and dowry, two major banes of our society. Her story became an inspiration for many young girls facing similar challenges in the course of societal pressure to be married off. Smt. Pratibha Patil expressed her great pride in Bulti and encouraged her to continue her studies to become economically independent. The State Government and other organizations offered financial aid, help with housing for the family and employment opportunities. All the organizations that came forward to lift the family of Bulti out of their poverty did so upon hearing of her situation after the President expressed interest.

Laxmi Indira Panda

In a similar vein, to her humanitarian service to others, Smt. Pratibha Patil also helped Laxmi Indira Panda, a freedom fighter who had fallen in hard times. Trying to eke out a living on a meagre pension, she came to meet President Smt. Pratibha Patil to seek her help and assistance. She was not disappointed. Smt. Pratibha Patil looked into the matter and made sure that her pension was revised and that she was taken care of.

To Sum it All Up…

Addressing a huge gathering on the 14th of April, 2011, at the golden jubilee celebration of Ahilyarani Mahila Vikas and Shaikshanik Sanstha at Ganesh Kala Krida Manch, Smt. Pratibha Patil again stressed the importance of empowering the women of our nation.

"Creating the environment which imparts equal status to women in family, society and country is the sole motive behind various facets of programmes being run for women empowerment. We have to work towards making them able to take their own decisions," she said. During her speech, the President touched upon a number of topics related to women empowerment. "Sex determination is a cruel exercise and the way we have to protect trees in order to save environment, protection of female child is important to save human race."[35]

Reviewing the role of women who had participated in the freedom struggle, Smt. Pratibha Patil remarked that there were several women who had played a crucial part in the achievement of India's independence.

"Can't we create a movement on the lines of the independence movement to address contemporary issues?" she asked. Stressing on the importance of education, the President said, "Education is the first tool of empowerment. Right to Education and Sarva Shiksha Abhiyan have ensured that education is available to children between the age group of 6 and 14. Be it a boy or girl, every child must get education. It's only women education that can challenge the traditions such as child marriage, dowry, social injustice and other sorts of discrimination. It is these educated women who can in turn educate other women and teach them independence and self-confidence."[35]

Reiterating some of these sentiments in her speech on the eve of India's 63rd Republic Day, she once again spoke of the subject closest to her heart: "I strongly believe that women need to be drawn fully into the national mainstream. Empowerment of women will have a very big impact on creating social structures that are stable. The National Mission on Empowerment of Women set up in 2010, should help in the co-coordinated delivery of women-centric and women-related programmes. An important component of women's development is their economic and social security. Social prejudices prevalent in our society which have led to gender discrimination need to be corrected. Social evils like female foeticide, child marriage and dowry must be eradicated. Status of women is an important indicator of progress in a society."[36]

Looking Back with Satisfaction

Reflecting on her tenure as the First Woman President of India, Smt. Pratibha Patil said that she was pleased at the increased elected representation of women, especially at the grass-roots level, and further said that once elected, she noticed that women naturally rose to the top and this "sent a good signal".[37] Smt. Pratibha Patil expressed her desire to see the long-pending Women's Reservation Bill being passed in parliament. "Women's Reservation Bill is already in Parliament… but it will be a happy moment if some consensus emerges. I won't say what, but some good formula should be arrived at. Let Parliament do its job, but I do hope they come up with something that is acceptable to all political parties."[37]

Looking back upon her experiences in Rashtrapati Bhavan, she said that they were deeply gratifying as she had had the opportunity to interact with a whole gamut of people from different social backgrounds, various ethnicities, a range of economic strata and also a plethora of avocations. "I have met so many people from a cross-section of society, school children who have shown bravery, women who have stood up against social problems like female foeticide, dowry and addiction. It has been an experience. There is a vast pool of talent in this country, there are people who are brave and have the guts to take a stand to face circumstances, there are people with great energy and we need to draw on this energy and talent for nation-building."[37]

Smt. Pratibha Patil said that the women of our country had come a long way since the early days of her political career. However, she admitted that there was still a long way to go. True emancipation had to come to women on many fronts. Far greater participation in the government, the judiciary and other public spheres is the need of the hour. Women need to be encouraged to take their place in all these areas. "I have seen a new confidence in the eyes of the women in rural areas, in the gram panchayats where women want to do something. The question is who is to empower them. There are schemes for women that need proper implementation, there should be education and information available to them," she said.[37]

While conceding that much has been accomplished, the comment hints at the vast ocean of work in the area of empowerment that still needs to be done. Probably, any individual watching the socio-economic scene unfolded in India in the last 20–30 years cannot help but agree with her. Exhibiting the wisdom that comes only from experience, she reflected that the social evils of dowry and female foeticide could not be banished by the passing of legislation, but rather they require a deep, sea-change in the attitudes and thinking of our people. Such transformation could only come from education, she said. Education along brings the enlightenment that can permanently rid our people of denigrating notions that are at the foundation of gender-bias.

Speaking on the occasion of International Women's Day, on the 7th of March 2012, Smt. Pratibha Patil once more said that while she appreciated the leaps and bounds taken by women in response to the government's attempts to empower them, "more work needs to be done to empower women."[38] "Women can play an important role in focusing on issues related to gender inequality, ways to eliminate poverty and on social practices that are disadvantageous to the development and empowerment of women and the girl child. Women's empowerment is an important field where more work needs to be done".[38] Pointing out its importance, she said that it is important to mark the day to celebrate the spirit of ordinary women, who have played extraordinary roles in shaping their families, communities, society and countries.

"At the same time, it is a day to reflect on the progress made in achieving the goal of all-round development of women, and of implementing a pro-active agenda of change," Smt. Pratibha Patil said, while greeting them for their continuing role and relentless effort in shaping the destiny of country.[38]

Smt. Pratibha Patil has left the office of the First Citizen of India with a deep sense of satisfaction: the happiness that comes from having done what one could. From implementing a wide range of reforms to assisting harassed women, Smt. Pratibha Patil spared no effort in stretching a helping hand out to fellow-women in need. Her tenure as the First Woman President of India will be remembered by the women as a time when one of them tried very hard to help all of them!

It may be pertinent to note here that Smt. Pratibha Patil as the supreme commander of the three Armed Forces, visited the Indian borders near

Pakistan and China to boost the morale of the soldiers. She also dared to take sortie in the fighter plane Sukhoi 30 which flies at a Supersonic speed at the age of 74 with the GI suit on and became the first woman in the world to fly a fighter plane.

References

Note: If a reference number occurs twice or more in the chapter, it is another reference to the same source.

[1] Chaube, Rasika and Chhaya Mahajan. Foreword of "An Inspirational Journey: Pratibha Devisingh Patil the First Woman President of India". New Delhi: S. Chand Group, on behalf of Shram Sadhana Delhi, 2011.

[2] Ibid.

[3] Ibid, p. 4.

[4] Ibid, p. 51.

[5] Ibid, p. 60.

[6] Ibid, p. 123.

[7] Ibid.

[8] Ibid, p. 123–124.

[9] Ibid, p. 153.

[10] Ibid.

[11] Ibid, p. 154.

[12] Ibid, p. 168.

[13] Ibid, p. 171.

[14] Ibid, p. 176.

[15] The Hindu—BusinessLine-New Delhi, Sep 2.

[16] PTI http://zeenews.india.com/news/nation/women-self-help-groups-should-be-supported-president_699632.html

[17] Chaube, Rasika and Chhaya Mahajan. "An Inspirational Journey: Pratibha Devisingh Patil, the First Woman President of India". New Delhi: S. Chand Group, on behalf of Shram Sadhana Delhi, 2011, p. 187.

[18] Ibid, p. 183.

[19] Rajesh Ahuja, The Hindu, 15th Jan., 2012. http://www.thehindu.com/news/national/article2801613.ece

[20] Chaube, Rasika and Chhaya Mahajan. "An Inspirational Journey: Pratibha Devisingh Patil, the First Woman President of India". New Delhi: S. Chand Group, on behalf of Shram Sadhana Delhi, 2011, p. 186.

[21] Ibid, p. 187.
[22] p. 6, of Mission Statement.
[23] The President's Speech on the eve of Republic Day.
http://ibnlive.in.com/news/full-texy-presidents-address-on-the-eve-of-republic-day/224282-3.html
[24] Chaube, Rasika and Chhaya Mahajan. "An Inspirational Journey: Pratibha Devisingh Patil, the First Woman President of India". New Delhi: S. Chand Group, on behalf of Shram Sadhana Delhi, 2011, p. 187.
[25] PTI-Times of India, 12th Oct., 2010.
[26] Smriti K. Ramachandran in "Electoral reforms need of the hour: Pratibha" in The Hindu, New Delhi, 15th April, 2012.
http://www.thehindu.com/news/national/article3315466.ece?homepage=true
[27] Danteshwari, 11th Feb., 2011 in "Women Empowerment a Must Says President Mrs. Pratibha Patil"
http://www.yreach.com/ahmedabad/news/breaking-news/flash-news/-women-empowerment-a-must-says-president-mrs-pratibha-patil.html
[28] Shoumojit Banerjee in The Hindu-March 23, 2011.
http://www.hindu.com/2011/03/23/stories/2011032355880800.htm
[29] Ananya Dutta—The Hindu, Dec. 14, 2010, New Delhi.
http://www.thehindu.com/todays-paper/tp-national/tp-newdelhi/article951211.ece
[30] The Hindu-Smriti Ramachandran, March 20, 2009.
http://blogs.thehindu.com/delhi/?p=16910
[31] ibnlive.in.com/news/wb-prez-awards-girls-for-opposing-child-marriage/209765-3.html
[32] http://pria.org/component/content/article/593
[33] New Delhi: Zeenews, March 17, 2010. http://zeenews.india.com/news/nation/six-year-old-s-noble-act-moves-president_611976.html
[34] Jhilmil Motihar in 'India Today', June 13, 2009.
[35] Express News Service: Pune, April 14, 2011.
[36] The President's Speech on the eve of Republic Day.
http://ibnlive.in.com/news/full-texy-presidents-address-on-the-eve-of-republic-day/224282-3.html
[37] Smriti K. Ramachandran, 'The Hindu', New Delhi, April, 15, 2012. 'Electoral Reforms need of the hour: Pratibha'.
www.thehindu.com/news/national/article3315466.ece?homepage=true
[38] PTI, New Delhi, March, 7, 2012.
http://news.oneindia.in/2012/03/07/more-work-needs-to-be-done-empower-women-president.html

Roshni: Lighting up Lives

"Give light and people will find the way."
—*Ella Baker*

"... Wherever I have seen paintings made by children, whether in India or abroad, the dominant theme of their drawing strokes, add up to a distinctly clear image of vibrant green trees; clear skies; flowing rivers and co-existence of animal and human life. It depicts the communion of man with cosmic nature, and this is what exactly resonates the essence of Roshni—the nurturing of a healthy environment around uses."
—*Smt. Pratibha Patil**

Environmental issues were first pushed to the forefront of the collective consciousness in the late 1900s, when people started realizing that their behaviour was having a negative impact on the environment, causing imbalance in the ecosystems of the world. Toxic waste, caused due to rampant abuse of natural resources, and other harmful bionetwork were since then increasingly questioned in the light of research and study available about how these activities hurt the environment. Proficient environmentalists and policy makers pushed for an awareness drive. Smt. Pratibha Patil, cognizant of the colossal damage to the fabric of natural world if corrective measures were not propagated, has been an ardent advocate of conservation and sustainability of the ecology for the common good of the human kind. Her pioneering endeavour of creating an eco-friendly environment in India started with her concerted effort in modulating and shaping the Rashtrapati Bhavan as a paradigm of eco-friendly urban habitat. Her indomitable challenge in persuading the residents of the Rashtrapati Bhavan to become more mindful of the environs surrounding them has fetched creditable appreciation. Today, Rashtrapati Bhavan stands as an

---

*Speech by the President of India, Smt. Pratibha Devisingh Patil at the Seminar on 'Universalisation of Roshni', Rashtrapati Bhavan, New Delhi, 19 May 2011.

inspiration for all the citizens of India to make the country environment affable, for future generation of the nation.

An ingenious brain child of Smt. Pratibha Patil, 'Roshni' is a groundbreaking green conception aimed at the holistic development of Indian urban habitats. She conceived 'Roshni' with the objective of creating an immaculate environment in which people can have unsullied breath of air; with proper and sustainable management of ecology; and empowerment of local communities of people to develop eco-friendly sustainable urban habitats through the active participation of stake holders and residents. Smt. Pratibha Patil has been a great champion of an eco-friendly environment since her growing up days, and after assuming the highest office, it was an opportunity to embark on the mission to realize and concretize her vision of a sustainable ecological environment. She looked no further than her home, the President's estate must be a symbol of a green, energy efficient and zero waste model township. The estate was turned into an ideal location and a metaphor for experimenting with her vision of an unpolluted and untainted green India.

Her resolute efforts in developing the Rashtrapati Bhavan as an eco-friendly urban habitat began with educating and convincing the residents of the Rashtrapati Bhavan to be receptive to their surroundings, this not only yielded triumphant result but enlightened and added 'Roshni' into their lives. Rashtrapati Bhavan now stands as an inspiration and guiding force for the people of India to make the country environment friendly. The President's Estate is a living heritage located on the Raisina Hills in the heart of Delhi, over an area of three hundred and forty acres, encompassing offices, residential buildings and green open terrain of rich biodiversity. She formally launched the 'Roshni' initiative on 25 July 2008, with the active involvement of the residents and partner organizations. She thought the best way to bring about awareness is to hold a conference at Rashtrapati Bhavan to initiate a series of dialogue and debate by bringing the best minds from across the country to discuss the potential relevance and benefits of such an endeavour. In the inauguration, Smt. Pratibha Patil expressed her conviction and credence that a clean and unpolluted environment can only lead us to a healthy and harmonious life, apart from enhancing our competence level and providing the best ground for the knowledge and awareness of our skills. To her, the basic objective of 'Roshni' was to make the President's Estate an eco-friendly, green and 'model urban habitat'. The larger goal of the initiative, is that this inventiveness will work as a role model and eventually percolate down to the grass root level, impacting and inspiring others to make their surroundings environment friendly and sustainable.

In her speech at the colloquium on 'Universalization of Roshni', she focused on her plan: "Nestled amidst green surroundings with rich bio-diversity, the President's Estate enjoys an unusual blessing. We realized that the well-being of our residents is closely linked with this wonderful gift of nature and that we must necessarily conserve this living natural heritage". She acknowledged that her efforts generated effectual awareness, enthusiasm and involvement amongst inhabitants to manage the local environs responsibly, "the time and energy devoted by them in ensuring the success of 'Roshni' is commendable. It demonstrates volunteerism at its best, and I congratulate them for their hardwork and dedication in embellishing the Estate with the radiant glow of Roshni". Environmental issues and ecological concerns were earnestly raised, discussed and debated in the symposium. It was noted that most of the countries of the world through many awareness campaigns, publication of literature on the subject and much propaganda made people realize that environment sustains human life. The rampant destruction and devastation of natural resources by the people in their selfish and unregulated pecuniary pursuits will continue to have a harmful impact on the environment. If we fail to regulate and ensure effectively, it will perhaps lead to the destruction of the world and human life. And hence, some eco-friendly ways of living were devised by the resolute efforts of the leaders of the world. Unfortunately, the destruction and obliteration of the environment continues, therefore, a continual discussion on awareness and sustainability of environment must be part of a globalized world. Highlighting on these issues of environmental decay Smt. Pratibha Patil in her speech at the 'Universalization of Roshni' program at Rashtrapati Bhavan on 19 May 2011 said "the need to foster this spirit has arisen as the impact of environmental degradation is clearly apparent, whether it is the rise in global temperatures; haphazard weather patterns; depletion of the ozone layer; change in sea-levels or the growing spate of natural catastrophes. With urbanization emerging as one of the most significant drivers of global environment change, for those of us living in concrete dominated city environments, we cannot afford to remain apathetic or indifferent to the mounting degradation of our natural ecosystems. In today's world, with cities being engines of economic growth, the phenomenon of urbanization has come to stay. The need of the moment is to evolve a comprehensive, integrated and cost effective strategy of management of urbanization.... As protection of the environment knows no boundaries, we must assume at the earliest, the responsibility to improve our local environment". The 'Roshni' map evolved as a concrete step in this direction.

The rapid pace of urbanization has undoubtedly led to the hasty ruin of the environment. In order to make our living matrix healthier and leave a better place for the future generation we need to love, respect and nurture the nature, only then can nature nurture us. Thus, the vision of 'Roshni' as visualized by Smt. Pratibha Patil is to make all urban habitats eco-friendly and sustainable. We should not lose focus of what the 'Roshni' project strives to achieve—"to equip us better to brave the challenges of living in harmony with nature".

To make the President's Estate an environmental friendly, green, energy efficient and zero waste model habitat, leaving minimum carbon footprint, through community participation, resource conservation and pollution prevention, an environmental improvement and sustained quality up-gradation drive was initiated with the active participation of the resident community of the President's Estate. Raising awareness and developing and building their capacities to make them more accountable and responsive in all identifiable areas with judicious use of water, electricity, paper and petroleum product, promoting eco-friendly products, and minimisation and management of waste became an objective.

Dynamics of Roshni

As symbol of growth and progress, 'Roshni' is the harbinger of an eco-friendly and environmental sustainable awareness. It strictly complies with the statutory regulatory requirements, encourages water conservation and augmentation of sources of water supply to make the Estate self-reliant and enforces energy conservation through energy audits, adoption of best practices and progressive use of new and renewable sources of energy, effective management of liquid and solid wastes through adoption of eco-friendly practices, improving the biodiversity through the conservation of flora and fauna. It adopts the convergence of ongoing government schemes to evolve a replicable model for the development of eco-friendly habitats. To ensure that the 'Roshni' initiative became entrenched in the system, it was decided to first get an external validation for its processes and standard operating procedures, thus laying the foundation for a strong and lasting institutionalisation process. Accordingly, the President's Estate became ISO-14001:2004 compliant on 25 July 2010.

The success of 'Roshni' initiative is linked with the stakeholder's participation and convergence of representation of partner institutions. The main pillars of 'Roshni' are President's Estate Resident's Welfare Association, Women Self-Help Groups (SHGs), Roshni Prachodaya Society and other partner institutions include the Bureau of Energy Efficiency, Department of Environment, Government of NCT of Delhi, University of Delhi, to name a few. The participation of stake holders and meeting of collective agenda of partner institutions bring about the realisation of 'Roshni'. The main leaders of 'Roshni' who took forward the mission are:

PERWA *(President's Estate Resident's Welfare Association)*

This Association was formed on 19 June 2008 with the intervention of Smt. Pratibha Patil to ensure the active participation of the residents of the President's Estate in the 'Roshni' enterprise. The idea is two pronged, to spread awareness as well as to prepare the next generation to be accountable and vigilant about the green sustainability of their habitats. PERWA is managed by a management committee comprising of ten members and a chairperson who is also a member of the advisory committee which is constituted to prepare an action plan for the 'Roshni' initiative. The members of the management committee of PERWA work as area specific officers of President's Estate assigned to them. They further nominate required number of block representatives in the ratio of one representative per ten houses for its smooth functioning.

Women Self-Help Groups (SHGs)

At the inauguration of 'Roshni' Smt. Pratibha Patil focused on the particular role of women in the success of the endeavour. The enormous possibilities the SHGs can initiate through 'Roshni', leading to women not only becoming economically independent but also in empowering them. The success of 'Roshni' would not be a reality without the active participation and support of the women SHGs thought Smt. Pratibha Patil, giving credit to them. But one cannot take away the fact that it is her endeavour that has given birth to many women SHGs. Some worth mentioning are the ones which have played a seminal role in the success of realizing her dream by shaping projects such as, vermicomposting and organic composting. It would be worthwhile to mention the major groups named after some inspiring women, Mother Teresa SHG—Vermicomposting; Rani Jhansi SHG—Organic composting; Sarojini Naidu SHG—Beauty culture; Kalpana Chawla SHG—Art & Craft; Indira SHG – *Masala* (Spice) grinding, spearheading the agenda of 'Roshni'.

Roshni Prachodaya Society

With the basic vision of creating an eco-friendly and sustainable urban habitat, the Roshni Prachodaya Society, was formed to conserve the President's Estate as an eco-friendly, green, energy efficient and zero waste model habitat, through participation of the community and stake holders, resource conservation, pollution abatement, environmental improvement and sustained quality upgradation, leaving minimum carbon footprint. The aim and objective of the Society is primarily to create a model of eco-friendly, urban habitat through active stakeholders' participation. It works towards capacity building of residents through skill development and institutional infrastructure like SHGs and also involves the PERWA actively in the planning and implementation of this policy. It promotes and spreads the concept of 'Roshni' in the cause of developing sustainable habitats. Pursuing the promotion of this concept with the sole aspiration to achieve the vision of making all urban habitats in the country eco-friendly and sustainable is a laudable endeavour.

Partner Institutions

Smt. Pratibha Patil through seminars, debates and discussions brought about a paradigm shift in Rashtrapati Bhavan; it became a hub of think tank looking for collaborative work in sustainable development. The conferences organized made effective recommendations for urban habitat, foremost being massive plantation as carbon sink; rainwater harvesting; implementation of vermicompost culture; solid waste management; and energy audit. It further focused specifically on government buildings and worked out measures towards energy conservation in buildings; green building architecture; renewable energy applications, particularly solar PV and solar water heaters; solar street lights, signals and signage; and solar parking. Some of the key players who saw merit in the endeavour and became part of 'Roshni' are: Cabinet Secretariat, Ministry of Urban Development, Ministry of Water Resources, Ministry of New and Renewable Energy, Ministry of Environment and Forests, Indian Institute of Technology, Delhi, University of Delhi, Indraprastha Gas Limited, National Environmental Engineering Research Institute, Department of Environment, Government of NCT of Delhi, New Delhi Municipal Council, Central Groundwater Board, Khadi and Village Industries Commission (KVIC), Bureau of Energy Efficiency, Central Electronics Limited, National Productivity Council and Bureau Veritas Certification India. If all the partners of this stature come together in working towards an ecological balance, India will certainly be rich in its resources, as well as be a prime source of inspiration to other countries.

Roshni Projects

Solid Waste Management

Composting of Household Organic Waste—Until 2007, traditional system of waste disposal was being followed in the President's Estate. The waste generated was collected and transported to the NDMC land-fill sites. With the arrival of 'Roshni' a waste generation system was put in place with the active support of NDMC. The residents of the President's Estate are trained to segregate the bio-degradable and non-bio-degradable waste generated in each house. Residents are provided with twin bins for segregating solid waste. Door to door collection of solid waste is undertaken. 400 kg of bio-degradable waste compost is collected every day. Organic manure generated is used in the President's garden. Women from SHGs carry out composting of biodegradable waste.

Vermicomposting of Garden Wastage—Garden waste generated in the President's gardens is being collected and utilized for making vermicompost. 96 vermicomposting pits have been constructed in an area of 3840 sq. ft, operated by the women of SHGs. These women have been trained with the help of National Centre for Organic Farming, Ghaziabad. More than 320 quintals of vermicompost have been prepared since October 2009. During *Udyanotsav* when the Mughal Garden was open for public viewing, the vermicompost and organic compost products produced by SHGs was put on sale which received tremendous response from the visitors.

Recycling of Waste Paper—Use of plastic bags is discouraged on the President's Estates. The members of SHGs are trained in making paper bags and envelopes in collaboration with an NGO, 'Literacy India' for the use of President's Secretariat and also sell to the residents and shopkeepers. The project provided employment opportunities to the members of the SHGs and helped in the reduction of plastic bags.

Energy Management

Rashtrapati Bhavan was selected as one of the six buildings by the Ministry of Power for the implementation of Energy Efficiency Measures (EEMs). An energy audit in the main building was conducted by the Bureau of Energy Efficiency. On the basis of its report, Energy Efficiency Measures were implemented in the main building. From 1 March 2009 to 1 March 2011 about 19,90,000 units of (kWh) were reportedly saved.

Energy Audit of Rashtrapati Bhavan and Estate—With the commissioning of the 'Roshni' initiative, the Bureau of Energy Efficiency was requested to carry out an energy audit of the President's Estate and submit the report for the adoption of energy efficiency measures in the

Estate. This was completed in December 2009. The effective metering and monitoring and conservation of energy have been institutionalized and substantial savings of electricity has been achieved. Traditional bulbs have been replaced by CFLs. Audit of air conditioning plant was carried out, and primary and secondary pumps were replaced, and BMS system was introduced. Due to the energy efficient measures, the corresponding electricity consumption from January to June 2010 has come down to 64.03 lakh units, which is a reduction of 14.92 lakh units.

Energy Conservation Measures—For the first time, with the intervention of the President of India, Smt. Partibha Patil, an electronic synchronization of street and security lights was achieved on the President's Estate. Energy efficient ACs with VRV/VRF technology was also installed. Use of energy efficient pumps, lights and equipment of occupancy sensors for automatic switching on-off of room lights has been installed.

Use of New and Renewable Energy Sources—Use of renewable sources of energy being one of the basic objectives of 'Roshni', a committee was constituted, including officials from the MNRE for studying the scope and use of new and renewable energy sources in the President's Estate. To harness the solar energy a 50 kWp SPV power plant consisting of 5 modules has been installed on the terrace of the auditorium. The street lights and the auditorium façade are lit by the SPV power plant. The electricity consumption was reduced by approximately 1 lakh kWh per annum. Three hundred and ninety eight living quarters in the President's Estate are also provided with solar water heating system.

Use of Battery Operated Vehicles—Five electric vehicles were purchased for the President's garage in 2009. These vehicles are charged by solar energy. They have been used for more than 12,500 km. These vehicles save fuel to the tune of ₹ 1.75 per km.

Bio-gas Plant for PBG Mess—A bio-gas plant of 25 cubic meter capacity has been set up at the cost of ₹ 4.45 lakh with the assistance from KVIC. It uses 600 kg of cattle dung every day and provides fuel for cooking purposes for about 70 to 80 persons. It also produces organic manure for the use in the gardens. Energy that is generated per day is equivalent to 15 liters of kerosene oil or 10.82 kg of LPG or 117.25 kWh of electricity.

Piped Natural Gas Connection—As part of 'Roshni' initiative, it was decided to replace LPG cylinders with Piped Natural Gas (PNG). Accordingly, a project covering all households within the President's Estate and the kitchen at Rashtrapati Bhavan, the departmental canteen and the President's laundry was taken up for providing PNG in consultation with Indraprastha Gas Ltd. (IGL). The President's Estate has now been provided with PNG which is 50% cheaper than LPG and is the cleanest burning fossil fuel. It has the basic advantage that it is available to the residents round the clock, without the effort for refilling. This has also led to the reduction in carbon footprint.

Water Management

Water, being a precious non-renewable resource, calls for diverse methods of recycling for conservation purpose, was asked to be studied and assessed by Smt. Pratibha Patil. The President's Estate requires on an average about 15 lakh litres of water for its residents and in addition 5 lakh litres of water per day for maintaining the gardens and the greens. This water is being supplied by NDMC and CPWD. The shortfall deficiency is met by pumping from borewells in the President's Estate. It was stipulated that a need for recycling waste-water within the Estate be explored. The liquid waste generated by the residents of the President's Estate flows into the NDMC drain. With the help of IIT Delhi, the CPWD has initiated a study for examining the possibility of treating the domestic waste-water in a Sewage Treatment Plant. Treatment of grey water was also explored.

Water Conservation/Rainwater Harvesting—Given the fact that less than 1% of total water available on earth is fit for human consumption, the conservation of water has become the focal point for sustainable development. Groundwater is one of the sources of water supplied in the Estate. To enhance the sustainable yield of the existing groundwater structure, and to arrest the decline in the water table, rainwater harvesting has been set up as a part of 'Roshni' initiative in Rashtrapati Bhavan. Smt. Pratibha Patil, keeping with her primary focus of getting research inputs and involving relevant bodies set up an Advisory Committee of the Centre for Science and Environment which developed a plan for rainwater harvesting in the Rashtrapati Bhavan. This scheme was implemented by the CPWD and the Central Groundwater Board.

The President's Estate receives an average of 700 mm of annual rainfall. This rainwater is captured from roof tops and storm water drain, besides surface run off from non-paved areas and used for recharging the existing dry dug wells. In addition, one injection well, one recharge shaft and two recharge trenches with borewells and allied structures were constructed. Meter readings were taken. In the first year of the project, there was 97 cm net increase in the groundwater levels. As a result of these rainwater harvesting structures, the rate of diminution of groundwater levels has been checked.

With the 'Roshni' inventiveness in place, it was felt water harvesting could be further augmented in collaboration with the Central Groundwater Board. Run offs from areas which were earlier not covered in the first phase of the programme were collected and rainwater from the new areas was diverted into specially constructed recharge structures. Recharging of 2 dug-wells and 4 dry borewells in the President's Estate were undertaken in the second phase, thereby utilizing 100% run off in the President's Estate. This has helped to raise the water table to 2.33 metres in September 2010.

Impact Assessment—Substantial rise in the water column with rainwater harvesting in place, the sustainable yield of the existing groundwater structure is enhanced which arrests the decline of the water table. The rainwater harvesting measures have resulted in a substantial rise in the water column.

Rise in Water Column

Year	*Compared to Previous Year*	*During Monsoon*
2009	0.35 meter	0.88 meter
2010	0.92 meter	2.33 meter

The Ecosystem Bionetwork

With the implementation of bionetwork, there has been a considerable transformation in the ecological system of the President's Estate. In many of the Raj Bhavans and some other places, this initiative is under implementation.

Increase in Green Cover—Under the 'Roshni' initiative, efforts have been made not only to increase the green cover but also to protect the ridge area in the President's Estate and to mend and replace the dry and dead trees. Plantation of various species of trees has been undertaken. During the last two years, 8000 saplings of different species have been planted in the President's Estate and their survival rate has been found to be around 90%. This has increased the green cover of the President's Estate to 50%, as on March of 2011 as compared to 41% prior to 2008. In terms of acreage, 170 acres of land in the Estate have been covered under green cover. With approximately 8000 trees planted, the likely increase in the green cover would be 52% by the year 2013.

Tree Census—The original plantation of trees in the President's Estate was undertaken during the construction of Rashtrapati Bhavan, between 1911 and 1931 under the supervision of Mr. W.R. Mustoe, the then in-charge of Horticulture. Initially, major emphasis was given to the species like, Putranjiva, Laurel Fig, Pilkhan, Jamun, Khirni, Kiegelia etc. Several species of trees were added subsequently. However, no tree census had ever been carried out. It was decided that a survey of trees would thus be undertaken as a part of the 'Roshni' project with the help of Department of Forest, Government of NCT of Delhi and Horticulture wing of NDMC. A total of 5387 trees belonging to 150 species have been recorded during the field survey of the Estate.

Field Survey of the National Bird—The President's Estate is the abode for the glamorous Blue Peafowl better known as the Indian Peacock, our National Bird. Their population in the President's Estate is sizeable. It was felt necessary to conduct a field study of the National Bird in order to get recommendations for exploring better protection and conservation methodologies. The field study was carried out by the World Peasants Association, India Chapter and a report was submitted by them wherein the population of the peacocks in the President's

Estate has been estimated to be 100 in 2010. The recommendations of the study are under implementation.

Development of Nature Trail—One of the best ways to create awareness on nature conservation is through direct interaction with the nature. Landscapes and diversified habitats harbouring rich flora and fauna are ideal sites for interactive nature education. President's Estate anchoring rich biodiversity serves as an ideal location for creating environmental awareness. The Nature Trail was piloted and inaugurated on 13 December, 2008 by President Smt. Pratibha Devisingh Patil. It is spread over an area of 75 acres, which is located at the western end of the manicured gardens of Rashtrapati Bhavan. The Nature Trail showcases the biodiversity of the President's Estate, and displays rare old trees and a variety of animals and birds etc. It encompasses both the managed and natural ecosystems of the site and is connected to a myriad of gardens of the Rashtrapati Bhavan. The Nature Trail includes Pond ecosystem, Butterfly corner, Ber grove, Mango orchard, Wilderness habitat, Peacock point, Orangery, Organic composting pit, Vermi composting pits, Vineyard, Temperate fruit orchard, Jack tree grove, Pomegranate orchard, Bio-fuel plantation, Tropical vegetables, Cereals and Millets, Litchi tree grove, Spice yielding plants, Teak grove, and Shrub land bird point etc.

The empowerment of community has been a major offshoot of the implementation of Environment Management System. Major beneficiaries are women and children. A number of women have gained employment/financial independence. Their average earning is ₹ 3000/- per month. This has led to opening up of associated/subsidiary business enterprises. Children of the labourers are provided with shelter, nutritious food, pre-school and primary school education. The successful implementation of the 'Roshni' project hinges on the active participation and involvement of the main stakeholders, the residents of the President's Estate. Thus, one of the main components of the 'Roshni' initiative was to generate awareness and consciousness and develop capacity building of residents so as to make them more responsible and responsive to all identifiable activities of environment management. This was brought about through Information Education Communication (IEC) efforts and also through interactive sessions, training, painting competitions, etc. The capacity building exercise was especially done for the women leading to gainful outcomes for the women, both in monetary terms as well as in terms of enhancing their confidence and self-esteem. 'Roshni' initiative has also embarked on setting up a crèche called 'SOPAN' for children of labourers working in the Estate. The crèche provides pre-school and primary education, nutritious meal, uniforms and a clean and healthy environment to the children when their parents are away at work.

Women at the Estate felt empowered, while working in the vermicompost plant, when interviewed, one of them said that they were initially apprehensive of handling the earthworms but gradually it became easy, now they earn some money for their own expenditure as well as they use this money to pay fees or to buy some household things. They feel self-sufficient and have a sense of achievement. Setting up of SHGs has added to the confidence and self-respect of the women on the Estate. Kalpana Chawla SHG women make paper bags, Indira SHG and Sarojini Naidu SHG women are making *masalas* (spices) and so on. Different SHG women are assigned varied assignments which they do with utmost sincerity and professionalism.

Roshni Expansion: Bhopal and Odisha (Orissa)

Greatly influenced by 'Roshni' initiated by Hon'ble President of India Smt. Pratibha Devisingh Patil for the creation of an ecofriendly and environmentally sustainable urban habitat, Governors across were inspired. In pursuance, Raj Bhavan, Bhopal has started executing environment friendly measures such as energy conservation; use of renewable sources of energy through installation of 20 kw Solar Plant and other stand alone systems, waste management, vermicomposting and energy audit of the complex were effectively implemented. Increase in the green cover and also improvement in biodiversity became the goal. The solid waste management encompassed the objective of imparting training to the residents of Raj Bhavan by segregation of the biodegradable and non-biodegradable waste generated in each house, thus ensuring proper disposal of solid waste at Raj Bhavan, Bhopal.

With the objective of establishing the concept of energy savings through power efficiency measures and installation of NRE devices in buildings and demonstrate it lively, the Raj Bhavan, Bhopal created eight vermicompost pits within an area of 1000 sq. ft. These pits consume 5000 cubic feet of garden waste; the pits are operational and produce 20000 cubic feet of manure of value over 3.2 lakhs per annum. The activity is being undertaken under MNRE scheme of Central Financial Assistance to Special Area under Category-I (SADP). It makes an analysis of energy supply demand pattern and measurement and analysis of power consumption of different gadgets/utilities of the Raj Bhavan. It has taken lead in the field of newer and renewable resources. In its first phase it has installed solar-wind hybrid system and biomass plant of total 36 kw capacity.

In the Raj Bahvan, Odisha (Orissa), Roshni was implemented with the objective of empowering the community to create eco-friendly sustainable habitat. It aimed at holistic development of habitats through environment management initiatives; improvement of Raj Bhavan garden; waste management; energy conservation; use of alternate source of energy; rainwater harvesting; and gender empowerment were focused and monitored towards the agenda for progress as visualized and initiated by Smt. Pratibha Patil.

Achievements of Roshni

From its humble beginning in 2008, 'Roshni' has scaled many milestones, and it needs to be further pursued. 'Roshni' perhaps can be seen as the individuals making the family, families making the villages, villages making districts, districts making states and states making countries and countries forming the globe. 'Roshni' began as a simple enterprise where one is required to think of making the environment of his/her locality green and eco-friendly, and this small step of improving the environment at the locality will eventually lead to the improvement at the larger level. Highlighting on the achievements of 'Roshni' in the brief span of three years of its initiation, Smt. Pratibha Patil said, "Roshni has sought to transform this Estate into a green, eco-friendly place, energy-efficient and a zero waste model township. From a humble start, today it encompasses a shelf of 13 activities, which I understand would be elaborately discussed. As Roshni spread its wings, we felt the need to institutionalise 'Roshni' as a regular environmental management system. We have in place an Environment Policy for the Estate. All activities which impact environment have been put to audit, and our environmental practices have been subjected to external validation. We crossed the first milestone in 2010 when we received the ISO 14001 certification. Carbon-emission reduction is also being monitored, and carbon footprint reduction potential is being analyzed to show the way forward".

Perhaps the remarkable aspect of this inventiveness is the gender empowerment. By involving the women in domestic activities like making paper bags, preparing spices, etc. it not only makes the women economically independent but also makes them inclusive in the economic growth fabric of India. In a very simple way it empowers women, while involving them in the cause of preserving the environment. In her speech on 'Universalisation of Roshni', Smt. Pratibha Patil highlighted the pivotal role played by women in the success story of 'Roshni' and in turn how the enterprise of 'Roshni' helped in transforming their lives: "With challenges, unexpected opportunities often come gift-wrapped. The ordinary women of our Estate, by investing their capabilities as environment resource managers through the 'Roshni' initiative, created new livelihood opportunities for themselves. The SHGs managed by them have not only triggered their capacity-building abilities and economic empowerment, but also enhanced their self-esteem in society. 'Roshni' has thus taught that in a fast-urbanizing environment, by striking the right balance between environmental and developmental needs; such initiatives have the potential of becoming success stories of the inclusive growth model. It is these learning experiences that have inspired us to meet at a common platform today, to harness our collective energy and commitment on how to replicate 'Roshni' in each others' local context, with on-the-spot variations. The thought, policy and action embracing 'Roshni', must spill over our boundaries to give impetus to a collective drive to create eco-friendly sustainable urban habitats".

Such a splendid concept and endeavour at creating an ecofriendly and sustainable environment and making people aware about the environmental hazards, and teach them to love the nature should percolate to all levels. Smt. Pratibha Patil's remarkable initiatives in taking this idea to the grass root level and making people aware about their safe and sustainable surrounding is to be translated into a policy initiative. A comprehensive and analytical understanding of the essences of 'Roshni,' led to a one day colloquium at Rashtrapati Bhavan on May 19, 2011 at the behest of Smt. Pratibha Patil for discussion and knowledge flow of this noteworthy concept among the academia, bureaucrats, statesmen, business organizations, the think tank and the policy makers. In her inaugural address Smt. Pratibha Patil focused on the environmental putrefaction brought about by the self-seeking economic interest of people. She also warned that the natural resources of the world are finite and any more attempts at the decomposition of the environment will certainly end in the great devastation. We cannot afford to remain apathetic or nonchalant to the mounting degradation of the natural ecosystems. She emphasized the need to foster the spirit of 'Roshni' in view of increasing impact of environmental degradation on global temperatures, haphazard weather patterns, changing sea levels and growing spate of natural catastrophes. Sheila Dixit, Chief Minister of NCT of Delhi, Dr. Farooq Abdullah, Minister of New and Renewable Energy, Mr. Kamal Nath, Minister of Urban Development and people from premier universities, bureaucracy, governmental agencies etc. were among the host of dignitaries participating in the seminar. The concept and initiative will hopefully continue to resonate in policy decisions.

Rashtrapati Bhavan is a town in itself; it houses school, hospital, bank, post office etc. It requires a lot of resources to run this town efficiently and it also incurs a lot of expenditure. To run this town efficiently in a cost effective manner, it needs a lot of planning and that is where President Smt. Pratibha Devisingh Patil stepped in and pioneered 'Roshni'. To her, goes the credit in establishing that it is not just a venture, but thinking and a way of life that must be inculcated in daily life. It's a vision that encompasses environment management and empowerment of local communities to create eco-friendly, sustainable, urban habitats with the reduction of carbon foot print, through the participation of stake holders and convergence of partnership program. Dr. Rasika Chaube (Internal Financial Advisor to the President), recalls that initially there was a lot of resistance from the local residents towards

'Roshni' but gradually once the National Productivity Council was also roped in they started understanding the benefits of 'Roshni'.

In her interview with Jyotika Grover for the Doordarshan Program titled *'Roshni'—Ek Soch*, Smt. Pratibha Patil said that she took the initiative of 'Roshni' to make all urban habitats eco-friendly and sustainable. It was possible due to the help of the local residents and the various partner institutions who made 'Roshni' possible. After three years of its implementation 'Roshni' is a success story because of the dedication of the residents and the partner institutions who made the President's Estate an eco-friendly, green and sustainable habitat. Accenting on the role of women in the success of her mission she said, "'Roshni' is a message of empowerment and socio-economic transformation, which can only happen if efforts are put in. Women have an inherent power in them, they need to be motivated and trained so that they are empowered to do wonders. This has been possible through 'Roshni,' they are involved in vermicompost generation, running the crèche, beauty culture, etc. which has added to their confidence. The project is called 'Roshni' because it lights up the lives of people not only within them but also lights up the society. People are encouraged to think in a positive way and make their habitats eco-friendly".

The environment that we live in is not sterilized, and life cannot sustain long in this unhygienic locale. The ecological squalor has led to many kinds of diseases and health hazards. Though there might be rise in the life expectancy, yet the existence per se has become diseased and hazardous. In her speech at the inauguration of the 'Roshni', she raised the serious concern that: "Preservation of nature and environment is the need of the hour. Sometimes we think and ask, why there is the rise in the temperature, and why the wind has become so polluted? Why the water in the river is not clean, and why do we see so few number of stars in the sky? For all these queries one answer comes to our mind, the environment has become very much polluted. If it continues like this, then what kind of world shall we leave for the coming generation?" She further reiterates the serious concern about the ecological imbalance: "With more than six billion people depending on the resources of the Earth, we must remain ever-vigilant, that we are drawing from finite reserves. The toll will rise higher with each new generation. For the sake of our coming generations, we have to work harder to leave behind a legacy of a cleaner, greener environmental landscape.... It also goes to prove that each one of us realizes that we have the potential to make a difference in our community, and to our environment. People do care about the planet they live on, and are willing to step out of their comfort zones to act as trustees of this planet, and create a sustainable habitat with all its mystery and its wonder. What is needed is to show them the way, and inspire them with confidence that they can do it". She highlighted on two gainful insights in the debate on 'Universalisation of Roshni'. "Firstly, we must not view environmental degradation as a problem without a solution. The creativity, ingenuity and innovation of humanity is always at hand to redress human-beings' self-created problems. We must look at the future with a hope, which rests on the confidence that our existence never poses problems that humankind cannot resolve. Secondly, we must appreciate that our human resource is our biggest strength. Our human capital if creatively galvanized with the right kind of management, and right modicum of participative decision-making, can find effective and practical solutions to the most formidable of problems". 'Roshni' could be an effective answer to all our ecological concerns. As a concept, it awakens us to our local habitat, forcing us to ponder on the ecological imbalances that we generate and are surrounded by. The mission is simple and direct, how do we as the populace improve upon the environs and make it eco-friendly. 'Roshni' can be implemented in all habitats and this is possible by formulating some governmental policies with legal and regulatory measures, help from the local residents and private players. Proper deployment of our resources is important so that the balance in the environment is maintained.

'Roshni' as a laboratory scale initiative has successfully been implemented and accomplished on pilot basis at the Rashtrapati Bhavan. There is a need to take this concept to the grass root level with the involvement of the Central and State governments, local bodies, civil society organizations, SHGs etc. Through the enterprise of 'Roshni', knowledge and experience of best practices can be shared. There should be investment in capacity building through training and R&D efforts, ensuring of inclusion of environment management system in the school/university curriculum, evolving of guidelines for convergence of programmes of partner institutions, identification of agencies who can be involved in this cause, assessment of resource requirements, bringing about of changes in legal and regulatory framework wherever required, and introduction of an incentive scheme for commendable efforts in this direction. 'Roshni' has the potential to spark off the latent light and energy within the minds and hearts of the people of India thereby creating a green environment around them. If implemented properly and widely 'Roshni' in the coming years will create a clean and eco-friendly environment in which there is a harmonious interface between man and nature. It carries the promise of becoming a global concept.

References

Note: The following sources have been used for the preparation of the chapter. 'Roshni' is an innovative concept being implemented in the President's Estate, Raj Bhavans and some other places. In view of the limited literature available on the subject these sources have been used extensively.

[1] ROSHNI - A Green Innovation for Sustainable Habitats.
 URL: http://roshni-rb.gov.in/roshni.html

[2] Official website of President of India (during the period of President Smt. Pratibha Patil).
 URL: http://presidentofindia.nic.in

[3] Speech by her Excellency the President of India, Smt. Pratibha Devisingh Patil at the Seminar on 'Universalisation of Roshni,' Rashtrapati Bhavan, New Delhi, 19th May 2011. [Online: web], Accessed 10 April 2012, URL: http://presidentofindia.nic.in

[4] Speech (in Hindi) by her Excellency the President of India, Shrimati Pratibha Devisingh Patil at the Inauguration of 'Roshni' Programme, 25 July 2008. [Online: web], Accessed 10 April 2012, URL: http://presidentofindia.nic.in

[5] Universalisation of Roshni: The Green Innovation for Sustainable ...
 [Online: web], URL: http://delhigreens.com/.../seminar-on-universalisation-of-roshni-the-green-...

[6] Raj Bhavan, Odisha (Orissa): Project Roshni.
 URL: http://www.rajbhavanorissa.gov.in/roshni.asp

[7] ROSHNI—A Green Innovation for Sustainable Urban Habitats.
 URL: http://roshni-prachodaya.org

[8] ROSHNI—A Green Innovation for Sustainable Urban Habitats. URL: http://roshni-prachodaya.org/Institutionalisation.html

[9] ROSHNI—A Green Innovation for Sustainable Urban Habitats. URL: http://roshni-prachodaya.org/biomedicalwaste.html

[10] Roshni Prachodaya Society and all India Institute of Local Self ... URL: http://indiacurrentaffairs.org › Government.

[11] *An Inspirational Journey: Pratibha Devisingh Patil ...* URL: http://www.amazon.com › Books › Biographies & Memoirs.

India and Overseas Business Collaboration

"No country can remain in its own cocoon and it is necessary for countries to increase engagement with others."

—*Smt. Pratibha Patil*

The English poet John Donne has famously said in one of his poems: "No man is an island". This maxim is as true of nations as it is of individuals. Particularly so, in a world that has speedy air travel and instant connect through the internet and has shrunk in ways that were unimaginable until the amazing times we now live in. Under these circumstances, it becomes imperative that, as a nation, India builds its rapport with other national entities around the world. Of course, there are numerous ways in which this is accomplished. Not least among them is the visits of our State's representatives, so that they may present our nation's current achievements and our visions for the future. As development is a shared process, India has much to learn from some nations and much to give to others. Thus, President Smt. Pratibha Patil's trips to 24 nations during her five year term have been instrumental in showcasing many of India's proud accomplishments, while inviting investment and interest in our nation's growing economy. The details of her trips and the outcomes of her visits are presented in detail, in this chapter.

President Smt. Pratibha Patil has described her foreign visits as "serious business" and gone on to say that her trips have been beneficial in building the country's image internationally, and have also helped to promote better understanding of many international problems. It is essential to build a relationship with leaders of other nations in order to ensure that a platform for dialogue exists when the need for one arises. She stated that "these visits have been in the context of the growing profile of India at the international level".[1]

Further, she added, "India seeks to be a permanent member of the Security Council...things like this doesn't happen automatically, you need constant dialogue and discussion with the world".[1]

President Smt. Pratibha Patil has undertaken 13 trips, covering 24 countries, across 4 continents in her 5 year tenure as the First Citizen of India. Most of these have been undertaken at the invitations of foreign governments and at the behest of the Indian Government, keeping the diplomatic interests of the country as the paramount criterion of decision-making.

When asked how she would describe her foreign visits, President Smt. Pratibha Patil remarked that she considered them to be "very successful" as each of them have gone a long way in promoting India's image as a growing economy in the world market, and a political and intellectual force to reckon with.[2] She also emphasized the role that her trips had played in improving bilateral relations with several nations, and enhancing trade and commerce with others. President Smt. Pratibha Patil went on to say that ties between nations were no longer just political, but extended to educational, cultural and economic realms as well. It was all these facets of relationship with other nations that had been benefitted by her trips, she felt. The following is an overview of each of her trips and the outcomes that they led to, in chronological order.

Brazil: April, 2008

President Smt. Pratibha Patil chose the lovely and strategic Latin American countries of Brazil, Mexico and Chile for her maiden visit as Head of State, beginning with Brazil. She had a hectic itinerary lined up for her as she addressed the Parliament, signed agreements and facilitated meetings between business groups from India and the host countries. The President was accompanied on her first trip abroad, in her new role, by Union Minister of State, V. Muttemwar. A high-level business delegation comprising members of the Confederation of Indian Industry (CII), representatives of leading industries like Essar Steel, Bajaj Auto, NIIT, UP Hotels and United Phosphorus were part of President Smt. Pratibha Patil's team in her leg in Chile and Brazil, and this was the first time that business representatives were joining the President on overseas visit. She was slated to meet a business delegation of the Federation of Industries of the State of Sao Paulo (FIESP) and the National Confederation of Industry (CNI). Meetings between the business delegates and captains of Brazilian industries were hoped to lead to an enhancement of trade between the two nations. The Presidents of both nations had agreed to further strengthen the existing strategic alliance between the two countries to step up the bilateral trade from the current level of about $3 billion to $10 billion by the year 2010. The high level CEO Forum chaired by Ratan Tata on the Indian side, and Jose Sergio Gabrielli, heading the Brazilian team, worked on creating the road-map that the two nations would embark upon in order to enhance the growth of trade between them.[3]

Improved connectivity and greater interest in global trade in the private and public sectors of Indian business is resulting in a search for new markets for business. Brazil is not only the largest country in Latin America; it is also India's biggest trade partner. India and Brazil have entered into a trade partnership and both nations are working together in IBSA (India-Brazil-South Africa) forum.

President Smt. Pratibha Patil's visit to this nation was at the invitation of the Brazilian President, Lula da Silva. President Lula expressed happiness that India's first woman President has chosen his country for her first visit abroad. In turn, President Smt. Pratibha Patil said that she was happy that her maiden visit as Head of State was to a nation as beautiful as Brazil.[4]

The visit is perceived as India's proactive effort to strengthen bilateral trade in the region and consolidate relations with old partners.

Outcomes

- MOU signed with CII and FIRJAN (Federation of Industries of the State of Rio de Janeiro) to promote trade and investment between the State of Rio de Janeiro and India.
- MOU signed with SESI, an organization which facilitates corporate social responsibility and grassroot network for women to work together in the field of welfare and corporate social responsibility.
- Investments in infrastructure, mining, oil, gas, biofuels and tourism were also discussed by business communities of both nations.

- During her tour, India signed agreements with Brazil on an extradition treaty, civil defense and humanitarian assistance.

Mexico: April, 2008

On the second leg of her visit to Latin America, President Smt. Pratibha Patil visited the historic city of Guadalajara, the second most populous city in Mexico. Her three-day visit to Mexico was marked by a situation, the President would have found familiar. She was forced to cancel her proposed address to a joint session of Parliament as the opposition had laid siege to it. As the protests of Mexico's Leftists was against the Government's attempts at privatization in the petroleum industry, President Smt. Pratibha Patil found her hosts in a predicament similar to situations back home in India.

She was accorded a grand reception at the palace, hosted by Governor Emilio Gonzales Marquez. The entertainment offered a taste of Mexican music, dance and authentic cuisine. The President was also felicitated by the Mexican President Felipe Calderon, at the Presidential House, Los Pianos. President Smt. Pratibha Patil warmed the hearts of her hosts by opening her address with greetings in Spanish. She then went on to seize the opportunity to open up a dialogue on the growing Indian economy and the potential for Mexican investments in it. She updated the dignitaries on growing Indian investments into Mexico and invited Mexican investors to consider investing in the Indian market. "There are tremendous opportunities in the areas of infrastructure and tourism in India which can be exploited by Mexican entrepreneurs. We welcome investments being made by Mexican companies in India," she said.[5] She talked about values like democracy, faith in non-violence, belief in dialogue and a pluralistic society, and secularism that both nations hold sacred and as such open up the possibility for the two countries to work together as allies in combating the challenges of present day globalization. "Our over-riding challenge is inclusive growth, not simply growth," she said.[5]

President Smt. Pratibha Patil referred to the upcoming meet of the India-Mexico High Level Group on Trade, expressing her confidence that the meeting scheduled for June, 2008 would lead to the establishment of clear guidelines for speedy development of trade between the two nations that would in turn solidify the Indo-Mexican economic relationship. She further added that the privileged partnership between India and Mexico was founded not only on the basis of common shared values that they cherished, but also "on the vision what we share for the future for our bilateral relations and also for the world".[5]

The interactions between Indian and Mexican business representatives were extremely fruitful, leading to the signing of agreements in the energy and aviation sectors. Vilas Muttemwar, the Indian Minister of State for Non-Conventional Energy Sources, formally signed the agreement with Mexican Secretary of Energy, Georgina Kessel.

In reply, President Calderon described President Smt. Pratibha Patil's visit to Mexico as "historic" and stated that the privileged partnership between the two countries would be mutually beneficial to both, taking them to new levels of economic growth. He said that bilateral and multilateral issues would be addressed in a "constructive and positive" way, as the rapport between the leaders had led to open lines of communication. President Calderon felt sure that the President's visit would establish India as a country to reckon with in the Latin American region. He added that both countries were now poised for greater collaboration in the filed of education and better avenues of partnership in the G-8 group.

President Smt. Pratibha Patil and President Calderon signed agreements on behalf of the two nations on technical cooperation in renewable energy and air services.

Outcomes

- One part of the delegation participated in the Post-World Economic Forum at Cancun, organized by PROMEXICO (CII's counterpart in Mexico). The main agenda of the meeting was the discussion of a strategy to achieve a US$ 5 billion target for bilateral trade between India and Mexico by 2010.
- CII and COMCE (another Mexican Chamber) signed an agreement in Mexico City to set up joint business forum for increasing trade and investment between the two nations.
- SEWA tied up with CII partners, India Mexico Business Chamber, to start a Mexican chapter of SEWA.

- Industry members of both nations had discussions concerning entering into joint ventures in bio-fuel, mining, tourism and agri-business.
- United Phosphorous had successful investment discussions with the Ministry of Agriculture.
- In Guadalajara, the CII delegates were exposed to business opportunities in Mexico, in the areas of IT, ITES and tourism.

Chile: April, 2008

The existing good relationship between the nations of India and Chile received a boost from President Smt. Pratibha Patil's three-day visit to Chile. Besides having talks with the leader of the Senate and the Chief Justice of the Supreme Court of Chile, the President also addressed the Indo-Chilean Chamber of Commerce.

President Smt. Pratibha Patil had high level summit talks with the Chilean President, Veronica Micjelle Bachelet Jeria, with whom developed a personal rapport. She signed four agreements with Chile, covering air service links, science, sports and expeditions to Antarctica.

President Smt. Pratibha Patil also visited the Republic of India School, an establishment where Indian culture is highly honoured. Our national anthem 'Jana Gana Mana' is sung every day after the Chilean national anthem and the Indian flag is hoisted at school ceremonies. She addressed the staff and students, commending them for their "continuing interest in our culture and the respect shown for India".[6]

Outcomes

The Chilean Chamber of Commerce organized a business interaction with the CII delegation in which joint ventures and investment opportunities in the fields of mining, IT, ITES and educational sectors were discussed. NIIT entered into a joint venture with a Chilean company for IT education. The following areas of business were successfully explored:

- Biofuel—opportunities for setting up and acquiring integrated biofuel plants in Brazil and Mexico were discussed.

- Tourism Sector—joint ventures in functional food plants in hotels, ayurveda, yoga centres and wellness centres were explored.
- Chemical and Fertilizer sector—detailed discussions were held for setting up of plants in Mexico and Brazil.
- Infrastructure and mining—opportunities for investments in joint ventures were discussed.
- Social Entrepreneurship—tie ups were entered into with local partners for developing social entrepreneurship.

Bhutan: November, 2008

President Smt. Pratibha Patil visited the Royal Kingdom of Bhutan on the auspicious occasion of the coronation of the King's son as the fifth Monarch of Bhutan. Bhutan was also celebrating the centenary of the Wangchuck Dynasty and the establishment of democracy through a democratically elected government. It was also the golden jubilee of Pt. Jawaharlal Nehru's visit to Bhutan in 1958, which founded long and fruitful relations between the two neighbouring nations. The many visits of Indian dignitaries to Bhutan and ministerial trips of Bhutan's officials to India had cemented the relationship leading to an increase in bilateral ties and greater cooperation across various fields of enterprise.

Bilateral relations between India and Bhutan have always been characterized by total trust and mutual understanding that has been sustained by regular interactions at the highest levels of governance. India has been the largest trade and development partner of Bhutan and the President reiterated India's commitment to developmental efforts begun by Prime Minister Nehru in the 1960s. She expressed India's continued support of Bhutan's Five Year Plans and assured the country of Indian aid in the development of a 10,000 MW hydropower that could be ready to export to India by 2020.

Vietnam: November–December, 2008

President Smt. Pratibha Patil made a 10-day visit to Vietnam and Indonesia in November, 2008, to explore the possibilities of expanding India's bilateral relations with these nations. It was generally felt in the political circles that the visit would strengthen India's economic presence in the South-East Asian region.

The President was accompanied by a business delegation and several meetings were on the agenda for increasing trade and exploring the possibilities of joint business ventures with these nations. The high level visit was aimed at infusing new enthusiasm and energy into bilateral relations extending across political, economic and cultural areas. In Vietnam, meetings had been scheduled between the President and her Vietnamese counterpart, Nguyen Minh Triet, as well as the Prime Minister of Vietnam, Nguyen Tan Dung.

In order to facilitate healthy interaction between the Indian business delegation and the stake-holders of business in the host nation, meetings had been arranged between the Federation of Indian Chambers of Commerce and Industry (FICCI) and the Vietnam Chambers of Commerce. Business delegates representing sectors like chemical industry, hydropower industry, mineral exploration and processing companies, steel and pharmacy industries, agricultural products processing industry and the energy sectors were all present.

The Vietnamese Minister of Industry and Trade addressed the joint forum of FICCI and VICCI (the Vietnamese counterpart of the FICCI) and recommended that Indian business houses increase their investment in oil and gas, petro-chemistry, mining, and food processing industries in Vietnam. He extended a special invitation to all Indian business houses to augment their present investments in Vietnam, contending that investments in that country benefitted them as Vietnam practised a free market economy and the country boasts a 95% literacy rate, having an extremely youthful population of which more than 50% is under the age of 25. This was seen as very encouraging to the growth of Indian investments in Vietnam.

Representatives of business houses from both nations went into detailed discussions in areas of business hitherto unexplored like ethanol, renewable sources of energy, pharmaceuticals, breweries and distilleries, education and tourism.

The platform provided for FICCI and VICCI to interact as a result of the Presidential visit was seen to be an ideal mechanism for close communication ties to be set up for the facilitation of commercial agreements for the future. It helped in establishing a framework for a strategic partnership and for long-term import-export strategies.

The high level meetings were seen by both nations as being extremely fruitful as the outcomes were optimistic on all sides. Representatives of both countries seemed enthusiastic to increase trade and commerce between them. The two nations decided to increase the trade target to US$ 7 billion by 2015, from the present level of US$ 2.7 billion. The fact that both nations felt an increase of more than double to be feasible augurs well for the future, it was thought. Officials from both nations felt the need to expedite the drafting of the India-ASEAN Free Trade Agreement in Service and Investment. India and Vietnam also discussed significant issues related to the situation in the Vietnamese Eastern Sea (South China Sea). Both nations also decided to launch a Biennial Security Dialogue to facilitate quick solutions between the home ministries of the countries.[7]

India and Vietnam entered into several agreements in a wide range of areas. The following are the most significant:

- India and Vietnam signed an extradition treaty.
- Oil exploration agreement in South China Sea.
- Friendship pact to celebrate the 40th anniversary of the diplomatic relations in 2012.
- Agreement in the field of agriculture and fisheries.
- Cooperation in sports and tourism.
- Agreement on cultural exchanges.

Outcomes

- All the companies that accompanied the President have expanded their operations in Vietnam.
- Bohra Industries have set up a US$ 20 million project in Vietnam.
- Essar Group has signed a joint venture agreement with Vietnam Steel Corp. and Vietnam Rubber Corp., to set up a US$ 527 million hot strip mill in the Phu ME Industrial zone in Baria Vung Tau province.

- Essar Exploration and Production Ltd. has won a contract for off-shore exploration in Vietnam's Song Hong Basin, with an investment of approximately US$ 60 million.
- KCP Ltd. has set up a new sugar plant.
- Angelique International and Futurelinks have been awarded a few infrastructure projects in Vietnam.
- Several Indian pharma companies like Torrent have entered into the Vietnamese markets.

Indonesia: November–December, 2008

On the second leg of her tour, President Smt. Pratibha Patil visited Bali and Jakarta, in Indonesia. On this phase, she was not accompanied by any business delegation.

Spain: April, 2009

In April 2009, President Smt. Pratibha Patil embarked on a visit to Spain and Poland. This was the first ever state visit by an Indian President to Spain. The trip aimed at further boosting the existing good relations between India and several European countries.

"President's visit to Spain and Poland will not only improve bilateral ties with these two nations but also with the European Union," an official said.[8] The official underlined the strategic significance of this trip in strengthening India's links with the European Union.

President Smt. Pratibha Patil's official delegation included the Minister of State for Industrial Policy and Promotion, Ashwani Kumar and sizeable business delegation comprising members of Confederation of Indian Industry (CII), the Federation of Indian Chambers of Commerce and Industry (FICCI) and the Associated Chambers of Commerce and Industry of India (ASSOCHAM).

Sensitive issues like the economy and the world's fight against terrorism were on the agenda for discussion between the President and her counterparts.

The CEOs of five diverse sectors, including IT, infrastructure and development and construction, financial services, railway applications, dyes and chemicals, energy, agri business, heavy engineering, high technology electronics, textile and automobiles, accompanied the President on this trip.

The CII had presented a report pointing to potential areas of joint development and cooperation between Spain and India and suggested that there are certain crucial areas that should be the focus of deliberations. These would include IT, environmental technology, aerospace, automobiles, infrastructure, transportation, pharma, SMEs and textiles.

Outcomes

The high level meetings and discussions were considered to be extremely fruitful as they were instrumental in the signing of several MOUs between the Indian Government and the Spanish Ministries in the areas of agriculture, renewable energy and tourism.

The specifics of the MOUs are as follows:

Agriculture
- Transfer and sharing of knowledge between the two nations.
- Development of bilateral cooperation, focusing on technical and technological fields.
- Constitution of a monitoring committee.
- Identification of areas of cooperation for institutional, legislative, regulatory aspects and legislations in the field of agriculture.

Renewable Energy
- Collaboration in the field of new and renewable sources of energy.
- Joint development in the field of renewable energy, particularly wind, solar, hydropower and biofuels.
- Exchange of expertise through holding seminars, workshops and other meetings.
- Establishment of a body to review and monitor matters related to this MOU.

Tourism
- Recognition of the importance of tourism as a factor of sustainable development.

- To mutually encourage the development of tourism in both countries.
- Promotion of HRD in tourism and travel-related industry in both countries.
- Promotion of cooperation in areas of tourism administration and management, product development, marketing and private sector cooperation.

In addition to these MOUs, a few other sectors were identified as potentially highly beneficial to both countries. They are: infrastructure development, Research and Development, and access through Spain to the Latin American market.

The Indian delegation evinced a high degree of interest in other sectors like infrastructure management and control. Indian business houses visited the Highway Control Centre of Madrid to study it.[9]

Areas identified where there is scope for cooperation in the future:
- Exchange programs at university level.
- Cooperation between Spanish and Indian hospitality training institutes.
- Investment relationships through mergers and joint ventures.
- Technology transfer for infrastructure development.
- Research and technology transfer in the public health system.
- Joint programs on entrepreneurship development between Indian and Spanish SMEs.
- Discussions with Spanish immigration authorities to facilitate free movement of Indian skilled manpower, intra-company transfers and business cooperation.

Poland: April, 2009

President Smt. Pratibha Patil made a four-day visit to Poland, the fourth by a high level Indian dignitary. Her visit was seen as being highly significant in view of India's increasingly high profile image in Eastern Europe, in the last five years.

The President's trip came after a long gap of thirteen years, the last President to visit being Shankar Dayal Sharma, in 1996. President Smt. Pratibha Patil was received by her Polish counterpart Lech Kaczynski. A hectic agenda drawn up for the two Presidents and several agreements lined up to be discussed and finalised, particularly in the realm of tourism and health.

The same business delegation, comprising 24 members, including well-known Indian industrialist Prakash Hinduja, that accompanied the President to Spain was with her on her trip to Poland. The Poland-India Chamber of Commerce and Industry (PICCI) had arranged a big meeting for them with Polish entrepreneurs. Several Polish business houses had expressed tremendous interest in partnering with Indian business houses.

"The profile of India has gone up tremendously in Poland in the last five years. Everyone still sees India as a huge market even in these recessionary days," said J.J. Singh, president of PICCI.[9]

President Smt. Pratibha Patil also met Polish Prime Minister Donald Tusk, Parliament Speaker Bronislaw Komorowski, and Senate Speaker Bogdan Borusewicz.

Janus Krzyzowski, President of the India-Polish Cultural Committee, expressed his surprise that no Indian Prime Minister had visited Poland after the fall of Communism in that nation.

However, the prospects of trade appeared bright in view of the rising figures for commerce between the two countries. Trade had risen from a humble $200 million in 2003 to a staggering $800 million in 2008. In the previous five years, Poland had become a strategic base for several Indian computer companies by virtue of its positioning in Eastern and Central Europe. Tata Consultancy Services and Reliance, among others, had made it the centre for their operations.

There has also been an increase in Indo-Polish exchanges in the area of military cooperation subsequent to the visit of the then Defence Minister and current President Pranab Mukherjee in December 2004. This had been followed up by a visit to strengthen defence alliances by Army Chief Gen. Deepak Kapoor.

President Smt. Pratibha Patil also made a tour of scenic places in Poland, universities and the infamous Auschwitz Concentration Camp where six million Jews were killed in obedience to Hitler's orders.

The major areas of focus of the business delegation were as follows:
- Economic cooperation with Poland to benefit Indian entrepreneurs.
- Facilities and promotional packages being extended by Polish SEZs.
- Cooperation in the fields of Food Processing, Mining, Chemicals, Renewable and Geothermal Energy.
- Encouragement to Indian private enterprise to participate in the Polish power Generating Sector.

In addition, scope was felt for economic cooperation in the knowledge-based industries, bio-technology, pharmaceuticals, automobiles and auto components, infrastructure, health tourism, higher education, and the establishing of centres for alternative medicine like Ayurveda and Yoga.

Some members of the delegation also felt that collaboration with Poland for the upgrading of roads and railways in India would be beneficial to our country.

Outcomes

- Indian entrepreneurs set up a project with Polish counterparts under Public Private Partnership (PPP), for infrastructure projects like sporting facilities, roads, water and sewage infrastructure, waste incinerators, schools, etc.
- CII, along with the Polish Trade and Investment Promotion body organized an advisory workshop in Delhi. Speakers expounded the advantages of Indo-Polish collaborative projects.
- Cooperation in areas like education, tourism and hospitality institutions, business and professional services, and renewable energy development to be stepped up.

Russia: September, 2009

In Sep., 2009, President Smt. Pratibha Patil undertook a weeklong visit to Russia and Tajikistan. It was the President's maiden trip to Russia in which she sought to further consolidate the good relationship that India has sustained with the "close friend and partner".[10] The trip was an important step to strengthen bilateral ties between these two nations and India. In fact, this agenda topped the President's list. In order to take some strident steps forward in the direction of greater collaboration between the nations, the President was accompanied by the Minister for Petroleum and Natural Gas, Murli Deora, and the Minister for Textiles, Panabaka Lakshmi.

Meetings had been scheduled first with the Russian President Dmitry Medvedev and Prime Minister, Vladimir Putin, to discuss regional and international issues, including the global acts of terrorism. Moscow described its ties with New Delhi as being defined by a "special trust". In response, President Smt. Pratibha Patil said that "the time-tested relationship between India and the Russian Federation has been marked by continuity, trust and mutual understanding".

Once the formal meetings were concluded, the President met with the Chairman of the Federation Council and the Speaker of the Duma.

Russia has a huge Indian presence. President Smt. Pratibha Patil met the Indian community and Friends of India, and witnessed the Indian cultural performance put up by them.

President Smt. Pratibha Patil in her speech made a note that the economic relations had become the "cornerstone" of the bilateral ties between the two nations and after the talks, there was a general agreement that the volume of trade must be raised to US$ 10 billion by 2010. The leaders of both nations felt that this was feasible in spite of the economic slowdown. The target figure was realistic in view of the continued growth in bilateral trade.

At a formal reception hosted in her honour by the Russian President, President Smt. Pratibha Patil remarked warmly on the tested relationship between Russia and India—"Indeed, our friendship has stood the test of time as our two countries have come to each other's aid in times of difficulty".[11] Speaking of strengthening cooperation in areas such as energy, space and defence, mutual investments in industries, high technology, IT, banking and finance, the President said there was immense scope for mutual development through partnerships.

For his part, Mr. Medvedev expressed Russia's need for Indian cooperation in the fields of energy, metallurgy, mechanical engineering, knowledge-intensive industries, the on-going construction of the Kudankulam nuclear plant and ONGC's involvement in the Sakhalin-I project.

Nirupama Rao, Foreign Secretary affirmed that "our wide-ranging cooperation on defence, nuclear energy and space formed the solid bedrock" of ties with Russia.[11]

India and Russia have a history of cooperation in the nuclear and defence areas. Russian involvement in the Kudankulam nuclear plant and a Russian designed power plant at new locations in India were initiatives already under way. Several joint Research and Development, and training and service contracts had also been entered into.

ONGC-Videsh Ltd. had acquired a 20% share in the Sakhalin-I oil and gas project in Russia by investing around US$ 2.8 billion. This is one of the biggest investments made by India, abroad. This makes the energy sector very important in the Indo-Russian bilateral relations.

The bilateral trade in 2007–08 was USD 3.41 billion, highly favourable to Russia.

Outcomes

- The two countries have completed the design of an unmanned lunar orbiter due to be sent to the Moon in 2011-2012.
- Russia is due to build an additional four reactors for the Kudankulam nuclear power plant in India under a deal signed in 2008.
- At the recent MAKS-2009 air show in Moscow, Russia's state arms exporter, Rosoboronexport and India's Hindustan Aeronautics Ltd. (HAL) signed a contract for 26 RD-33 series 3 engines.
- The first batch of ten T-90 Bhishma battle tanks, assembled in India under Russian license, was handed over to the Indian Army.

Tajikistan: September, 2009

From Russia, President Smt. Pratibha Patil travelled to Tajikistan, from 6–8 September, 2009. President Smt. Pratibha Patil made history as she was the first Indian President to visit this nation. President Smt. Pratibha Patil held talks with Tajikistan President Emomali Rakhmon on a wide range of issues, including efforts to tackle terrorism, promote bilateral relations, and developments in and around the region aimed at consolidating ties between the two countries in the political, economic and other spheres.

An important part of her agenda was the inauguration of the India-Tajikistan Joint Business Forum, while in Tajikistan. President Smt. Pratibha Patil had high level discussions which also focussed on trade relations with the Tajik President, and the Prime Minister, Oquil Oquilov.

Tajikistan's strategic location has made it even more important for India to maintain good relations with this nation. It shares borders with Uzbekistan, Kyrgyzstan, Afghanistan, and China, and is located in proximity to Pakistan-occupied Kashmir (PoK). Jihadis and human trafficking are two major concerns that India shares with Tajikistan. A joint working group on counter terrorism is working on controlling terrorist infiltration along with Russia and Iran.

During Tajik President's visit to India, four bilateral pacts were signed to enhance cooperation in fighting terrorism, and to work together in the fields of science, technology and energy. Although no treaties were signed during the Indian President's visit, the trip itself was seen as indicative of Tajikistan's critical importance to India. India and Tajikistan have maintained a good relationship of mutual goodwill and understanding and President Smt. Pratibha Patil's visit underscored the nation as being on the priority list of India. In her speech, the President spoke of the importance of working together to stem the onslaught of terrorist activities.

President Smt. Pratibha Patil also dealt with bilateral issues like cooperation in the development of the hydroelectric power generation in Tajikistan. As the country had the potential to develop its hydroelectric capacity to a much greater extent, this is where the possibility for Indian involvement existed. Russia, Iran and China are already playing a major role in the hydroelectric sector in Tajikistan. India is also helping in the Varzob-I Hydro Power Station. Indian companies like National Hydro Power Corporation (NHPC) and BHEL are already involved but there is scope for enhancing their participation. This would be mutually beneficial to both nations.

Tajikistan also has rich deposits of gold, silver and more than 40 semi-precious stones. India could be involved in setting up units for the excavation and for the manufacture of jewellery that would contribute substantially to the economic growth of both countries.

India has provided training for Tajik forces and there is a high level of cooperation between the two nations in the realm of defence.

However, the trade statistics between the two countries remain unsatisfactory. Tajik-India trade relations accounted for $15.50 million during 2006-07 and $22.11 million during 2007–08. Officials from both nations agreed that there was immense potential to increase the volume of trade to mutually benefit all concerned.

The President stressed that Tajikistan's deposits of oil and gas are not fully exploited at present and the government there is seeking to tap this potential. Tajikistan's abundance of metals and minerals makes it the country with one of the richest natural resources in the region.[12]

During the visit of the President to Tajikistan, the CII organized a 14 member delegation to Dushanbe, comprising representatives from the Sur Group, Mahindra & Mahindra, KEC International Ltd., Dynamic Logistics Ltd., Shyam Telecom Ltd., Ravi Energie, Stylrite Optical Industries, Annapurna Hing Pvt. Ltd., Ambo Exports Ltd., Marvis Pvt. Ltd. and Atlas Cycles Ltd.[13]

The primary objective of the business mission was to study the potential to enter into business and enhance bilateral trade between the two countries. The Coordination Council of the Business Association of Tajikistan organized visits to various sites to enable the delegation to study the opportunities.

The sectors identified for cooperation between India and Tajikistan include hydro-electric power generation, agriculture, mining, infra-structure, IT, banking, financial services, commodity trade, food processing, pharma, tourism, education and automobiles.

Outcomes

Attempts to establish business in Tajikistan by Sur Group and Atlas Cycles are facing major challenges from Chinese and Russian competitors.

United Kingdom: October–November, 2009

President Smt. Pratibha Patil embarked on a three-day visit to Britain in Oct., 2009. This would be the third visit by an Indian President, but after a long gap of almost twenty years. The President's trip was organized in response to an invitation by Queen Elizabeth.

Indian diplomats noted that a great change had taken place in the economic relationship between the two countries, with India now having become the second largest investor in the UK, following closely after the US.

Among the many important issues in the agenda for the President's visit, these would definitely include political, economic and environmental situations. The President met with British Prime Minister Gordon Brown and they worked through the Afghan issue, the situation in South Asia, climate change, WTO trade talks, and the world financial crisis. Not far behind were also the areas of cooperation in education, research, counter-terrorism and economic alliances that the two leaders and their delegations considered.

The President was also scheduled to attend a business meeting organized by the UK-India Business Council. In addition, she met the Lord Mayor of the City of London and British Members of Parliament.

The President's visit was also considered significant as it was the first State visit after the relation between the two countries was strengthened by the Strategic Partnership Treaty signed in 2004. She addressed business delegations of both countries and emphasized the need for greater cooperation between India and the United Kingdom in areas of education, climate change and health care.

The Indian business delegation that accompanied the President was organized by FICCI and consisted of CEOs from India's top business enterprises, cutting across sectors. It was led by Harish Patil Singhania, President, FICCI.

A summit on 'UK-India Partnership in Action' was organized by the UK-India Business Council (UKIBC). The summit was addressed by dignitaries from both countries. At the end of the deliberations, the speakers felt that some of the key areas where cooperation between the two nations would yield high results, were: infrastructure financing, small and medium enterprises, IT and ITES, S&T, biotechnology, pharmaceuticals, health environment protection and conservation. The President stressed that, if the business communities of both countries worked together, much development could be achieved in both nations.

The President of FICCI said that he believed that the economies of UK and India were showing signs of recovery and because of this, doubling the level of bilateral trade between the two countries in the following three to five years, was a real possibility.

Outcomes

- The Commonwealth Business Club of India (CBCI) was launched.
- A MOU was signed between FICCI and the organization committee of the Commonwealth Games 2010.

The shared agenda of these fora was to enhance business outreach and promote India as an attractive investment and business destination.

Cyprus: October–November, 2009

From the UK, President Smt. Pratibha Patil made a two-day stop-over at Cyprus, where she met with President Demetris Christofias.

Meetings had been arranged between the business delegation that accompanied the President and members of the business community in Cyprus. President Smt. Pratibha Patil stated that the bilateral trade between the two nations was US$ 68 million. She said that this was far below the potential for trade and that members of both business communities must resolve to remedy this situation to the benefit of both. The President went on to enumerate the vast possibilities open to business people for making alliances in the fields of Information Technology and knowledge-based industry. This, she said, was important in view of the emphasis being placed on these two areas of development for the economy of Cyprus.

Before leaving the nation, the President paid a floral tribute at the statue of Mahatma Gandhi.

China: May, 2010

In May, 2010, President Smt. Pratibha Patil made a trip to China to consolidate trade relations with that nation. During her six-day visit, the Presidential agenda was tightly knit with the inauguration of a Buddhist temple, a visit to the India and China pavilions at the Shanghai Expo 2010, and several high level meetings with the India-China Business Forum, which she addressed and also participated in discussions.

The two countries pledged to intensify their strategic alliances through political dialogue, cultural diplomacy and economic cooperation. The President's visit revolved around these three key areas. Foreign Secretary Nirupama Rao further emphasized this fact by stating that the visit "signals our unequivocal commitment to deepen and expand our strategic and cooperative partnership with China".[14]

The President had several meetings with senior Chinese leaders including her counterpart, Hu Jintao, and other Chinese officials. All these talks were aimed to "upgrade China-India relations to higher levels". A Chinese ministry spokesman commented on the President's visit as the "time to deepen bilateral understanding and cooperation".[15]

The President also addressed a business conference that was well attended by industrialists from both countries. China considered the President's visit as "Fruitful and successful" primarily because it would go a long way in the promotion and development of bilateral ties between India and China.[16]

The Chinese Foreign Ministry spokesman Ma Zhaoxu said that the two countries had "entered into a period of stability and steady progress".[17] This could be assessed by the fact that, the officials of both nations were able to reach a consensus on many major long-standing issues.

The President was accompanied on her trip to China by a high level official delegation including a Union Minister, Member of Parliament, Secretaries of various departments and senior officials. There was also a 57 member Business Delegation—representatives of India's biggest business houses—the largest contingent that had ever accompanied the President. An India-China business Forum was organized by the China Council for Promotion of International Trade (CCPIT) for the contingent. ASSOCHAM was directed by the Government of India to coordinate the Indian business delegation, the largest ever, to accompany a President on a foreign tour. The India-China Business Forum utilized the opportunity to meet India's President to acquaint her with issues relating to being involved with business with China. There was also a lively discussion related to prospects for further enhancement of trade exchanges between the two countries. Businessmen from both nations came away feeling that the visit of the Indian contingent had been a success.

Some major thrust areas for business identified were:
- Pharmaceuticals
- IT
- Infrastructure
- Education
- Minerals
- Agriculture

Observations made from the visit:
- Need for confidence building
- Promotion of Chinese language to facilitate comprehension
- Increase in jobs in IT sector
- Development of pharmaceutical sector.

Outcomes

- Business Chambers trying to get concerned Chinese ministry to sign MOU to enable Indian banks to clear banking transactions in China.

Lao PDR/Laos: September, 2010

With a view of further strengthening India's presence in the Far East, President Smt. Pratibha Patil paid a state visit to Laos and Cambodia in

Sep., 2010. The visit was part of India's 'Look East Policy', aimed at the unveiling of hitherto untapped, but potential markets to drive India's economic development at an even faster pace.

The President's visit to Laos was in response to the invitation of the President of Laos, Choummaly Sayasone, who had extended this invitation on his visit to India in Aug., 2008.

A delegation of senior officials accompanied the President on the trip. Her visit is considered significant as it is only the second visit of an Indian President to Laos after Dr. Rajendra Prasad's visit in 1959. The delegation travelled to the Laotian capital Vientiane, and then also visited Luang Prabang.

Meetings between President Smt. Pratibha Patil, President Sayasone and the Prime Minister Bouasone Bouphavanh were held, in addition to official talks between delegates from both nations. President Smt. Pratibha Patil stated that her visit was intended to affirm India's commitment to the strengthening and consolidation of bilateral ties between Laos and India. She also asserted that it was the intention of her government to enter into joint ventures that would help in socio-economic development of both nations as well as assured India's desire to engage in greater economic assistance to Laos.

The President was accompanied by a business contingent representing 25 Indian companies, who attended the Forum, in addition to the CII, FICCI and ASSOCHAM, the Lao National Chamber of Commerce and Industry and the Indian Chamber of Commerce in Laos.

The President addressed the India-Laos Business Forum and called upon Indian businessmen present to avail of the opportunities provided by the investment environment in Laos. She urged Indian businessmen to consider entering into the hydropower, mining, construction, roads, railways and agricultural sectors in this growing nation and be a part of its development. She called the attention of the business investors to the simplified laws in Laos that make dealing with this nation easy. The President stated that several changes that had taken place in recent years had facilitated bilateral trade, like the Duty Free Tariff Preference Scheme for Least Developed Countries and the India-ASEAN Free Trade Agreement. In spite of this, trade was still at a very low level, running below US$ 7 million. The President appealed to all the businessmen attending the Forum to make strident moves to change this situation.

Outcomes

- Letters of Intent signed between the Indian Chamber of Commerce in Laos and the Lao National Chamber of Commerce & Industry, the CII and the ASSOCHAM.
- India agreed to extend a line of credit to Laos for US$ 72.55 million for two hydropower projects.

Cambodia: September, 2010

From Laos, President Smt. Pratibha Patil travelled to Cambodia, where she was a guest of the King of Cambodia, Norodom Sihamoni. The visit was considered highly significant as India and Cambodia share close cultural ties and a historical affinity that goes back a long way. The trip was also aimed at giving a fillip to India's "warm and cordial relations" with Laos and Cambodia.[18] President Smt. Pratibha Patil was accompanied by Minister for Tribal Affairs, Kantilal Bhuria. Cambodia and India are also important members of the ASEAN countries. At the present time, Cambodia is the coordinator for India-ASEAN relations, hence the visit took on an even more important dimension. Along with Laos, Cambodia supports India's bid for Permanent Membership of the UN Security Council.

The President visited the Cambodian capital of Phnom Penh and then travelled with a high level delegation to Siem Reap, the location of the world-famous temples of Angkor Wat. At both cities, meetings were held between delegates from India and officials from the host nation. The platform provided a great opportunity for consolidation of strong bilateral ties between India and Cambodia. Several discussions were also held to explore the possibilities of commercial and investment relations between the business communities of both countries.

The President told the Indian media that she was sure her visit would do much to chart out the means for promoting greater stability and security in the region. She added that there would be individual gains for the three nations in cooperating with one another to combat terrorism and extremism.

In addition, the President was accompanied by a business delegation which was on the look-out for business opportunities in both countries.

UAE: November, 2010

To boost India's relationship with the Gulf region, President Smt. Pratibha Patil made a visit to the UAE and Syria. The President's trip was in response to an invitation from the President of the UAE, Sheik Khalifa bin Zayed Al Nahyan.

The President was accompanied by a business delegation and had structured into the agenda of the visit, a number of interactions with industrialists of the UAE. This was seen as a significant move to take forward the existing figures of trade between the two nations. The Gulf has emerged as a top destination for India's exports, registering a whopping 13.41% of the country's total export volumes in 2009–10.

Discussion between the two Heads of State focused on bilateral issues in every sphere, political, economic and cultural.

Several platforms were made available for the members of the business delegation to interact with captains of industry in the UAE and potential areas of commerce were deliberated upon. Both nations were looking to enhance their investment opportunities with the other.

The delegation had in-depth interactions in Abu Dhabi and Sharjah. At Sharjah the contingent had the opportunity to visit the Harariyah Free Zone, Dubai. Here, they were well-received and acquainted with market opportunities and made aware of immense untapped potential for trade and commerce in a wide range of sectors in the UAE.

The delegation had meetings with the Abu Dhabi Chamber of Commerce over lunch and these discussions continued at the reception hosted by the Indian Ambassador, who had also invited the crème-de-la-creme of the Indian business community in Dubai.

The President also organized a meeting between the business delegation and renowned business leaders from the UAE. The group brain-stormed together and came up with innumerable ideas for furthering trade and business relations between the two countries. Several companies whose representatives were present during the sessions were able to begin the process of forging alliances at these meetings. Among them were: Apollo Hospitals (healthcare) HCL Infosystems, (IT & ITES), Raheja Developers (real estate), Punj Lloyd (EPC projects), and Rashtriya Chemicals and Fertilizers.

Several areas of business were identified by the group, like: education, oil and gas, banking, infrastructure, real estate, healthcare, skill development and IT & ITES. A general consensus emerged that the scope for business alliances was immense. Most felt that the best way to start would be cooperation in Small and Medium Enterprises (SMEs), in order to increase economic cooperation.

One evening, Deloitte organized a presentation entitled 'Doing Business with UAE'. Its content and informative value received high commendation.

Outcomes

- Indian delegates impressed UAE counterparts, resulting in a number of possible partnerships and JVs across sectors, starting up in the near future.
- Decision taken to hold India-UAE Joint Business Council to revitalise existing bilateral relations.
- The interactions at Abu Dhabi and Dubai Chambers of Commerce led to a focus on promoting bi-directional exchange of business delegations and dissemination of business-related information to members.
- BEML had a successful meeting with Dubai Metro for contributing their expertise to prestigious infrastructure projects in the Emirate.
- The visit and the business interactions received wide media coverage in the UAE.
- Apollo Hospitals have mooted discussions for establishing referral centres in the UAE.
- UAE participated in CII at the IETF in Feb., 2011 as the focus country. India did business events with Sheikha Lubna, Minister for Foreign Trade of UAE, who was the Chief Guest.

- CII is working closely with the IBPC in Delhi to organize business events in India and in the UAE to promote bilateral trade and investment.

Syria: November, 2010

President Smt. Pratibha Patil's visit to Syria was the first ever by an Indian Head of State. After a ceremonial welcome that was accorded to her at the Presidential Palace, she held talks with Syrian President, Bashar al-Assad. During his visit to India in 2008, bilateral political and economic relations were strengthened. India's involvement in the Syrian economic sphere had increased substantially. President Smt. Pratibha Patil's visit was seen as a further augmentation of those ties already established by President Assad's earlier visit to India. Her aim was to focus on bilateral issues—political, economic and cultural. She would also be looking at investment opportunities in both countries, to ensure mutual development.

Trade levels with Syria had not seen much enhancement—they stood at a modest US$530 million. Blueprints were being laid by the Indo-Syrian Joint Commission to increase this figure to twice as much by doubling the volume of trade. The Presidential visit was expected to boost these figures substantially. President Smt. Pratibha Patil also, officially launched the India-Syria Business Council to look into areas of possible development of trade and commerce that would drive bilateral trade to a new high.

Outcomes

- Possibility of cultural agreement between Doordarshan and the Syrian national broadcaster.
- Possible agreement between the Press Trust of India and the official Syrian news agency.
- IT centre being established in Syria with Indian assistance, to be functional shortly.
- Indian organization, MECON, to submit feasibility study on utilization of Syria's phosphate resources.
- Power project partly funded by India, being executed by BHEL.

- Apollo International, India, upgrading a steel plant in Hama, for which India has extended a credit facility of US$25 million.[19]

Mauritius: April, 2011

President Smt. Pratibha Patil visited the beautiful island nation of Mauritius from 24–28 April, 2011. Her tightly packed itinerary included an address to the national assembly and bilateral talks with the nation's top leadership. During her meetings with her counterpart Sir Anerood Jugnauth and Prime Minister Navinchandra Ramgoolam, issues of regional and international interest were looked into, in some depth.

The External Affairs Ministry said in a statement that, "India-Mauritius partnership today is mutually beneficial, comprehensive, deep and diverse. The commitment of the two countries to democratic ideals, values and pluralism reinforces the close ties that they enjoy". The Ministry further said that the President's visit was "part of the process of exchanges at the highest political level between India and Mauritius", as the alliance between the two countries was "firmly rooted in history, tradition and cultural affinities".[20]

The President's visit, it was felt, would give a thrust to the further consolidation of this bond, while enhancing the India-Mauritius trade partnership.

A high level business delegation comprising of 57 Indian businessmen were also on the trip. They were there to study opportunities to increase the economic ties between the two nations.

The delegation was headed by Navin Raheja, Managing Director, Raheja Developers Ltd. The Indian business persons hailed from a whole range of sectors like the cement industry, telecommunications, real estate, education, IT, agriculture, agri-inputs—agrochemicals, fertilizers and seeds, infrastructure, finance and legal services, cable manufacturers, industrial granites, technical and higher education, art and design and IT applications in the healthcare sector.

There were several high-level meetings between the Indian delegates and the businessmen of Mauritius. Ample opportunities were provided for interaction between the business communities of the two countries to meet.

Outcomes

- Businessmen from both countries agreed to increase exchanges in the fields of IT, higher education, tourism, science and technology, hospitality, rural development and culture.
- The Board of Investment of Mauritius organized an interactive session between those involved in business in Mauritius and Mauritian ministers. It was the perfect platform to raise their concerns and get answers to queries. The high level ministerial delegation assured them of the local governmental support in all their ventures.
- The Mauritian Board of Investment made a presentation highlighting investment opportunities in that country. The Board deputed officials from government agencies to work out specifics for the Indian delegates, if need arose.
- The Mauritian President called for a meeting with members of the business delegation in the presence of the High Commissioner of India in Mauritius to take note of business issues that do crop up, and take his inputs on resolving them.
- The Minister of Tourism organized a cultural show called 'Soul of the World' for the Indian delegates. The ministry expressed its aim of doubling the number of tourists from India by the year 2015.
- Stressing on the strong Indian presence in Mauritius, the Minister of Industry and Commerce of Mauritius noted that Indian companies like the State Bank of India, Bank of Baroda, Life Insurance Corporation of India, Indian Oil and the Oberoi Hotel were well established. He announced that an investment project by Binani Cement was under consideration. Members of both business communities were able to interact one-on-one at the networking lunch hosted jointly by the JEC and the MCCI.
- The Federation of Mauritius Business Chambers (FMBC) held a meeting with a hundred of their delegates, for the Indian side. It emphasized the opportunities for business development and acclaimed Mauritius as an investment-friendly country.

Interestingly, Mauritius is the single largest source of foreign direct investment in India, accounting for 40% of FDI flows in the last ten years. According to the Reserve Bank of India, the amount of FDI flows from Mauritius to India was US$ 49.11 billion from 2000 to 2009. For the year 2010 alone, the figures stood at US$ 10.37 billion. The bilateral trade volume at the time of President Smt. Pratibha Patil's visit in 2011 was around US$ 465 million.

Another important aspect of the bilateral talks was the sharp increase in the use of Mauritius as an offshore base for terrorists and other entities that wish to target India. This was part of the discussion points related to the 'Bilateral Investment Promotion and Protection Agreement', signed by the two nations in 1998.

President Smt. Pratibha Patil said that she hoped her visit would enhance the scope of the "dynamic and ever-expanding bilateral cooperation" between India and Mauritius.[20]

The President also met with the large Indian community in Mauritius and assured them of the Indian Government's desire to expedite initiatives for the benefit of its diaspora, like the right to vote, and plans to merge the PIO (Person of Indian Origin) card with the OCI (Overseas Indian Citizen) card. She said that plans were afoot to work out a mechanism whereby overseas Indians could have the benefits of one card.

Republic of Korea (South Korea): July, 2011

In 2011, President Smt. Pratibha Patil went on a three-day visit to the Republic of Korea in which she scheduled discussions on a wide range of issues like civil nuclear cooperation, trade and defense.

It is believed that her visit is part of India's 'Look East Policy' to garner further support from nations in our eastern neighbourhood. These nations are established as manufacturers of a variety of home appliances as well as being rich in mineral resources.

A number of important agreements were signed at Seoul and Ulaanbaatar. These were seen as an important follow-up to the Comprehensive Economic Partnership Agreement (CEPA) concluded by the Joint Task Force, which was signed in 2009, but came into force in 2010.

The purpose of this agreement was for signatories to boost trade and investigate new commercial opportunities.

Apart from meetings and high level discussions, the President also met with business delegates to expand the business base between the two nations. India also sought to explore the possibility of strengthening its nuclear understanding with South Korea and the Indian Atomic Energy Commission. President Smt. Pratibha Patil said that she would "push for a civil nuclear cooperation with South Korea".[21]

"It was important to be able to strike this deal with Korea, in the wake of such a pact with Japan falling through", nuclear scientists said. South Korea was also keen to enter into this deal as it would mean that its firms could construct reactors in India. This deal came as a result of the strong relationship that India has been able to build with its East Asian and South East Asian neighbours.

Deep Kapuria, the leader of the Indian business delegation, pointed out that Korea is fast emerging as an important trading partner of India in the Far East. Bilateral trade between India and Korea had grown nine times since 2001, but there was an imbalance in favour of Korea that needed to be addressed by Indian business. After studying the potential in Korea, he suggested that the following areas had good business potential: IT, pharma, auto components, etc.

Sandeep Tiwari, regional manager, State Bank of India, observed that there were no Indian banks operating in Korea and this lacuna could easily be filled in the near future.

The Chairman of the Indian Chamber of Commerce in Korea, Jong Kim stated that the bilateral trade between India and South Korea was around US$ 13 billion. There was tremendous potential to increase this, he said. It was expected that the CEPA would further boost bilateral trade, up to the tune of US$3.3 billion. Industry partners felt confident that the target of US$ 30 billion for bilateral trade between the two countries should be achieved by 2014.

Outcomes

Luncheon session was held for businessmen to discuss possible areas of trade and investment. These included IT, pharma, automobile parts and education.

- Suggestion was made that, Indians establishing business in Korea learn the language as not knowing Korean can be an obstacle.
- SBI was in the process of opening a branch in Seoul.

Mongolia: July, 2011

President Smt. Pratibha Patil's visit to Mongolia was aimed at finding new avenues in trade and forming tie-ups in defense, IT, trade and mining. It was the first visit of an Indian President in 23 years. India already has a strong export base in Mongolia, chiefly comprising pharmaceuticals, veterinary medicines, automobiles and parts, thereof. Trade between the two nations has touched the US$ 16.9 million mark. However, the Indian President asked Indian industrialists to exploit the immense opportunities in the mining sector in Mongolia, as the country has huge reserves of yet untapped gold, copper and uranium. She felt that "Mongolia's mineral wealth...reserves of coal, copper, gold and uranium, offer investment opportunities for Indian companies", that our business people must take due note of.[22] She urged the business delegation travelling with her to observe that development in mining could have a cascading effect on requirements in the areas of construction, mining equipment, power generation, water-supply and rail transport. Indian companies could get involved in all these areas, she suggested.

Outcomes

- Business meeting with interactive sessions were organized by the industrial bodies of both nations, and attended by entrepreneurs.
- Bilateral agreements on defense cooperation. This agreement is seen as highly significant as it involves a range of cooperation including training, high-level military exchanges and joint exercises.
- Bilateral agreements on media exchange.
- The President invited her counterpart, Ts. Elbegdorj, to become joint-investors in India's socio-economic transformation as financiers or traders.

Switzerland: September, 2011

President Smt. Pratibha Patil went on an eight day visit to Switzerland and Austria. The main agenda for the visit was to build economic cooperation with Switzerland. Speaking to reporters on board the Air India One, enroute to Geneva, President Smt. Pratibha Patil said, "Both countries will look forward to further boost ties in areas of scientific research, educational exchanges and people to people contacts".[23]

The President also emphasized the growing importance of Switzerland as a trade partner, as this nation had emerged as one of the top investors in India. Trade between the two nations had risen by 36% between the years 2006 to 2010, touching an all-time high of US$ 3.7 billion. The President had wide-ranging discussions with her Swiss counterpart Calmy Rey and other members of the Federal Council of Switzerland, while in Berne.

The President visited the prestigious European Organization for Nuclear Research (CERN). It is believed to be one of the most important bodies involved in the research of particle physics.

Outcomes

- A MOU was signed between the University and the Indian Council for Cultural Relations on setting up a Chair of Indian Studies.

Austria: September, 2011

President Smt. Pratibha Patil proceeded from Switzerland to Austria on the second leg of her tour of these nations. From the 5–7th, President Smt. Pratibha Patil was on a state visit to Austria. She was accompanied by a high level business delegation from FICCI, ASSOCHAM and CII.

A meeting was held for the Austria-India Business Forum at the Austrian Federal Economic Chamber in Vienna, and the very fruitful discussions led to the signing of two MOUs between the two countries.

One MOU, that was entered into, was related to improving the railways in India, with particular attention to cooperation in the use of technology for the extension of India's rail capacity, extension of railway lines, modernization of infrastructure and rolling stock. The agreement extended to the provision of technical staff like professionals, technicians and also trainers to raise the standards of Indian staff.

The other MOU was more general in nature, and related to cooperation in science and technology, without being specifically restricted to any one area.

Outcomes

- MOU signed regarding improvement of the Indian Railways.
- MOU signed for cooperation in research in science and technology.

Seychelles: April, 2012

President Smt. Pratibha Patil embarked on what could well be the last foreign trip of her career as President, to South Africa and Seychelles, in April, 2012. President Smt. Pratibha Patil's first leg of her African visit began at the scenic island nation of Seychelles. This was the second presidential visit to Seychelles after that of President Venkataraman in 1989. The island is strategically located in the Indian Ocean. President Smt. Pratibha Patil had a meeting with her counterpart James Alix Michel in which they spoke of several bilateral issues of regional and international significance to both nations. The highlight of her trip was the President's address to the Special Session of the National Assembly. On behalf of India, the President vouched to help the small island country in tackling the menace of piracy, and also extended India's support in the form of a financial package of US$ 75 million.

Outcomes

- A MOU was signed under which police personnel of the island republic would receive training from India's Bureau of Police Research and Development.
- A MOU was entered into to cooperate with the Republic in the area of youth and sports affairs.

South Africa: April, 2012

President Smt. Pratibha Patil's visit helped to boost existing good relations with the African nation, as India's ties with South Africa are enjoined by a strategic partnership. The President's trip augured well for the growing relationship with Pretoria, coming in the wake of Prime Minister Manmohan Singh's visit of 2010, and South African President Jacob Zuma's visit to India in 2010.

A business delegation accompanying the President attended the India-South Africa Business Forum meet, that the President addressed.

The President also had discussions with her South African counterpart Jacob Zuma on key bilateral issues which were seen by the President as being "significant". The leaders talked of expansion of the cooperation between the two nations in several fields like power, IT, healthcare, tourism and infrastructure development.

President Zuma addressed the Indo-South African Business Council where the Indian President was in attendance. He said that bilateral trade could be enhanced to see greater profit sharing between the two nations, as they were already important trading partners.

Trade between the two countries had reached the US$ 11 billion mark in 2010–11. The two leaders hoped that with some intense efforts of the business community, this figure could be raised to US$ 15 billion by 2014.

There is already a long list of items that is being exported from India to South Africa, among them are mineral fuel, mineral oil, engineering goods, textiles, gems and jewellery, chemicals and drugs and pharmaceuticals. On the other hand, India imports large quantities of gold from South Africa.

Conclusion

With this visit to South Africa, President Smt. Pratibha Patil came to the end of her foreign visits as the First Citizen of India. In an interview to a national news channel, the President reiterated that the foreign trips she made were "serious business" and helped to build the country's image while resolving problems that are political or diplomatic in nature.[24] In her five year term as President of this nation, she has done much to make India known to the citizens of the world. She has carried the flavour of India to 24 nations across 4 continents. The President said that in an increasingly interdependent world, "no country can remain in its own cocoon and it was necessary for countries to increase engagement with others".[25] Visiting countries was essential, according to the President, to "make new friends and promote ties with old ones".[25]

She was the first President to start the tradition of taking along an accompanying Business Contingent, thus simultaneously opening up the vistas of commerce to the very individuals who would be pushing it forward. This one action of hers has probably helped many of India's leading businessmen or business aspirants to get a first-hand experience of high-level trade deals and enabled them to interact with fellow-business people from countries across the globe. If there were those imbued with abundant entrepreneurial spirit, then the platform was provided for them to go ahead and cast the net for their dreams.

The President said that in an ever-changing world, relations between countries is no longer only political in nature. Rather, the relationship has to be worked out at various levels, like social, economic and cultural levels as well. In such an environment, she said, high-level trips help in strengthening bonds between people and groups at all levels.

In addition to building good relations between India and several nations of the world, she has signed numerous bilateral trade agreements, negotiated deals for the nation and enhanced trade values for India. By how much? Only time or perhaps history will tell the impact of the foreign visits of President Smt. Pratibha Patil on the larger economy of India.

References

Note: If a reference number occurs twice or more in the chapter, it is another reference to the same source.

[1] http://ibnlive.in.com/news/misconception-over-foreign-trips-pratibha-patil/25531-3.html

[2] Asia Tribune (http://presidentofindia.nic.in/pr071108.html)

[3] http://www.andhranews.net/India/2008/April/12-President-Pratibha-Patil-41039.asp#ixzz1x74y9kB4

[4] http://www.andhranews.net/India/2008/April/12-President-Pratibha-Patil-41039.asp#ixzz1x74WvSlC

[5] headlinesindia.com

http://www.nowpublic.com/world/visit-president-pratibha-patil-india-mexico-defined-historic

[6] http://www.sify.com/news/president-visits-chile-s-republic-of-india-news-national-jegq0Uebhch.html

[7] http://www.jagranjosh.com/current-affairs/india-and-vietnam-signed-six-agreements-including-joint-oil-exploration-in-south-china-sea-1319190056-1

[8] http://www.newstrackindia.com/newsdetails/87642

[9] http://indiatoday.intoday.in/story/President+visits+Spain,+Poland+to+improve+bilateral+ties/1/37610.html

[10] http://www.thehindu.com/news/national/article15546.ece

[11] http://www.indianexpress.com/news/president-leaves-for-visit-to-russia-tajikistan/510763/

[12] http://www.idsa.in/idsastrategiccomments/PratibhaPatilsVisittoTajikistan_msroy_230909

[13] http://www.newstrackindia.com/newsdetails/120536

[14] PTI, May 26, 2010.

[15] Saibal Dasgupta, TNN, May 25, 2010.

[16] http://news.oneindia.in/2010/05/29/pratibha-patil-visit-louyang.html

[17] http://articles.economictimes.indiatimes.com/2010-06-01/news/27581980_1_president-patil-state-visit-loyang

[18] http://www.newstrackindia.com/newsdetails/178400

[19] http://www.thehindu.com/news/national/article915170.ece

[20] http://www.dnaindia.com/india/report_pratibha-patil-on-5-day-state-visit-to-mauritius-from-tomorrow_1535271

[21] http://www.asianscientist.com/topnews/indian-president-pratibha-patil-south-korea-nuclear-deal

[22] http://dailypioneer.com/nation/51600-pms-4-day-korea-visit-to-start-on-march-24.html

[23] http://articles.economictimes.indiatimes.com/2011-09-30/ne

[24] http://ibnlive.in.com/news/misconception-over-foreign-trips=-pratibha-patil/255311-3.html

[25] http://www.asiantribune.com/news/2012/04/29president-pratibha-patil-her-last-foreign-trip-dismisses-criticism

Agrarian Advancement

"Recent unrest in different parts of the world highlights the fact that the future will belong to nations with grains and not guns."
—*M.S. Swaminathan**

"The words of Mahatma Gandhi that, India lives in villages, holds true even today as nearly 70 percent of our population resides in rural areas. With more than six lakh villages, with millions of farm families and millions of farm workers, it is difficult to visualize a prosperous India without rural development."
—*Smt. Pratibha Patil***

In India, agriculture occupies an exceedingly significant site, not only for providing food bowl to the people thereby securing a livelihood for a large number of poor masses, but also because symbolically from ancient time it is an integral part of the socio-cultural and religious fabric of people of India. Agriculture in India is traced to a very ancient period. The Vedic literature and some Sanskrit texts speak volumes of the practice of agriculture in ancient India. Land is seen as the Mother Goddess providing the bountiful through the rain God *Indra*, if the people are virtuous and value driven. But, if the people are debased and have lost their moral moorings, this is manifested through the withdrawal of the rain God, leading to drought and hunger. This is seen as the natural justice. More interestingly, the Hindu religious traditions and festivals are very much integrated to the tradition of agricultural

---

* 37th Session of the Committee on World Food Security (CFS), Rome, Monday 17 October 2011, Statement by Prof. M.S. Swaminathan, Chairperson of the Steering Committee of the High Level Panel of Experts on Food Security and Nutrition.
[Online web] Accessed 1 August 2012, URL: http://www.mssrf.org/mss/CFS-opening-Draft-Statement-MSS.pdf.

**Speech by Her Excellency the President of India, Shrimati Pratibha Devisingh Patil, at the Foundation Day Lecture of the Indian Council of Agricultural Research (ICAR), NASC Complex, Pusa, New Delhi, 16 July 2008.
[Online web] Accessed 10 April 2012, URL: http://presidentofindia.nic.in.

practice; most festivals in India are related to land and crop—sowing the seeds, reaping, harvesting and so on, be they *Ugadi, Onam, Baisakhi, Ganesh Chaturthi* or even *Dussehra* when all the instruments/tools of farming are worshipped, they are all marked by different stages of farming, celebrating the beginning, the end and the onset of a new cycle. In Hindu mythologies like *Ramayan*a, the Saint King *Janak* finds an infant girl while cultivating his land, he adopts her as his daughter, as the gift of Mother Goddess, and names her *Sita*, the lady protagonist of *Ramayana*. Her eventual return and submersion into the land is also symbolic of withdrawal of grace. The key is that even a king could cultivate his land. In the ancient Hindu scriptures one also reads about the *Rishis/Gurus* (teacher) and their *Sisyas* (disciples) worked in the agricultural fields and fended cattle. Though the archeologists and agricultural scientists do not have the uniform view about the origin of agriculture in India, yet it can't be denied that agriculture in India can be traced to a very ancient period, perhaps one of the earliest in the world. Indian agricultural produce was of great demand during the period of mercantile trade in ancient world. It is the wealth of India, stemming from its agricultural prosperity and affluence that captured and beckoned the treacherous fanciness of many of the invaders to the '*Sone ki Chidiya*' (The Golden bird). However, some of the foreign invaders diversified Indian agriculture with their novel techniques of agriculture, while taking away from India their wealth, flora, fauna, cattle and other treasures.

But, in the period of British colonialism, agriculture in India was neglected as Britishers were primarily concerned with the production of that substance which was used as raw material in the factories in Britain. Also, Britain was engaged in shipping food grains to different parts of the world, where their soldiers were fighting wars with other European powers, for the possession or restoration of colonies. The British brought in calamities, as well as, natural disasters which led to widespread famine in different parts of the country in which millions of people across the country died of hunger and starvation. In the post-independence era, Prime Minister Jawaharlal Nehru's foremost concern was to provide food to the millions of hungry hands knocking at his door. In the First Five Year Plan, Nehru significantly focused on the development in the agrarian sector, investing in the construction of dams, enhancing irrigation facilities etc. Though many measures were taken by subsequent governments for the development of agriculture and enhancement of agricultural produce, they were not sufficient to cope with the demands of the mounting population. With the increase in population, which was escalating more rapidly than the growth in agriculture, in the 1960s, this became a very serious concern for the government. During the period of crisis, Prof. M.S. Swaminathan ushered in a new era in the agro-sector, later labeled as the father of 'Green Revolution,' he focused on the scientific use of the modern techniques and introduced technological innovation in the field of agriculture. The green revolution credited to him, was gradually circulated to different parts of the country, which resulted in the substantial production of food grains, an effort to eradicate poverty and hunger. This was accomplished to a large extent, changing the face of India at the world level, as a poor and hungry country.

But we still do not have a complete answer to augment the production of grains to cater to the growing Indian population. While framing and initiating policies, the policy makers in India are very much conscious of the fact that agriculture contributes a significant portion to the GDP of the country and most prominently majority portion of Indian population are dependent on agriculture for earning livelihood for themselves and their families. It is to be remembered that land is constant, and the population is rising, so we need to devise new techniques and innovations to provide food to the growing population. And the global recession has proved that no country in this world can dare to neglect its agricultural sector, it's the food security that will be the biggest concerns of the nation-states in the coming years. In the millions of hungry bellies in Africa, Asia, Latin America and Caribbean, one can feel the agony of human suffering. In the present day scenario, in spite of many initiatives, the problems of the farmers has not ended. Every year farmers in many parts of the country are committing suicide. So, it seems that there are certain basic issues, concerns and problems that need to be addressed, so that the farmers of the country who toil in the scorching sun and subject themselves to untold suffering can feed their families.

Smt. Pratibha Patil's political career, right from her first assignment has been more of activism, trying to tackle the social evils. Her concern for the underprivileged and the deprived in the society took her to the grass root level in the society, grappling with the harsh realities in which the masses live became a priority. Hailing from an agricultural home town herself, Smt. Pratibha Patil has always been aware that the bulk of the Indian population is dependent upon agriculture. Cognizant that a greater part of the cultivated land in India is rainfed, and also about 80% of the farmers involved in this rainfed farming are small farmers. She stressed the need for urgent attention for improving rainfed farming in India, along with the need to be aware of the local realities of a rural life. The farmers in rural areas are still captives in the hands of the village money lenders who exploit the financial helplessness of the farmers. And if the monsoon is cruel and there is no harvest, the farmers land in many kinds of difficulties and exploitations. This primarily leads to the farmer suicides in the country. The farmers need to be provided with easy interest free loans, which the farmers should be allowed to pay at their convenience. Most significantly, the general perception about the farmers as a poor, hungry and ignorant man needs to be changed and should be accorded respectability as the provider of food. These are some of the basic issues that Smt. Pratibha Patil has raised and worked while in Maharashtra politics and carried this forward as the President of India. Smt. Pratibha Patil also aspires for a second green revolution, but the parameters need to be set as it ought to be environment responsive, sustainable, broad-based, and inclusive.

In view of the persistently mounting demand for food grains in India, there is an urgent need to augment the productivity of rainfed areas. Smt. Pratibha Patil, as the President of India has evinced immense concern in this area of dryland farming. She has spoken on the fundamental need and potentiality of rainfed farming on various occasions and has endeavoured to provide a broader mechanism and framework to develop the rainfed farming in India. There is a need to explore Smt. Pratibha Patil's goal, vision and insight on the agrarian scenario of the nation. Her seminal contribution on the mechanism, policy frameworks, farming-industry partnership and the involvement of the corporate sector in the development of dry and rainfed farming and agriculture in India needs a strategic mapping.

Situating the priority line that agriculture segment must occupy in the Indian economy, she had observed that a growing nation like India requires a regular review and a constant renewal of commitments built into our work ethos. Particularly in the agricultural sector, it is time for another great leap forward. This will be possible with a clear recognition of the many existing inter-linkages and a clear roadmap.[1] She posits on the immediate need of "… measures to enhance productivity, profitability, sustainability and competitiveness of the agriculture sector in India, with special reference to rainfed area farming, which is very important for our country in many ways—food security, agro-processing industries, great employability capacity, greener environment and many others."[1] Synergising diverse sectors is the key to growth and advancement, with this as the objective, Smt. Pratibha Patil invited a committee of Governors to plan a road map for 'farmer-industry partnership'.

Indian agriculture is traditionally a system of rainfed agriculture encompassing a huge part of the country. And some of the significant crops like cotton, oil seeds, pulses and coarse cereals are cultivated and grown in most regions. Out of 143 million hectares of net cropped area in India, about 72% is rain reliant production, about 45% of food grains and 75–80% of pulses and oil-seeds and a number of important industrial crops are all rain nourished. But such rain dependent land masses possess the threat of climatic inconsistency. This climatic variability affects the crop, livestock, and food systems. Considering the present rate of development of irrigation facilities and also water potentiality of the country, it can be estimated that at any point of time 50% of harvested area in India will remain below the rainfed category. Such vast areas as of now consume hardly 25% of total fertilizer consumption of the country. Due to poor level of management, crop productivity is also very low, resulting in socio-economic backwardness of the people. At the Committee meeting of Governors on farmer-industry partnership, Smt. Pratibha Patil stressed on the need to be mindful of ground realities, "There are about 145 million rural households in over 6 lakh villages. 82% of total land owners are small and marginal farmers. Can we afford to neglect them? Agriculture remains the largest employer of our national workforce, providing livelihood to about 60% of our people, with 65% of farm work undertaken by women."[1] We have to learn to interrogate and focus on the sustainability of the agriculture and to realize its latent potential, full scale.

She highlighted the statistical data to underscore the significance of dryland farming, "About 60% of the cultivated area in India is rainfed. It provides 44% of food production in the country that includes 85–95% of coarse cereals, 89% pulses, 80% oil seeds, 65% cotton and 45% rice. It supports about 40% of the population, mostly belonging to the poorer sections of society. It also supports nearly 60% of the livestock population."[1] In the Workshop on 'Policy Initiatives for Promoting Partnership between Stakeholders in Agriculture' with particular reference to Rain-Fed/Dryland Farming (RFDF), she emphasizes on several specific features of rainfed and dryland farming: "… It has very low investment as compared to irrigated areas and I think urgent attention to RFDF is warranted, as broadly 80% of farmers in RFDF areas are small farmers. A willingness to look at out-of-the-box solutions is necessary to usher in a noticeable change in handling the subject."[2] Smt. Pratibha Patil strongly believes that, "urgent attention to dryland farming is important—The important point now is to identify, in a comprehensive manner, what is doable, workable and implementable, so that the necessary thrust can be given to the holistic development of rainfed farming."[1]

Reiterating the conviction of Smt. Pratibha Patil, Dr. J.S. Samra, CEO, National Rainfed Area Authority speaking at the conclave of Governors on farmer-industry partnership, organized at the behest of the President of India at Rashtrapati Bhavan on 15 December 2011, stated that only 40–50% of the area will continue to be rainfed in India and the green revolution has bypassed this area, and there is need for a more focused emphasis on the phenomenon. Dr. Samra referred to the Food Security Bill Draft which states that India needs 65 to 74 tonnes of food procurement to serve the food security requirements. The coarse cereals are also included in this draft. There is a subsidy commitment of rupees 1 lakh crores in this bill and this also needs to be reviewed. The rainfed produce commodities like, coarse cereals can help to keep the expenses at moderate costs. In the past, rice and wheat were procured. Highlighting the prospect in the production capability of rainfed farming,

Dr. Samra affirmed that, "the productivity of the rainfed areas has more opportunities, than the productivity of the irrigated agriculture. As the percentage of irrigated area decreases, the productivity also decreases. On the other hand, though the productivity of the rainfed area is only 50–54% of the irrigated area, but it is increasing at a much faster rate as compared to the irrigated area."[3]

The issue of farmers' suicide was a matter of immense concern for the country. Smt. Pratibha Patil opened up deliberations on the issue of debt waiver for farmers, as she felt it is essential that as a nation we need to posit on the concern as a policy matter. 60% of the total cultivated area in India is rainfed, 40% of the agricultural production is from rainfed area, and interestingly 60% of the livestock depend on rainfed areas. This is clearly indicative of the significance of rainfed areas in Indian agriculture. She also laid particular prominence on two aspects: (i) the importance of area farming, (ii) farmer-industry partnership. This becomes necessary as the economic index indicates how the share of agriculture in GDP is going down over a period of time. While it was 18% of GDP five years ago, it has come down to 14.5% last year. The share of agriculture is coming down and this has to be looked into. The President Smt. Patil asserted that all the efforts made should be farmer centric, industry driven and knowledge based which can reengineer the agricultural sector in India.[4]

Smt. Pratibha Patil averred that it should be the objective to ensure that the potential of the rainfed farming is realised most effectively and there is enhancement in the productivity of the rainfed farms. For the effective realisation of this objective, technology has to be used extensively, micro-financing should work successfully at the local level, farmer friendly loans with cheap rate of interest should be provided to the farmers. The marriage of different sectors will be the key to success, an effective collaboration between the farmers and the industry; the corporate sector playing a proactive mandatory role in the development of the rainfed farming can augment the agrarian sector. Also genetic engineering can be used for the maximization of agricultural yield. Expressing her pleasure to address the session on the "Prospects of rainfed farming with special reference to engaging the Corporate Sector," she complimented the people for their interest in such a prominent issue of rainfed farming, for being a part of this initiative, and for recognizing the relevance of this issue in the prosperity of our country's economy. Farmers are the backbone of India's economy, and more than 70% of the Indian population depends upon agriculture. So, farming is one of the key sectors and farmers are one of the key players of the Indian economy. No country can grow without its due respect and share to its farmers. In this speech she noted that though, "During the last few years, there has been a commendable growth in the corporate and service sector performance, yet the plight of the farmers engaged in dryland farming, continues to be less encouraging. The aspiration of ascending GDP cannot be sustained unless the incomes of the farmers, the landless and the disadvantaged in the rural areas get an upward boost; I am convinced that it is time to embark on a sustained Second Green Revolution."[5]

The well anticipated and conceptualised second green revolution should endeavor to focus on the underdeveloped areas such as the irrigation facilities and lack of modern technologies for cultivation. As she says, "Unlike in the 1970s, the green revolution cannot remain confined to the well-endowed irrigated areas only. It has to spread out to rainfed areas which continue to face the challenges of low productivity, lack of technological breakthrough, scarcity of water, absence of better agronomic practices, absence of crop diversification and agricultural extensions. Small fragmented land holdings, which are unable to take advantage of economies of scale, further add to their woes. ... Unless we make the areas the cradle for a second green revolution, these will continue to remain underinvested, undermining the full potential of the agriculture sector as a whole."[5]

Policy Framework

At the first level she emphasised on the policy initiatives to remove factors impeding rapid development in RFDF and to suggest measures to expedite growth. Smt. Pratibha Patil believes that the development of rainfed farming in India will help us in feeding the poor masses of the country. Since most livelihoods are dependent upon agriculture and majority of the lands in India are rainfed, we should develop mechanisms and policy frameworks at the government level involving the civil society organizations to develop and sustain rainfed farming in India. Smt. Pratibha Patil expresses a strong belief that by the Twelfth Five-Year Plan, "it is necessary to give a thrust to RFDF areas that will generate a sense of urgency at the government level to promote partnership between various stakeholders to revitalise Indian agriculture".[6]

Workshop on 'Policy Initiatives for Promoting Partnership between Stakeholders in Agriculture with particular reference to Rainfed/Dryland Farming,' was an enormous step in the direction of policy initiatives. Addressing the think tank, Prime Minister Manmohan Singh affirmed that although farmers had produced an estimated record 250 million food grains this year, but cautioned that the nation cannot remain complacent as demand for agricultural products had been increasing rapidly. "Although food production has regained the momentum in the recent years, we cannot afford to be complacent since the demand of horticulture and animal products are increasing very rapidly. ... A strong agriculture sector is necessary for our food and nutritional security," the PM said.[7]

The participation of agricultural institutions in research inputs for growth cannot be underestimated. Taking this line of thinking forward, Smt. Pratibha Patil has expressed concern over "very low investment" in RFDF areas as compared to integrated areas and called for paying urgent attention towards it.[8] In her address at the College of Agriculture of the Mahatma Phule Krishi Vidyapeeth, Smt. Pratibha Patil reiterated the need to implement extensive programmes to resolve problems faced by rainfed agriculture in the country. She also said agriculture universities should focus on research and see that improved varieties of seeds and crops suitable to local weather conditions are made available to farmers.[9] For the development and sustainability of rainfed farming, Smt. Pratibha Patil spoke about the greater need of a policy framework. She emphasized on an integrated approach in this regard. She claimed that agriculture cannot be perceived as an exclusive activity. For a healthier development and greater production we need an inclusive approach in which the industry, corporate sector, research organizations etc. are collectively together.

Water

Water conservation, creation design and utilization are crucial to a farm sector. Smt. Pratibha Patil's roadmap is simple and could be effective if policy measures are put in place. "One of the most important factors in RFDF is the accessibility of water to the farmer and ensuring its optimal use.... Water and soil conservation activities along with de-silting of the existing water reservoirs will have to be undertaken on a big scale. Proper harvesting of rainwater will also be of great use. I would like to mention here that I know in Rajasthan where there is shortage of drinking water, people used to, and in some places they continue to, dig wells of particular depth and circumference and store rainwater hygienically in the dry wells, to be used later. So, I think why not use the same idea for RFDF. The drywell could be dug in any low lying part of the land for harvesting rainwater. The rainwater collected can be used for crops in dry spells between two rains, particularly when there are delayed rains, during the sowing and crop growing periods as dry spell is what hits the crop the hardest. The water can be taken to the fields through pumps and sprinklers which can be provided to farmers individually or jointly through some mechanism which can be worked out. I understand that a drywell of 5 meter diameter and 10 meter depth can be useful in irrigating crop on one acre and also it is not an expensive proposition and a onetime investment. The wells could be dug under MNREGA and in this way funds under the scheme can be put for productive use in agriculture. There are also instances in RFDF where water in the wells was limited, it was brought by tankers and put in the well, along with some use of manure and drip irrigation was used. Through this practice, yields went up four times. This is another method that can be looked at. I think a down to earth approach needs to be taken into account."[2]

Soil

Another important aspect that she focuses on is the maintenance of soil health which is critical to RFDF. Her concern and guidelines framework for farmers are indicative of the research interest at personal level, "Farmers need to know about the use of appropriate fertilizers at the right time and in adequate quantity. Certain cropping patterns also help the soil retain its nutrients. Vermi-compost and organic manure are better known nature's produce for rejuvenating soil health. Compost pits in every village, as also common facility centers for customized services in agriculture machinery could be thought of. We need to look at innovative methods of providing farm based services through public-private-partnership also. Policy support is needed for such partnerships."[2] Her initiatives in this direction, while setting the tone for development also indicate that much more needs to be accomplished.

Food and Fodder Bank

One of the most significant matters she got the think tank to interrogate on is the synergy between government, financial division, businesses, food processing industries, farm sectors to arrive at a 'food and fodder bank', a concept Smt. Pratibha Patil was keen to explore and institute, "how to coordinate the allied sectors in RFDF? Improved livestock management can lead to huge accretion to milk yield which will increase business opportunities and at the same time result in improved nutritional levels. Also food processing industries can give option of value addition, improving the viability of farming activity, and leading it to an 'enterprise mode', enhancing purchasing power of the farmers and boosting the economy as a whole. This requires the whole-hearted support of the governments and financial institutions and proper guidance. However, can all this be systematically done and made a reality? Greater coherence and coordination of different schemes under different ministries, both at policy formulation level as well as implementation level is important. And there should be planning from village level to block and district levels. A block, generally the administrative unit for all developmental activities, could monitor, coordinate activities in the block. Each block could also be a nucleus of a "food and fodder bank" where food and fodder, is stored as per requirements to ensure food guarantee for people and livestock. Local storage of grains with easy availability in any season would reduce the distribution cost and would be a low cost option that also cuts on wastage during transportation. This will facilitate PDS too."[2] All the allied sectors need to synchronize and work together to achieve this goal.

The integration of agriculture with other sectors will certainly help in the development of agriculture. Smt. Pratibha Patil, a great believer in the integrated approach, for the agricultural development too, she maintained the significant role that the corporate sector can play. She said, "In terms of an approach, I have been advocating a move away from an isolationist attitude whereby agriculture is considered as an activity that happens in distant rural areas. Without integrating agriculture with other sectors it will not benefit the farmers or nation. Industry, big and small can have a mutually beneficial symbiosis with agriculture. I have been speaking about industry-agriculture interface over the last two years. I am glad that some formats are emerging where the farmer is also stakeholder and can also keep his land in his possession. We need to draw lessons from these and see how to further strengthen these models. Indian corporate houses have emerged as major investors in agriculture, in other countries. Why then the hesitation to engage with the agriculture sector and rural areas within the country, which has a huge potential?"[2] A crucial question that needs to be addressed at the policy level.

Industry-Agriculture Interface

It is highly important to devise ways to engage the farmers in the process of synergy and linkages. Smt. Pratibha Patil recalls and refers to her address at the National Corporate Awards Function organized under the aegis of the Corporate Affairs Ministry on 23 December 2009, in which she stressed the need for forging healthy linkages between the industry and the agriculture sector, especially in rainfed areas: "I had exhorted the industry to evolve suitable models for a farmer-industry partnership, whereby we could harness the full potential of the rainfed areas, take advantage of economies of scale, and provide farmers a durable arrangement of production and marketing. While evolving the model, I had prescribed a word of caution, that the model must be transparent so that the farmers are confident about retaining their interest in the ownership of land.... While working on and conceptualising these models, our primary intention should be to positively encourage farmers and primary user organizations, for better price realisation, value addition, branding and marketing."[5] A seminal endeavor which needs effective policy oriented thinking leading to regulation.

Another vital stride Smt. Pratibha Patil marched ahead with was in the direction of initiating discussions on the development of some of the basic models to bring farmers into partnership arrangements with SMEs and the corporate world. Highlighting the prominence of the model which will be helpful she said, "The farmer-industry partnership can include crop specific and region specific models by making farmer associations, shareholders or co-operatives or organizing farmers into primary producer bodies, or any other desirable and viable model between farmers and industries. Also, these agreements should, on one hand, safeguard the ownership of land of the farmer and, on the other hand, ensure tenure security during the agreement period for the industrial establishment. This would create a conducive environment for the establishment of a viable industry-farmer partnership." And this partnership is a "farmer-centric, industry-driven and knowledge-based partnership."[1]

The farmer-industry partnership will certainly be beneficial to the farmers. The technological expertise and advancement that the industry will bring up to the farming will maximize the yielding. She said, "...Agreements of farmers with industrial establishments could cover production, processing, value addition, storage and marketing, all of which contribute to better price realisation. In fact, in a broader term, the integration of agriculture with other sectors of the economy is important for sustainable development. India is one of the largest producers of food grains, fruits and vegetables in the world. Yet, food processing is not even 10%. Storage facilities like building silos, warehousing or cold storage facilities; and promoting value addition of food products so that their shelf-life increases, will bring better returns to farmers. The Agricultural Produce Market Committee Act and such other issues also need to be reviewed for making agriculture remunerative."[1]

She also highlights the superb role of many Indian companies like, IT enabled pilots of e-chaupals of ITC, Tata Kisan Sansars, Primary Producers' Companies of Tata Chemicals and Haryali of Mahindra and Mahindra, which have greatly transformed the lives as well as enhanced the income of the farmers. She focused on the need and the scope "for more crop and product specific, region development specific, multi-crop and livestock development specific models to be evolved to enhance the overall productivity in these areas. I urge the corporate sector to take this as a challenge, and evolve commercially viable business models in respect of food crops, also ensuring food security in the country. Such models can work well for both food and commercial crops, as well as in combination."[5]

The corporate sector has to play a prominent role in the development of rainfed farming. In the speech at the policy debate on "Prospects of Rainfed Farming with special reference to engaging the Corporate Sector," Smt. Pratibha Patil aired her thoughts and ideas on the value of corporate sector's linkage with the rainfed farming, "A collaborative approach from the corporate sector would go a long way in adding to the capacity building exercise, very urgently needed in the pursuit of bringing agriculture and industry together. Corporate houses can set up dedicated funds for entrepreneurship development and capacity building among farmers in dryland areas, and create replicable models of group formation and leadership among farmers. Innovative approaches to help organize growers groups, can mobilize resources, receive benefits from the government and have better bargaining power in the market. The Government has already put in place a three-tier model for skill development in 2008, with the Prime Minister's National Council at the apex level. To ensure that labour forces, especially those in the unorganised sector like agriculture benefit from such initiatives, full cooperation from the corporate world is also required. Various business chambers like CII, FICCI, etc., in collaboration with the National Skill Development Foundation, are already working in this direction. Such efforts will promote inclusive growth with reduction in skill shortages within the country and globally. We are also faced with the issue of scarcity of farm labour, which is increasingly becoming a hindrance in cultivation of land. Support in the form of mechanised farming, is becoming a necessity in rainfed areas, and business houses can play a major role in this."[5]

Majority of the Indian population depend upon agriculture and majority of the cultivated land in India is rainfed. The poorer sections of the Indian population are dependent upon these areas. So, special focus needs to be put on these areas. Smt. Pratibha Patil refered to the available statistics to vindicate her conviction. She said, "…About 60%

of cultivated area in India is rainfed. Of the total production in the country, 44% is from dryland farming and also supports around 40% of the population, belonging to the poorer sections of society. ... It is expected that when all water resources have been developed, between 45–50% of net cultivated area will continue to be rainfed. Unfortunately 85% of the farming community in this area has less than 5 acres of land. If these small farm holdings are brought together under one umbrella, it will change their productivity, thereby changing the scenario entirely. I recall a poem which I had learnt as a child which said, 'If all the trees were one tree, what a large tree it would be; if all the rivers were one river, what a large river it would be.' Similarly, if small holdings of farms are consolidated into optimum farm size, how efficient and easy could it be to apply modern technology for better yield? It could be thought of to take-up a village or a group of villages and carry out operations such as soil conservation, sowing, to crop planning, to the end product and storage, as well as processing. This could be done as an ideal village development programme. It will set an example for others."[5]

Processing is another significant issue in farming and the corporate sector can play a very crucial role in this. The corporate sector should now urgently focus more on agro-processing in a massive manner as a new policy approach. As on date, the percentage of processing that takes place in the country, as compared to the overall percentage of production is only approximately 10%. We aim to increase this figure substantially in the coming years. This is possible only with the active involvement of the corporate sector. Rainfed areas offer good scope in this, and should be tapped by business houses. With the shift in India's demographic profile in favour of a younger population, double income families and changing food habits, this area offers tremendous potential, and can be of advantage both to farmers and corporate houses.[5]

The corporate sector can play a very proactive role in integrating the small land holdings into larger ones. It will be very easy to irrigate and use modern technologies in these larger units. These larger holdings will be owned by many agriculturalists who will work in a cooperative way. "It is often said that the agricultural economy in India is the biggest private enterprise of many small producers, which constitutes about 80% of the rural household. These small producers, with their sub-optimal size farms are unable to take advantage of modern technology for intensive agriculture. The corporate sector can help remove this handicap, possibly by linking them through joint cooperative efforts. I do not recommend any particular format for partnership farming, because what suits one region may not suit the other. But the basic ingredient is to bring together farmers with different farm holdings, to reap the benefits of economies of scale, assured remunerative prices, improved agricultural practices, new technologies and better quality produce, so as to make them competitive in the open market. Partnership farming has other advantages as well. Availability of agricultural loans becomes comparatively easier, it creates more employment, migration to urban areas gets reduced, better quality life is assured, and development activities are given a thrust, making the rural economy prosperous."[5] As a paradigm shift the 'partnership' farming can open many avenues for both debt management as well as augmenting social growth.

Smt. Pratibha Patil strongly believes that the government, corporate sector, agricultural research institutes and universities and many civil society organizations pertaining to agricultural research should work in an integrated way for the development of agriculture. "Today we are discussing how best to engage the corporate sector in improving the prospects of rainfed farming. I believe it is possible to address the issues of dryland farming through joint efforts of the government, research institutions as well as the corporate sector. I must share with you that even uneducated farmers in rainfed areas, are doing a good job in adopting better cropping patterns, developing new seeds and improved implements, which institutions like the National Innovation Foundation are attempting to identify, promote and patronize. Farmers are indeed responsive to adopting innovations and change, if found beneficial."[5]

"It is decidedly critical that government, corporate sector, civil society, academics, and bureaucracy etc. should come on a common platform to develop common framework in this regard", she said in her speech at the Workshop on 'Policy Initiatives for Promoting Partnership between Stakeholders in Agriculture with particular reference to Rainfed/Dryland Farming'. It indeed was a big gathering enlisting their support to the cause. Smt. Pratibha Patil thanked all the participants who hailed from the different corners of the entire country—from the North, South, West and East, including states from North-East region representing different agricultural zones. She was very happy that the Prime Minister Dr. Manmohan Singh was there to inaugurate the workshop, and his cabinet colleagues, Governors, and Chief Ministers were present, as also were farmer organizations, agricultural organizations, agricultural universities, institutions like KVKs, representatives of industry, experts, scientists, bureaucrats and academicians. As she said, this workshop was an attempt to bring all stakeholders on one platform so that they can put their heads together for a sort of convergence of various important aspects to make agriculture prosperous and productive.

The corporate sector with its modern technological tools can play a significant role in the rainfed farming. It can be engaged as the facilitator and augmenter. This complimenting and enhancement role of the corporate sector is a way to fill the wide gaps that exist in various aspects of agriculture. The new technological developments can be expanded with the use of new tools, and the packages of allied activities, which the corporate sector can bring in, would aid in the increase in productivity in a magnificent mode. By bridging the fissure that exists between agro-based rural enterprises and the corporate world, the corporate sector can facilitate and make the farmers more capable of maximizing their produce and income. However, it should be ensured that the sensitivity of the farmer is well taken care of and the benefit and interest of the farmers is of primary significance.

Disseminating Knowledge

The other significant aspect that she highlights on is to take this initiative to the grass root level. Articulating her concern, she states: "Another issue is the convergence of schemes at the local level. We are reaching out to the farmer through various institutions, under different ministries to make available agricultural inputs like credits, seeds and fertilizers. Knowledge inputs like climate parameters and weather forecasts, market situations must be made available to farmers. Also farmers need information on water management and modern irrigation technologies, particularly drip and sprinkle irrigation, new user friendly technologies for many agricultural operations, new scientific methods of crop planning, warehousing and food processing technologies as well. It is nearly impossible for a farmer to engage with a multitude of agencies. How can all this coordinate? You may please ponder over this. I think that this co-ordination should be done by involving Panchayati Raj Institutions. Gram Sabhas must move centre stage to play a leading role in this. In the three tiers Panchayati Raj System also, a block is generally taken as a unit for all developmental activities. Agricultural operations, especially crop planning, expenditure planning, and also planning all-round livestock development with supporting activities of veterinary doctors and fodder etc., may be carried out with block as a unit, taking into account local conditions and requirements. Each block can be a nucleus of a "food and fodder bank" where food and fodder, is stored as per requirements to ensure food guarantee for its people and livestock. Local storage of grains with easy availability in any season would reduce the cost of distribution under the PDS system, and at the same time, it would be a low cost option that also cuts on wastage during transportation. To co-ordinate these activities and to ensure farmers' participation, Block Level Committees can be thought of. Infrastructure like warehouses, food processing units like dal mills and oil mills etc., could be set up at the Block level. This will facilitate the creation of local jobs and occupation opportunities for the youth. Individuals and SHGs can benefit out of it. However, how can all this be systematically done and made a reality? We have to find the answer."[1] Crucial issues that need to be reflected upon by the partner stakeholders to arrive at a policy decision.

Knowledge, information, technology and expertise are highly essential in the development of RFDF. Smt. Pratibha Patil, taking position on this, states that extension mechanism in the country being weak, there is an urgent need to strengthen it to expedite the transfer of innovations from laboratories to fields, becomes mandatory.[10] It is quite crucial that various institutions, scientists, farming experts and agricultural universities can develop modern techniques and methods and make the farmers learn how to use the modern technologies and scientific method. As she says, "The various agricultural institutes and universities in the country should focus on farmer oriented technologies. Similarly, the extension machinery needs to be far more pulsating so that the results of research quickly reach the farmers. Farmers have traditional wisdom and practical ideas. Knowledge partners can also build on this wealth. At the local level, how can the Panchayati Raj Institutions, agriculture officers and the Krishi Vigyan Kendras play a proactive role to firmly weave knowledge and technology into the fabric of agriculture? This needs fresh thinking."[2]

She emphasizes that the Krishi Vigyan Kendras can be used for the dissemination of agriculture knowledge and the new developments in agricultural technology. She referred to her speech at the 5th National Conference on Krishi Vigyan Kendras, in which she had asked "whether it is possible to enroll an army of trained "Kisan Bandhus" attached to Krishi Vigyan Kendras across the country, who could help farmers through extension activities. Knowledge and knowledge management have to be leveraged effectively for the benefit of the farming community. Results from agricultural research are sometimes too academic to guide intermediary organizations and extension agencies. If that is the case, farmers do not gain anything, as knowledge is not being transferred to them in an understandable and doable form. Therefore, there is a need to start programmes that create or reinforce partnerships between intermediary organizations and research institutes, to produce accessible content in local languages and, at the appropriate technical level. Apart from this top down approach, there also is a need to look for small-small innovations made by local people in farming communities. Over the past few years I have seen many grassroots innovations, some such exhibitions were put up at Rashtrapati Bhavan also. It is important that these innovations can be refined and made marketable, by developing knowledge partnerships. How this can be done should be discussed. The role of agricultural universities and research institutions, both at the central and state levels, need to be looked into, as also the involvement of agriculture related Public Sector Undertakings."[1] Roadmap initiatives have been part of government priorities.

Marketing Farm Products

The ladder for the development in agriculture, sustainability in cultivating the land and enhancement along with refining the agricultural produce should go the length of the plans, procedures and actions to eradicate the impediments and empower them through marketing, finances and association of farmers. Smt. Pratibha Patil suggests, "How can farmers get better marketing options? We need to look at building more open marketing systems including through suitable amendments in the Agriculture Produce Marketing Committees Act, which are operative in some states. More useful and better enactments are necessary. It is observed that even regulated markets are not able to serve the intended purpose. These have to undergo structural changes in tune with the changing market conditions. The development of warehousing and cold storage are also essential. Ware-house receipts have recently been made negotiable instruments; but the reach is very limited in scope and the system is yet to stabilize."[2]

Financial Aid

Smt. Pratibha Patil provides a framework, "how to empower farmers through financial inclusion and access to credit. Indeed, financial exclusion has been a bane for Indian agriculturists. As of now, only five percent of more than six lakh villages in the country have bank branches. This coverage must expand rapidly…. Farmers continue to go even now to money-lenders as the money is lent to them easily and quickly. This is a ground reality. So, it may be useful to find out whether individuals or micro-lending institutions can be registered and given some incentives and with some regulation, allowed to finance agriculture under the supervision of a suitable regulatory agency. Let these be woven into the banking system so as to facilitate speedier disbursement of loans to farmers. Sowing and other farming operations go as a cycle, and farmers cannot wait for paper-work to be completed by banks. Therefore, lending time to farmers with some degree of flexibility is basic to rural credit systems. This reality needs to be taken into consideration. And, I think at various stages new laws need to be enacted and readiness to do so has to be shown, for the growth of the agriculture sector."[2] Obsolete laws and regulations must be reviewed in the changing contexts of time.

The organizations or co-operatives of the farmers will not only help them in raising their issues and concerns but also it will provide them an opportunity to share their expertise to develop agriculture in a co-ordinated way. "When farmers organize themselves into farmers' organizations or cooperatives or producer organization, it gives them the advantage of dealing with their problems and engaging other stakeholders through a collective approach. The SHGs have demonstrated that with a pooling of resources, their bargaining power increases."[2]

Government Schemes

Smt. Pratibha Patil stated that various schemes initiated by GOI aimed especially at the rural population can be used for the development of rainfed farming, "government schemes like the Mahatma Gandhi National Rural Employment Guarantee Act have had a major impact in rural India. It has opened up many opportunities for work and employment which is very important. Its further utilization for agriculture needs to be looked at, in a deeper way, to see how to maximize the potential of this scheme, for rural development and agricultural operations, in the context of the emerging scenario of farm labour shortages and food security."[1]

Smt. Pratibha Patil focused on the institutional changes which are required for addressing certain issues and specific problems and empowering small farmers in RFDF, "An administrative set up in the form of a separate Directorate for RFDF in the states under the Ministry of Agriculture would be useful for focused and coordinated action. In the Twelfth Five Year Plan it is necessary to give a thrust to RFDF areas that will generate a sense of urgency at the government level and promote partnership between various stakeholders to revitalize Indian agriculture."[2]

A Case Study

Dr. Samra refered to "five districts such as Nilgiri, Kullu, Shimla, Lahaul and Spiti where the productivity is much more than the districts of Punjab and Haryana although they are 100% irrigated states. In the rainfed areas there are some special attribute crops which especially need to be taken care of like the coarse cereals, gaur gum, soya bean and moth bean. Most of the coarse cereals are nutritious and have great nutritious value, so what is required is some industry comes in and processes the products of the area, brand them and sell them. It is bound to be profitable for farmers. Similarly 65% cotton is rain-fed, but it is a traditional industry. Unfortunately, the textile industry has not done anything for cotton. Livestock has traditionally been used as a safety net in the areas because when everything fails the livestock come to the rescue. Similarly, solar energy and wind farming can be promoted in the desert areas."[3] Dr. Samra greatly appreciated companies like, Godrej and Ruchi who are extending their services by starting many nurseries, especially in Mizoram.

Summing up

The common perception and attitude towards the farmers that they are unaware, uninformed and mere cultivators of the land need to be changed. The image of the farmer as a poor man begging for alms at the door of the money lenders and an archaic man arranging traditional ploughs to till the land has to be altered. Another significant aspect is that in India there is the wrong notion prevalent among people that only illiterate people should do agricultural work. Agriculture is being perceived commonly as a debasing work for an educated person. "In India, there is a misconception that only illiterates should be farmers. This is wrong. In many other countries, I have seen, highly educated people are involved in farming using modern technology. In our country, too, we need to increase the use of modern technology. This can be effectively done if the educated lot takes up farming," said Smt. Pratibha Patil.[10]

Smt. Pratibha Patil was highly critical of this perception and attitude rather the effort should be "how to engage the farmer is another question? Our approach will have to change from one where the farmer is viewed as a "tiller", to one where we look at the farmer as an 'agri-preneur' who is eager to look at new forms of engagement with other stakeholders, to enhance productivity and profitability from agriculture. Much like the industrial entrepreneur, the farmer takes risks, sows seeds and puts in tremendous effort in manning it. The farmer today requires inputs of knowledge and scientific research, access to markets, credit support and insurance coverage and management techniques for effective utilization of various resources. These are very much the inputs for running a successful business operation! So linking industry and the farmer is very much a viable option."[1]

It is to be remembered that farmers are the real backbone of India. They feed us. We have to be sensitised to the plight of the farmers in India. Farming is a noble profession as the farmers feed the entire population. Farming also has all the potentiality of becoming a profitable enterprise. Smt. Pratibha Patil appeals to the masses in India to give up this prejudice against the farmers. Once the tag of prejudice is removed, the educated will not hesitate to do farming. Once the educated people enter into farming, it will be easier for them to get acquainted with new developments and handle new technologies in agriculture, and they can also help their other fellow agriculturists to be trained in modern technologies.

Another major aspect that needs to be realized and raised is that of the involvement of the women in the agricultural development of the country. For the awareness and sustainability of the growth of the country, women should not just be a part but also an equal partner of the men in the process of growth. There are many women who work in the agricultural fields but their contributions have hardly ever been acknowledged. Smt. Pratibha Patil strongly recommends recognition of the full involvement of women in agriculture in India. As the Chief Guest in the Global Conference on Women in Agriculture she, while delivering valedictory address emphasised the need to empower women with new knowledge and skills to bring women into the mainstream of agricultural development and reduce gender disparity. "Today, much of the scientific knowledge and technologies does not reach rural women for various reasons. This needs rectification. Research systems must also seek the inputs of women, as they have historically been the source of much traditional knowledge and innovations at the grassroots level", she said.[11]

Smt. Pratibha Patil spoke about the need to form 'Mahila Kisan Mandals' in every village to educate and make women aware of different aspects of agriculture and related activities. "I also believe that tapping the potential of rainfed and dryland farming is necessary. In this, water management would be essential, again an area where the role of women is crucial, and needs to be supported", she added.[11] Smt. Pratibha Patil hoped that the women centric schemes, researches and developments of technological innovations in agriculture would certainly contribute immensely in enhancing agricultural production, and in bringing a transformation in the lives of women engaged in the sector.

Smt. Pratibha Patil's focus on the need for more investment in agricultural research so that new technologies can be developed to increase profitability in farming is a policy matter today.[10] Government of India's investment in the research in agriculture has also been amplified. To cater to the needs of such a huge sector of Indian economy, many of the agricultural universities and institutes pertaining to researches in agriculture will also be established in different corners of the country. Another important aspect of agricultural research is the use of technology and the dissemination of the knowledge of technology to the grassroot level. Smt. Pratibha Patil said the use of modern technology can bring in a drastic change in the way farming is carried out. She added that the need of the hour for states was to invest more in development of farming technology.[10] Indubitably the farmers are the real backbone of Indian economy. Smt. Pratibha Patil's views of farmers will perhaps surmise her vision for India:

> *'Let us together with our farmers toil.*
> *Let us make our dryland fertile!*
> *Let us walk one more mile!*
> *To let our farmer smile!!* [2]

References

Note: If a reference number occurs twice or more in the chapter, it is another reference to the same source.

[1] Speech by Her Excellency the President of India, Shrimati Pratibha Devisingh Patil at the "Meeting of the Committee of Governors on Farmer-Industry Partnership", Rashtrapati Bhavan, New Delhi, 15 December 2011.
   [Online: web] Accessed 10 April 2012, URL: http://presidentofindia.nic.in.

[2] Speech by Her Excellency the President of India Shrimati Pratibha Devisingh Patil at the Workshop on "Policy Initiatives for Promoting Partnership between Stakeholders in Agriculture with particular reference to Rainfed/Dryland Farming," Rashtrapati Bhavan, New Delhi, 15 February, 2012.
   [Online: web] Accessed 10 April 2012, URL: http://presidentofindia.nic.in.

[3] Speech by Dr. J.S. Samra, CEO, National Area Authority at the "Meeting of the Committee of Governors on Farmer-Industry Partnership" organized at behest of Her Excellency the President of India, Shrimati Pratibha Devisingh Patil at Rashtrapati Bhavan, New Delhi, 15 December 2011.

[4] Speech by Dr. Christy Fernandez, Secretary to the President of India at the "Meeting of the Committee of Governors on Farmer-Industry Partnership" organized at behest of Her Excellency the President of India, Shrimati Pratibha Devisingh Patil at Rashtrapati Bhavan, New Delhi, 15 December 2011.

[5] Speech by Her Excellency the President of India, Shrimati Pratibha Devisingh Patil at the Brain Storming Session on "Prospects of Rainfed Farming with special reference to engaging the Corporate Sector," Bangalore, Karnataka, 5th August 2011.

[Online: web] Accessed 10 April 2012, URL: http://presidentofindia.nic.in.

[6] *The Financial Express*, Monday, 25 June 2012.

http://www.financialexpress.com/news/need-to-give-thrust-to-dryland-farming-prez/912527/0.

[7] "President urges innovative solutions to curb food inflation," *The Times of India*, February 16, 2012.

http://articles.timesofindia.indiatimes.com/2012-02-16/india-business/31066184_1_food-inflation-food-production-dryland.

[8] "Prez for looking at out-of-box solutions for dryland farming," *APN News*, February 15, 2012.

http://apnnews.com/2012/02/15/prez-for-looking-at-out-of-box-solutions-for-dryland-farming.

[9] "Plan needed for rainfed agriculture: President Pratibha Patil," *The Times of India*, Pune, June 11, 2012.

http://articles.timesofindia.indiatimes.com/2012-06-11/pune/32174422_1_agriculture-president-pratibha-patil-rainfed.

[10] "Focus on agri research to boost profitability," *The Indian Express*, Pune, Monday June 11, 2012.

http://www.indianexpress.com/news/focus-on-agri-research-to-boost-profitability/960350/0.

[11] "President Called Upon Scientists to Bring Women into the Mainstream of Agricultural Development," *Global Conference on Women in Agriculture*, New Delhi, 15 March, 2011.

http://www.gcwa.in.

Social Milieu: Issues and Concerns

"The time has come for us to take a closer look at our social milieu. Is there growing criminalization of our society? Is there increasing apathy towards each other? Are we becoming too materialistic, shortsighted and unconcerned about the impact of our actions on our brethren, society or the environment?"

—*Smt. Pratibha Patil**

Terming the tenure of Smt. Pratibha Patil as a 'quiet legacy', Praveen Swami aptly quotes the social scientist and essayist Walter Bagehot, who famously wrote in the nineteenth century that in the United Kingdom, the monarch "has the right to be consulted, the right to encourage, and the right to warn. In the quietest possible way, President Smt. Pratibha Patil has sought to exercise all three of these rights, while avoiding public controversy of any kind."[1] Since the beginning of her career in politics she has endeavoured to develop the vision of a democratic, liberated, peaceful and harmonious India where every citizen of the country is respected, where women are treated with equality, and the country is free of social ills and tribulations. After stepping into the highest office in the country this calm and quiet woman, maintaining a low profile has fought with resolute conviction to uproot the social ills like female infanticide, child marriage, ragging, dowry, drug addiction and alcoholism etc. and she has succeeded in much bigger ways in purging these evils from the society.

Her method of combating against these tribulations has been based on the Gandhian principle. Smt. Pratibha Patil believes in the democratic ethos of proper implementation of legislations against the social evils and the involvement of all the sections of the society. To fight against

---

*Speech by the President of India, Shrimati Pratibha Devisingh Patil to the Nation on the eve of 62nd Republic Day of India, New Delhi, 25th January, 2011.

these problems, she significantly highlighted on our cultural and civilizational notion of peace and nonviolence: "I appeal to my fellow citizens to never resort to violence. Our nation won its freedom by travelling on the high path of non-violence and truth. In our journey as an independent nation too, we must adhere to it and demonstrate moral courage. Societies evolve in a positive direction when people work to bring about constructive changes and to eliminate social evils."[2]

Womb Speaks Out: Stop Female Foeticide and Female Infanticide

Laying the foundation of an independent India, Mahatma Gandhi had said, "Salvation of India lies in the elevation of her women."**

"A world without women is a world without, those members of the family who bring so much joy and gentleness in our lives. Life will become dry if women disappear. It is a world without grandmothers, it is a world without sisters, it is a world without mothers and if there is no mother—the human race will come to an end."***

—Smt. Pratibha Patil

The 'positioning' of women in Indian society has been quite interesting as well as very startling. The status of the women has varied from that of respecting and worshipping women as mothers, sisters, goddesses etc. to that of burden, torture, torment and oppression. The history of positioning of the women has been quite eventful in India. Our religious and civilizational traditions and ethos place the women above the men in the ladder. Though there may be contrasting views, some scholars believe that in ancient India women enjoyed equal status with men, and some women were placed above the men for their distinctions. As we know Indian history is replete with many foreign invasions and aggressions, and these foreign atrocities brought with them many

---

**Speech by the President of India, Shrimati Pratibha Devisingh Patil at the Dr. V.N. Tewari Memorial Oration at Panjab University, Chandigarh, 17th March, 2011. [Online: web] Accessed 1 May 2012, URL: http://presidentofindia.nic.in.)

***Speech by the President of India, Shrimati Pratibha Devisingh Patil at a function being organized by the Nanhi Chhaan Foundation, Gandhi Darshan, Delhi, 9th April 2011. [Online: web] Accessed 1 May 2012, URL: http://presidentofindia.nic.in).

forms of outrages on women, sometimes covet, sometimes open. Also at home, kings were at war with each other for territorial possession which was considered to be the hallmark of one's supremacy. In that, women used to be the easiest prey. The winner king used to take pride and thought it best to satiate his revenge in subjecting the women folks of the defeated one to many forms of violence. The condition of women became dreadful in the medieval period, as well as, during the period of colonialism. All these developments led to the evil practices like, child marriage, sati, purdah etc. and religious sanctions were granted to these practices.

During the colonial period our social reformers like, Raja Ram Mohan Roy, Mahatma Phule, B.R. Ambedkar, Mahatma Gandhi etc. took up very strongly the cause of the women in the society, fought for the total elimination of these evil practices and the upliftment of women in the society. They sought the participation of women in every sphere of life and also strived to change the mindset and the prevailing discriminations against the women which limited their role and participation in the society. They succeeded to some extent in their fight. The nationalists and reformers of India believed that once India becomes free, manages its own affairs, and its legislature and judiciary are in effect, the status of women in our society will be strengthened. But we seemed to have made little progress.

In the modern day India, the status of women lies in a paradox. The largest democracy of the world has seen one of the most dynamic Prime Ministers in the form of a woman, Smt. Indira Gandhi; how gentle, humble, impartial and democratic the first citizen or the highest post of the country should be has been set by the first woman President of the republic, Smt. Pratibha Patil; and the current Speaker of Lok Sabha, President of the biggest political party in India, Leader of the opposition of Lok Sabha and Chief Ministers of some states are women. Indian women have excelled in all the walks of life and every sphere of the profession like, defence services, civil services, academics, medicine, engineering, managing public and private firms etc. But in spite of the achievements, women of this country are still considered as bad omen and burden, and face much discrimination and numerous challenges stemming out of the rooted social prejudices and evils.

The recent trend in the decline of the female sex ratio as shown in our census is quite disturbing as well as dangerous. In the economically developed states like Punjab and Haryana, the problem is quite acute. Some of the states in India have started reaping the devastation of these evil sowings. The survey conducted by the UK-based Thompson Reuters Foundation states that India is the fourth most dangerous country for women.[3] So, we need to correct the basics and change the perception about the women. Here, Smt. Pratibha Patil steps in and raises the core issue, "why are there still female foeticide incidents in society, why are girls considered as a burden, why the practice of dowry, why the helpless condition of widows? All these issues are very much there on the horizon, and need to be handled by Governments, by society and by people themselves."[4] It is time that the deeply rooted and widely prevalent social prejudices and biases which have resulted in the gender discrimination need to be totally deracinated and eliminated from the society. The evil practices of female foeticide, child marriage and dowry must be stopped. The mindset of the society towards the women needs to be changed. The citizens of the country, government, civil society organizations, NGOs etc. should come forward and work in a co-ordinated manner in the fight against this evil.

It is to be remembered that the status of women in the society speaks of how developed and progressing a country is. On one occasion Smt. Pratibha Patil quotes the first Prime Minister of India, Jawaharlal Nehru who said, "You can tell the status of a nation by looking at the status of its women."[5] There is no second opinion that women of India or of any country play a very crucial and critical role for the development and progress. As Smt. Pratibha Patil said, "It is because of the many roles that a woman plays, that she is a critical determinant of the future. As a mother, she imparts values to the future generation. As a member of the society, she makes it stable and more humane, and imparts an emotional content to society. As a citizen of the country, she can contribute to its productivity, its growth, prosperity and well-being. This places her in a position to be a driver of change and growth in a rising India."[6] Women in India have indeed entered and excelled in every sphere of society. They have undertaken leadership roles with splendid accomplishments and success in the political, economic, social domain of India, and they have also started proving their worth and bravery in the new arenas and professions once unthinkable for women. In fact in some spheres women have fared better than men. All these developments will certainly transmit into, as Smt. Pratibha Patil says, a 'silent revolution' in the status of the women in our country.[7]

But in spite of such key and determinant role played by women for the all-round progress and prosperity of this country, in some parts of India, girls are still considered as undesirable arrival in the family, some foetus are destroyed before they could see the light and if some come out they carry the burden of being labeled as 'nakushi' (unwanted). These immoral acts and practices have led to India's pathetic sex ratio in 2011, of 940 females per 1000 males, and more alarming has been the female population ratio in the age group of 0-6, which stands at 914, the lowest since independence.[8] At the root of this lies the prevailing social prejudices against the girl child and the preference for the boy child which have given rise to the most distressful and condemnable evil practices of female foeticide and female infanticide. The time is quite mature that the whole society should come forward united to fight against this monstrous practice.

The younger generation with the support and motivation from the older generation should develop a new social consciousness against this. Smt. Pratibha Patil rightly points out the necessity of a "new social movement for gender equality—a movement that changes society's attitude towards women and promotes an understanding, that women and men have a complementary and supplementary role to play in building a happy home, a peaceful society and a prosperous future."[9] Another significant aspect that she focuses on is the prevention of the misuse of diagnostic tests for the purpose of pre-natal sex determination which ultimately leads to the destruction or abortion of the female foetus. In her address at the inauguration of the 64th National Conference of the Indian Radiologist and Imaging Association, New Delhi, 28th January, 2011 she brought to the notice of all the laws and special legal provisions that forbid the medical practitioners from pre-natal determination of the sex of the child, and she also claimed that it is not only illegal but also unethical and highly detrimental to the society.

She urged the medical fraternity to adhere to the medical ethics and prevent the female foeticide.

It is not that legislation of our country is not sufficient enough to fight and eliminate this evil. It is essential that the common people of this country should be made aware of these legislations. But the serious concern is that it has become a mindset in the society. We need to change this. She strongly feels that right from the primary education children should be taught lessons of gender equality to change their mindset. It requires the concerted efforts from all the strata of the society. Smt. Pratibha Patil appealed, "... We have a social responsibility to bring about an end to prejudices and discrimination against the girl child. We must encourage all such steps that will contribute to the welfare of the girl child—proper nutrition, education, opportunity to work and to be financially independent. A girl child is an asset to the nation."[10] Smt. Pratibha Patil urged every citizen of the country, the Government, civil society organisations, NGOs etc. to join hands to stop this crime. Education can also play a very significant role in this.

Citing the imagery of the wheels of the chariot she focused on how the men and women are complementary to each other, and it is only through their combined efforts that the society or country will grow: "For a chariot to move forward, both wheels have to be strong, and if one is weak, it cannot move forward. So to move the chariot of our country forward, both the wheels—men and women—have to be strong and move ahead jointly. Our full potential as a nation will only be realized when women, are given opportunities to fully realize their potential. As long as that does not happen, almost half the talent of the country would be lost. We as a nation cannot afford to do that."[11]

India can never become complete as a country unless its female population is given the proper chances to realise their full potential. Women should be the equal partners in the growth story of India. Quoting from a young Indian poet, written on the theme of a girl child, Smt. Pratibha Patil quoted a few lines from one of them titled 'कन्याओं को आने दो':[12]

खिलने दो खुशबू पहचानो, कलियों को मुसकाने दो
आने दो रे आने दो, उन्हें इस जीवन में आने दो।

Ragging

"... Ragging is violence. It is heinous and should not be tolerated, for it can cause irreparable loss to the parents and to the country. Our social fabric is deeply damaged by such incidents and it is essential that these tendencies are curbed in the interest of social harmony and cohesion."****

—*Smt. Pratibha Patil*

It is rightly said that education brings out the best in the body, mind and spirit. It is through the powers of education that a society or state can exterminate the darkness prevalent in it and grow. And yet we find that this modern menace has occupied the social space in higher education sector. For the most fruitful accomplishment and realization of education, the hazard of ragging which crumbles the pillars of peace, certitude, mutuality and reciprocity of the educational campuses in India needs to be uprooted. Ragging is generally being seen as an act of violence and aggression committed by a senior student or senior group of students who by virtue of their being seniors feel it a social, psychological and moral right and authority to commit such act over the junior student or group of students who are new to the institution, and hence to be shaped into the so-called code of the institution as devised by the senior groups. But the unfortunate story is that these new students perpetuate the same heinous act as they climb up the ladder. The tradition of ragging continues. Sometimes, ragging even takes the ugliest turns like, caste, communal and communitarian violence and sometimes losing precious lives.

It is to be remembered that in ancient times though learning was available to the few fortunate elite, yet the centres of learning in India during this period focused on peace, love, mutual respect and reciprocity. Though there were certain differences among the scholars on particular issues, yet they were amicably discussed and debated with good spirit. The modern day system of ragging seems to have roots in the British colonial education policy in India. The commencement of ragging or canning was the usual colonial practice of predisposition and practice of

---

**** Speech by the President of India, Shrimati Pratibha Devisingh Patil to the Nation on the eve of 62nd Republic Day of India, New Delhi, 25th January, 2011.

judging others by inflicting insult and subjecting to mental and physical torment. This diabolism though started in the English institutions gradually poisoned the whole of the Indian educational system. In the present day scenario, the terrible act of ragging is being practiced in almost all the educational institutions including the premier universities and institutions.

Smt. Pratibha Patil has been a great advocate of raising concerns over the issues affecting the society at large. She has exhibited her serious concerns and anguish over the rising menaces of ragging in the educational institutions across India. On many occasions and platforms she has raised the rising incidents and issues of ragging and appealed the student community to refrain from such heinous acts like ragging. She has urged the state governments to formulate appropriate legislations to deal with this hazard. The vice chancellors of all the universities and the heads of all the institutions in India have been appealed by her to strictly implement the available legislations and educate the students about the immorality of ragging. Smt. Pratibha Patil had personally written and communicated with the Governors asking them to use their good offices in annihilating ragging from the educational institutions in their respective States and Union Territories. With her personal interest, her office had taken up the issue with the Ministry of Human Resource Development (MHRD), GOI and University Grants Commission (UGC). She had also appealed to many civil society organisations and NGOs for their support in the fight against this social hazard.

At every opportunity to address the students and teachers, she has always pointed out that ragging is a highly degrading, disgraceful and criminal act which creates a psychological, physical and moral illness on the part of the victim which greatly obstructs in the growth of his or her personality. The student or group of students who perform this heinous act can also not escape from its disastrous effect. So, if these rising instances of ragging continue then it will certainly cripple the youth of this country. In her speech at the 25th Convocation of Ranchi University she called ragging as "most injurious, criminal and disgraceful practice which should be immediately stopped by the students with their junior colleagues. Institutions should be extra careful and prevent it forthwith. It brings bad name to the institution and our country."[13] She advised the students to pledge not to get involved in this dreadful act and to strive to develop self-discipline.

At the Convocation of Mizoram University, Smt. Pratibha Patil highlighted on the imbibing and use of socio-cultural nuances to eliminate ragging. She said, "I have often spoken against ragging, which is nothing but suppression of new entrants to the campus. I am glad to learn that this university is free from ragging and hope that it will continue to be so. It is encouraging that older students welcome the new students and help them to settle down. This is also a tribute to the Mizo moral code of *Tlawmngaihna* which imposes an obligation on all members of society to be hospitable, kind, unselfish, and helpful to others. While looking after those in your communities, as students, you must also appreciate our country as one that is enriched by its various streams. These bring to the nation a rich diversity of languages, dances and traditions. We must, therefore, work to preserve our unity in diversity."[14] And all this stems from our socio-cultural upbringing and an edifice based on love, peace, certitude, tolerance and respectability. The educational institution should be the place where the body and mind of the students are without fear and breezed by love and goodwill. The other important aspect is that educational institutions are not only the temples of learning but also the celebration of our unity in diversity.

Smt. Pratibha Patil in her speech at the Conference of Governors had expressed her grave concern on this issue of ragging and had appealed them to fight against this crime: "I will also like to focus your attention on the inhuman conduct on the part of senior students, inflicting physical cruelty and mental torment on freshers that have outraged society. The Apex court has taken a strong stand against ragging. The Ministry of Human Resource Development has endeavoured to build a credible architecture of deterrence. Many States have enacted laws, rules and regulations to prevent ragging. The regulatory structures have to be constantly monitored and all inadequacies removed. While it is the primary responsibility of the management of educational institutions and teachers to prevent ragging, parents and guardians have to be mobilized to counsel their wards to behave more responsibly. NGOs could be enlisted to foster a climate of awareness against ragging. Your persuasive influence, especially as Chancellors of State Universities can immensely help in wiping out this blot."[15] In June 2009, Smt. Pratibha Patil had written to the Governors urging them to use their good offices to totally ban ragging in the educational institutions of their States and Union Territories. In her letter she further brought to the notice that, the Supreme Court of India is very much serious on this issue and has taken a very strong stand, and rules and regulations including laws have already been enacted at different levels to deal with this menace.

As a result of the resolute conviction of Smt. Pratibha Patil, Governors and Lt. Governors instituted measures like the formation of Anti-Ragging Committees and Squads, State Level Monitoring Committees with Governor as its chairman holding meetings with the VCs of the universities falling under their jurisdiction. Subsequently, the Governors and Lt. Governors sent their actions taken reports to the President of India, on the measures or actions taken to stop this menace. The Governor of Goa informed the President's Office about coming into effect of Goa Prohibition of Ragging Act, 2008, with effect from May 29, 2009 in the State of Goa. The Governor of Himachal Pradesh informed about promulgation of Himachal Pradesh Educational Institutions (Prohibition of Ragging) Ordinance on March 25, 2009. The Governor of Tamil Nadu brought to the attention of the VCs the already existing the Tamil Nadu Prohibition of Ragging Act, 1997 for its strict compliance and held a conference of VCs, principals of colleges and Deans of hostels on July 23, 2009. The Governor of Uttarakhand also convened similar meeting and set up a Chancellor's Monitoring Committee at Raj Bhavan with a dedicated e-mail for this purpose. The Lt. Governor of Delhi informed about setting up of Anti-Ragging Committees in each district of Delhi by Delhi Police.

As a further follow-up measure, the President's Secretariat took up the issue on June 14, 2010 with the Department of Higher Education in the Ministry of Human Resource Development for the proper implementation of the existing legal and penal provisions in this regard. The matter was again taken up with the Ministry on December 3, 2010 to ensure effective functioning of the anti-ragging helpline portal. Smt. Pratibha Patil has also appealed the State Governments to formulate appropriate legislations to fight against this menace.

Her very keen and avowed resoluteness and dedication on this issue motivated and persuaded many aggrieved parents, activists and organisations fighting for this cause to come and visit her to seek her advice, help and counsel. Consequent to the death of Aman Kachroo, who lost his life due to ragging in a medical college in Himachal Pradesh, his father Prof. Raj Kachroo launched a movement in his son's name to fight against this socio-psychological problem. Prof. Raj Kachroo met Smt. Pratibha Patil twice on April 30, 2009 and again on August 26, 2010 and sought her help to launch an 'on the ground' awareness campaign using the good offices of the Chancellors of various universities. In order to support his cause and to highlight the pain of such incidents caused to the students and the parents, she directed her Secretariat to extend necessary help to Prof. Kachroo to help him reach out to the student community and keeping the Chancellors/Vice Chancellors office in the loop. She also ensured he got the opportunity to put his point across in the right forum. The President's Office took a very proactive role in helping Prof. Kachroo in his mission of eliminating this malevolence from the society. Prof. Kachroo has now been given the responsibility to manage the UGC-maintained call centre, helpline and also to create a database on the issue.

Smt. Pratibha Patil believes that films and various television and radio programmes highlighting on the issues of ragging can be significant tools to build social awareness. Film maker Manish Gupta called on Smt. Pratibha Patil on 2nd June, 2011 at the Rashtrapati Bhavan and presented her a copy of his film titled, "Hostel," which critically explores the psychological and physical dimensions of ragging and how it disastrously affects the student's psyche. She advised him that real incident victims who acted in the film should come on public forum and appeal to the youth to eschew violence. On the initiative of President's Office, DDK, Delhi, came forward to make a special programme involving all the stake holders, including the youth, to flag the issue. Many such programmes are in the pipeline.

Child Marriage

Though there is no concrete data on the inception of child marriage in India, yet it is believed that the child marriage was quite rampant during the medieval period in Indian history. It is argued that to protect the women from the lust of some of the barbaric rulers of that time this system of child marriage seems to have got wider acceptance and practice. The protection of the chastity of the women folk of the family was considered to be the honour of the family. This led to the repugnant practice of child marriage. Then the religious and cultural signification was imposed on these child marriages—that marriage is a sacred act and the children are the reflection of God. This evil led to other gross practice of 'bride price'. Some greedy parents sold their infant daughters in marriage to the aged purchasers who were willing to offer the best bride price. It was a kind of covet system of auctioning where a girl of age 6-7 years sometimes was forced to accept a man of 50-60 years as husband. This system was much in practice during the period of feudalism in India.

But in spite of India striding into the twenty-first century it is quite reprehensible that this practice of child marriage still haunts the socio-cultural mosaic of rural India. Though the child marriage affects both the children, it brings terrible disasters for the girls. It brings dreadful health, hygienic and psychological problems for the girls. Smt. Pratibha Patil raised a strong voice for the eradication of this anomaly by generating social consciousness, and involving the government, civil society, NGOs and common citizens of the country in this fight.

On learning about the stories of courage of five teenagers from West Bengal who with little education and almost no support fought social and family pressure and resisted child marriage and dowry, Smt. Pratibha Patil was decidedly impressed and invited them and felicitated them in the Rashtrapati Bhavan. She also presented the girls with cash purse. After meeting these girls, Smt. Pratibha Patil said, "economic progress is not the only indicator of a country's development, a nation requires its people to show courage against social pressures and overcome social evils."[16] Hailing them as icons, Smt. Pratibha Patil encouraged them to visit their nearby areas on holidays and narrate their courageous stories to other girls and refrain them from under age marriages. She urged the district administration to take appropriate steps to stop this atrocity committed on the young girls. It is not only these girls but also the whole society should come forward in this fight. Education of the girls will play the key role in this, as Smt. Pratibha Patil said, "while education opens up new avenues for the girl child, an early marriage brings with it a cycle of misery, poor health and poverty. A young mother with children often becomes the victim of poor health and mortality."[17]

Undoubtedly, the encouragement and motivation of Smt. Pratibha Patil had profoundly influenced these girls. These girls had in fact created tremendous impact in their locality by succeeding in their persuasion to others to refrain from these kinds of social ills. The father of one of the girls was a daily wage earner and an alcoholic, but after her persuasion her father gave up alcohol.[18] As the then Collector of Purulia said, "these girls have become celebrities. They are being revered in and around their village for asserting themselves against oppression. They are now being invited in big functions in cities like Kolkata to inaugurate cultural festivals and 'Durga pooja' celebrations."[19] In India we have much legislation to deal with these kinds of evils and Smt. Pratibha Patil appealed that it was high time that common people were made aware of these legislations and a social awareness needs to be created in villages to counter such practices.

Dowry

Dowry is the most treacherous and iniquitous act that has deeply intruded into the fabric of Indian society and engulfed the Indian psyche. When the men and women have contributed equally to the building and progress of India and, are complementary to each other, then why should the bride be asked to take dowry with her to the groom's family. By giving money and other items in the form of dowry the family members of the girls feel that they are dispossessing off a liability (girl), and on the other end the family members of the boys feel that they are bringing this liability home, so they need money and other items for her maintenance. But, as we know there is no end to the human greed. Once the girl is married, the demand from the in-laws increases, and if the gluttony is not satiated, the brides are subjected to many kinds of physical and mental torture leading to either bride burning or suicide. But the regrettable and reprehensible part of the story is that even the educated and so called enlightened are no exceptions to the malevolent practice. Even the girls who are highly educated and in good jobs are victims of this social conditioning. Sometimes it makes us feel duplicitous and shameful when we say that India is the largest 'Democratic Republic' of the world, and yet unable to safeguard the interest of women. We need to continue to ask ourselves whether the women of this country are liberated, until then, the reality will continue to haunt us. Smt. Pratibha Patil questioned the mindset wherein the girl is burdened with the inhuman, and hideous practice of female foeticide and male child preference, ironically both stem from the immoral desire of dowry. The birth of a girl heralds the trepidation of collecting and saving for the girl price, very often land and property is sold. The demands of the society rob the young girls of parental and family members' love and affection, leading to low slow esteem in girls/women.

It is time Smt. Pratibha Patil felt, that this mindset was changed and a mass movement was generated to build up awareness among the different sections of the society, both the rural and urban, to annihilate the curse called dowry. In this struggle, the men and the boys should take the lead. The girls should come forward to say 'no' to marry in a family which asks for dowry. The girl child should be educated and be made economically independent, which will certainly bring the long needed revolution in the society. The social consciousness of the people needs to be metamorphosed; they should recognize that girls and boys are equal partners in every sphere of life. The government, civil society, NGOs etc. should partner to awaken the society, particularly the rural India.

Absolute prominence should be given to bring about the change in the social set up where the status and honour of women will be elevated. Smt. Pratibha Patil said, "[Only] When fathers of the bride and groom participate in the marriage ceremony of their children with their heads held up would we witness the first signatures of the change in the mindset towards a society based on equality."[20]

Alcohol and Drug Addiction

Alcoholism and drugs are serious problems that have engulfed the country, robbing the nation of its pride. The recent research has found that there is a steady rise in the alcohol consumption in this country.

More seriously the young masses, the poor and labour class have very disastrously been affected by alcoholism and drug addiction. These vices not only make our youth hollow from within, but also bring with it economic destitution. The poor spend much of their income in alcohol. These peccadillo practices have led to many kinds of depraved acts committed by the youth and other sections leading to the loss of tranquility in the family life as well as the loss of the harmonious bonding between the husband and the wife. In her inaugural speech at the National Conference of All India Federation of Women Lawyers, Kerala, Smt. Pratibha Patil expressed grave concern that in spite of Kerala being a prosperous state in terms of the social achievement with a remarkable female sex ratio and female literacy ratio, the highest in the country, the state had not got rid of the problem of alcoholism: "… I am surprised to learn that in spite of this, alcoholism is rampant and women are the worst sufferers."[21]

Smt. Pratibha Patil believed that building up awareness at the grass root level about the disastrous consequences of the dreadful habits, a larger receptiveness can be created in the society. We do have legislations in place to deal with these kinds of hazards, but it is important that people should be made aware of these legal provisions and more significantly affected people should be made to realize of their catastrophic upshots. A case in point is, Roshni Devi, a Dalit woman from a village in Haryana had started, in spite of many hurdles, an anti-alcohol movement in her locality and succeeded in persuading many men to quit alcohol and succeeded in bringing a sharp decline in the alcohol consumption in her locality. Smt. Pratibha Patil invited this courageous woman to Rashtrapati Bhavan and applauded her efforts and courage, "her movement's achievement proved that the most difficult of challenges in society can be overcome with courage, dedication and confidence."[22] The people of this country should take the awareness initiatives like that of Roshni Devi.

In her interview to NDTV[23], Smt. Pratibha Patil narrated one experience of her dealing with alcohol consumption among the laboring class. "… and then you see I was always talking about that, and I feel very, very strongly and is passionate about it to remove the evils from the society. Child marriage, female foeticide, drug addiction, addiction to liquor or whatever, you see, that is spoiling the health of our country. I'll tell you one experience. When I was Minister in Maharashtra, one year there was a very severe drought and even farmers with 50 acres, 60 acres of land, they had to go on the field too, on the field there was no work, they had to go on the scarcity work started by the Government. Because crops failed, no rains, and the Government of Maharashtra started the scarcity works, giving work for everyone who comes for this, so the labourers who used to come to field for work, used to come for building roads and different tanks, percolation tanks and all that. And you see the wages were announced and you see a person going to the field to work, getting ₹ 50 per day started to get ₹ 70 to 80 a day, his wife also got it and his child, above the age of 18 years, that child also, boy or girl got, so their income was almost doubled. So then I was taking a round with the Collector to see work is being given or not and everything is being done properly. I said I'm interested to know what these labourers have done with this increased income. So you please make a survey and tell me next time when I come. After a week I went there and they told me that 50 per cent of the labourers, they have utilized their increased income, some have paid back their loans, some people have kept in the bank, some people have purchased jewellery for the marriage of their daughter, but 50 per cent of them have spent away the money in drinking and gambling."

Smt. Pratibha Patil went on to narrate, "And believe me that was a period when Indira ji was working for 'Garibi Hatao' programme and the 20 point programme. So it was an eye-opener for me that we think that 'garibi' will go away, poverty will go away if we give income in the hands of people. But that's not totally true. If they continue with these addictions and spend away their money, they are going to be what they are, even if their income is increased, probably they'll hamper their health more by drinking more. And therefore it's necessary to work against this evil and you see when I was the Governor in Rajasthan, I called a seminar of those who were interested in this, and said come on, let's think over, what we can do to save our people from this addiction. So I think along with all the economic progress we may make, whatever financial allocations we may make, but if it has to really move to over, and this is at the mass scale, labour classes are a mass scale, so we will have to have very constant and very well planned efforts to see that these evils are eradicated, and I've been talking about that at the Rashtrapati Bhavan...."

It is quite essential that the poor and illiterate labouring class should be made aware of their basic amenities and spends their wages on the essential items. Smt. Pratibha Patil appealed to the women, men, young population, the student community, government, civil society, NGOs etc. to make concerted effort in raising awareness against this perilous habit. She has a strong message for the nation, "Learn what is good and useful to society; unlearn what is harmful to society".

References

Note: If a reference number occurs twice or more in the chapter, it is another reference to the same source.

[1] Swami, Praveen, "The quiet legacy of President Pratibha Patil," *The Hindu*, May 25, 2012.
URL: http://www.thehindu.com/opinion/interview/article3453077.ece.

[2] Speech by the President of India, Shrimati Pratibha Devisingh Patil to the Nation on the eve of 62nd Republic Day of India, New Delhi, 25th January, 2011. [Online: web] Accessed 25 May 2012, URL: http://presidentofindia.nic.in.

[3] "India fourth most dangerous country for women: Poll", The *Indian Express*, New Delhi, Jun 15, 2011.
URL: http://www.indianexpress.com/news/india-fourth-most-dangerous-country-for-women-poll/803716.

[4] Speech by the President of India, Shrimati Pratibha Devisingh Patil at the Inauguration of the 125th Year Celebrations of the Isabella Thoburn College, Lucknow, Uttar Pradesh, 2nd November 2011. [Online: web] Accessed 1 May 2012, URL:http://presidentofindia.nic.in.

[5] Speech by the President of India, Shrimati Pratibha Devisingh Patil at the Dr. V.N. Tewari Memorial Oration at Panjab University, Chandigarh, 17th March, 2011. [Online: web] Accessed 1 May 2012, URL: http://presidentofindia.nic.in.

[6] Speech by the President of India, Shrimati Pratibha Devisingh Patil at the Dr. V.N. Tewari Memorial Oration at Panjab University, Chandigarh, 17th March, 2011. [Online: web] Accessed 1 May 2012, URL: http://presidentofindia.nic.in.

[7] Speech by the President of India, Shrimati Pratibha Devisingh Patil at the Dr. V.N. Tewari Memorial Oration at Panjab University, Chandigarh, 17th March, 2011. [Online: web] Accessed 1 May 2012, URL: http://presidentofindia.nic.in.

[8] URL: http://www.censusindia.gov.in/2011prov-results/data_files/india/Final_PPT_2011_chapter5.pdf.

[9] Speech by the President of India, Shrimati Pratibha Devisingh Patil at a Function being organized by the Nanhi Chhaan Foundation, Gandhi Darshan, Delhi, 9th April 2011. [Online: web] Accessed 1 May 2012, URL: http://presidentofindia.nic.in.

[10] Speech by the President of India, Shrimati Pratibha Devisingh Patil at the Inauguration of the 64th National Conference of the Indian Radiologist and Imaging Association, New Delhi, 28th January, 2011. [Online: web] Accessed 1 May 2012, URL: http://presidentofindia.nic.in.

[11] Speech by the President of India, Shrimati Pratibha Devisingh Patil at a function being organized by the Nanhi Chhaan Foundation, Gandhi Darshan, Delhi, 9th April 2011. [Online: web] Accessed 1 May 2012, URL: http://presidentofindia.nic.in.

[12] Speech by the President of India, Shrimati Pratibha Devisingh Patil at a function being organized by the Nanhi Chhaan Foundation, Gandhi Darshan, Delhi, 9th April 2011. [Online: web] Accessed 1 May 2012, URL: http://presidentofindia.nic.in.

[13] Speech by the President of India, Shrimati Pratibha Devisingh Patil at the 25th Convocation of Ranchi University, Ranchi, Jharkhand, 10th December, 2010. [Online: web] Accessed 25 May 2012, URL: http://presidentofindia.nic.in.

[14] Speech by the President of India, Shrimati Pratibha Devisingh Patil at the Convocation of Mizoram University, Aizawl, Mizoram, 24th September 2010. [Online: web] Accessed 25 May 2012, URL: http://presidentofindia.nic.in.

[15] Speech by the President of India, Shrimati Pratibha Devisingh Patil at the Conference of Governors – 2011, New Delhi, 29th October 2011. [Online: web] Accessed 25 May 2012, URL: http://presidentofindia.nic.in.

[16] Ramachandran, Smriti Kak, "Five girls who resisted child marriage hailed as 'icons' by President," *The Hindu*, New Delhi, December 7, 2011.
URL: http://www.thehindu.com/news/national/article2695939.ece.

[17] Ramachandran, Smriti Kak, "Five girls who resisted child marriage hailed as 'icons' by President," *The Hindu*, New Delhi, December 7, 2011.
URL: http://www.thehindu.com/news/national/article2695939.ece.

[18] "Prez Awards 3 Purulia Girls for Opposing Child Marriage," New Delhi, December 07, 2011.
URL: http://news.outlookindia.com/items.aspx?artid=743631.

[19] "Prez Awards 3 Purulia Girls for Opposing Child Marriage," New Delhi, December 07, 2011.
URL: http://news.outlookindia.com/items.aspx?artid=743631.

[20] Pandher, Sarabjit, "Pratibha Patil for movement against dowry," *The Hindu*, Amritsar, October 7, 2010.

URL: http://www.thehindu.com/todays-paper/tp-national/article817197.ece

[21] "Prez concerned about alcoholism."

URL: http://www.indusage.com.au/news/politics/11160-prez-concerned-about-alcoholism.html.

[22] Rahman, Shaikh Azizur, "India's women go to war against alcohol abuse," *The National*, Dec 31, 2009.

URL: http://www.thenational.ae/news/world/south-asia/indias-women-go-to-war-against-alcohol-abuse.

[23] "Full transcript: President Pratibha Patil's interview to *NDTV*," Updated: May 07, 2012. URL: http://www.ndtv.com/article/india/full-transcript-president pratibha-patils-interview-to-ndtv-207063NDTV.com.

Section–III
Reflections

Education:
The Highest Leveler of Inequity

"The task of the modern educator is not to cut down jungles, but to irrigate deserts."

—*C.S. Lewis*

"Literacy is not a luxury; it is a right and a responsibility. If our world is to meet the challenges of the 21st century we must harness the energy and creativity of all our citizens."

—*Bill Clinton*

Smt. Pratibha Patil has been a crusader in many spheres for India's growth and development. Education, one of her passions, is to her, the primary index of nation's advancement, heralding the real emancipation to the people, liberating one from the shackles of ignorance, poverty and deprivation. She has vociferously maintained that, "Education is perceived by us in India, as a parameter of the human development index essential for developing the nation, and for making every Indian individual, an invaluable asset contributing to the country's economic development". This chapter, taking from her diverse discussions and speeches thus, focuses on her reflections on the seminal role of education in the national character building. Her conviction that education is the only tool for the underdog to reclaim his/her self-esteem and a position in society is perhaps a pragmatic approach. At every opportune time she has spread the message that through the access to education, equality and common good can be brought in to the fabric of society. Education has not only the power of elevating the self into a liberal, free-thinking one, but also helps in creating a structured knowledge society by driving out the dark and monstrous forces causing backwardness, from the society. Martin Luther King Jr. had said, "Intelligence, plus character, is the goal of true education". The parameters of education vary from nation, to nation depending on their goals and road map for the country. The policy decisions on education is reflective of the HRD Minister's vision, the country's education system is certainly better focused than ever.

Smt. Pratibha Patil's primary concern has been with women's education. Inaugurating the International Conference on 'Women's Literacy for Inclusive and Sustainable Development,' she maintained that "education is critical for achieving growth and more so, in knowledge based societies, where lack of education is in itself an impediment to progress. … India has accorded high priority to meeting the education requirements of the country, and to extend the frontiers of literacy in the nation. India's policies and programmes are directed towards achieving the goal of education for all. All children from the age of 6 to 14 years are to be provided free and compulsory education. We are also expanding our secondary school enrolment and our higher education infrastructure."[1] Her belief that education is the highest leveler of inequities and the only source for bringing about change and progress in the human lives and society is constantly reinforced by her prioritizing of education. Every child must have access to education. She has always been happy to note that in India, free and compulsory education is being provided to children from the age of 6 to 14 under 'Sarva Shiksha Abhiyan'.

Universities in all the parts of the world have been perceived as the fertile ground where knowledge, wisdom, liberal ideas, insights and perception about the world are germinated. It is from the universities that ideas and perceptions about cultural revolution take root. Citing one of her ideals, Pandit Jawaharlal Nehru, at the University of Chile, she said, "Pandit Jawaharlal Nehru, the first Prime Minister of India used to say, and I quote 'universities are temples of learning and if universities are doing well the nation is doing well.' … A university is home for scholars, intellectuals, academicians, and scientists—who through their scholarly pursuits and imparting of knowledge, have contributed to the progress of societies and nations. A university is also home for students who define the future. It is here that the minds of the youth are moulded, ideas are born and the contours of the future shaped. The role of universities in the socio-economic development of a country in today's knowledge-based and technology-driven world has increased immensely. The biggest challenge for universities is how to prepare the youth for the opportunities and challenges of a globalised world that is constantly changing and ever evolving. Education must give to the students the ability to analyse, the capacity to think, to act with humility and be individuals willing to contribute to nation building as well as to preserving the planet for the future generations and working for the welfare of humankind. … Science and Technology profoundly influences the course of human civilization. Inventions and innovations help make our economies modern, more productive and competitive. Cutting-edge technology plays a critical role in agriculture, communications, biotechnology, and pharmaceuticals, automobile and other manufacturing industries. I believe that universities have a critical role to play in updating the knowledge base of our societies and economies."[2] Smt. Pratibha Patil strongly believes that it is the university that creates responsible citizens and human resources who carry the torch of progress of the nation. It is from the university that the future leaders of the nation are nurtured. It is the nature of the universities that determines the structure of the country.

On another occasion at the Ceremony Conferring Degree of Doctor Honoris Causa on her by the University of Mauritius, she talked about the role education plays in the quest for growth and success, "It is pertinent to note that the pursuit of knowledge and education finds a common strand in our endeavour to provide for the common good of our people. A university … contributes to the progress of societies and nations. … As a society transforms, the education system must respond to change. It is only then, that it will be relevant. Our institutions of higher learning must gear up for facing challenges of a knowledge-based and technology-driven world. … Education has a fundamental role to play in creating responsible, innovative and analytical citizens. I believe that as the youth acquire skills, they should also be made sensitive to the qualities of the head as well as of the heart. As Nobel Laureate Rabindranath Tagore said, 'The highest education is that which does not merely give us information but makes our life in harmony with all existence'. Our universities, therefore, should be symbols of learning, humanism, tolerance and balanced reasoning."[3] Society always remains in the process of change and progress, and the university should prepare the youth to meet and cater to these changes.

In India 'learning' has always been the focus of our Upanishadic tradition. In the tradition of learning, people have held the seers and sages in high esteem. Indian society is full of narrations about people from all walks of life, sacrificing material quest in their pursuit of knowledge. Smt. Pratibha Patil focuses on this legacy of Indian edification, "since ancient times there has been a great emphasis on learning. This tradition got translated into a vision, where establishing an educational infrastructure becomes a priority in our nation building process in the post-independence phase. It was due to the strength in our education system, with emphasis on science and technology, which India has been able to assume a leadership role in Information Technology and other knowledge based sectors. We continue to lay great emphasis on education. Primary education is now a fundamental right; we are working towards the universalization of secondary education and augmenting our tertiary education institutions."[4] It is the growth in education sector in India that has placed us as one of the key players in the global senario. Indian scientists, doctors, academicians, writers, etc. have excelled world over. India continues to provide highly professional human resource to the world which has been possible due to our civilizational importance to education as well as the conscious and continuous efforts by the government and the concerned agencies. It is education that purifies the body, mind and spirit, and creates the true human self. It is in the context of the primary significance to education and wisdom that the 'gurus' are revered as more than gods in India. As Smt. Pratibha Patil says, "In my country, we attach great importance to knowledge and wisdom and have profound reverence for teachers. We, in India, celebrate 5th September as Teachers' Day throughout India ...."[5]

Smt. Pratibha Patil believes that only through learning that a society or a country can be empowered. The social evils can effectively be eradicated through the dissemination of knowledge.

Education lends identity and character to the society. It needs to be mentioned that during the period of indentured labour migration from

India to the British and other European colonial plantation estates in the 1830s, it was felt by these labourers in the distant host plantation countries that it is only the power of education that can emancipate their younger generation from the drudgeries of colonial dispensation. One reads that the younger generations of the Indian indentured labourers in the Caribbean, Mauritius and Fiji etc. climbed the ladder of success in the 1940s–50s due to their focus on education. Focusing on the power of education in her speech at the University of Mauritius, Port Louis, Mauritius on 28th April 2011, she informed that "Mahatma Gandhi visited Mauritius in 1901 and his most important message to Mauritians was to educate their children so that they were in a position to rise against the indignity of oppression and servitude. Gandhiji used to say education could bring about results which no force can. The Father of your Nation (Mauritius), Sir Seewoosagur, always emphasized that salvation lies in educating and training our men and women."[6] It needs to be understood that the period when Mahatma Gandhi visited Mauritius, many Indian indentured labourers were getting transported to British plantation colonies in Africa, Caribbean, and Fiji etc. It was during this period that in India there was a huge hue and cry against this diabolic system of indenture slavery. Finally, with the momentous struggle by Mahatma Gandhi, C.F. Andrews, G.K. Gokhale and several others this system of new slavery came to an end in 1920.

Another important aspect that needs to move along with the education is the gender focus on education. The best way of empowering the gender is to take special care to educate the girl child. Smt. Pratibha Patil, a major advocate of educating the gender, believes that a society or a country cannot progress without educating its female population. In her view, "increasing female literacy has the potential of becoming a force multiplier in pushing forward the socio-economic development of the nation. If we make women literate, they will be self-reliant and the beneficial impact on society will be manifold. It is said that if you educate a boy, you educate an individual, but if you educate a girl, you educate the whole family. It has been observed that where women are literate, the rate of infant mortality comes down and the quality of life improves. Literate women are more aware about diseases and their treatment; with better capability to deal with sickness and disease, and the confidence to approach medical assistance when required. It helps in many ways in her domestic activities. Also, when women are taught how to read and write, they in turn begin to send their girl child to school, breaking the pattern of social gender discrimination, which is a strong barrier to girls' education. What they need is an opportunity to educate themselves. Ability without opportunity is of little account. If educated, and if opportunity is made available to them, they are second to none. It is important that in schools, girls must get equal opportunity to study and acquire necessary skills and knowledge."[7] Her endeavour has been to transform the perception of the people regarding female education, particularly in villages. Since the woman is the mother and nurturer of the child, her education is not only significant but also indispensable. A stable, prosperous and progressive country needs educated citizens, hence educated mothers.

Certainly in India, over the years, education has played a tremendous role in the empowerment of women. Women are no longer viewed in terms of their confinement to the assignments and roles prescribed by the patriarchy. Women in India have succeeded in many walks of life, "in India, we have had success stories of women moving out of poverty as a result of literacy movements. ... Imparting education to women and girls is important for bringing about social change and for the full development of societies. Our efforts in this field must continue relentlessly. Educated women can play a significant role in helping in promoting women's literacy programmes. They can also contribute by helping other women, who are not so fortunate to have been educated, in making them socially aware."[8] Women in India are emerging as equal partners in creating an accomplishment story as an economic world power and a key global player.

Smt. Pratibha Patil wants to see women from across the world coming to the forefront and participate in all walks of life. Especially in the developing and underdeveloped countries of the world, the participation of women in all the sectors of the society has been limited. In some countries they are still bludgeoned under the iniquitous wheels of patriarchy. Unless the country brings its women population to the forefront, the growth of the country will be stalled. The mindset and perception about the women need to be changed. She was very happy to note, at the Ceremony Conferring Degree Doctor Honoris Causa on her by the University of Mauritius, that Mauritius has special focus on gender empowerment. As she says, "I am pleased that there is a focus on gender empowerment in Mauritius, particularly in the educational sector. As the first woman President of India, this makes me feel happy and I am confident that this augurs well for your country. Gender equality and development provides an ideal platform for any country to grow and find its place with equality and dignity in the comity of nations. As everyone knows a chariot moves on its two wheels. So also, men and women are the two wheels of the chariot of the nation. If one wheel is weak, movement will be slow. Therefore, women, who are the other wheel, must be made equally strong for the nation to progress in a smooth, rapid and balanced manner."[9] She strongly believes that the true development of a country can only take place when the women are empowered, and they equally participate in the growth process. And the preeminent method to empower women is to educate them. Women do reinvent themselves and their leadership qualities given the challenging environment they are put in. Smt. Pratibha Patil is a primary example.

In her acceptance speech at yet another honour of conferring the Doctorate Honoris Causa to her by the University of Chile, Santiago, she observed that, "another aspect I would like to highlight is the need to provide emphasis on the education of women. From an early stage, mothers can deeply influence their children to develop respect for knowledge and learning. ... There has been some progress on gender equality issues worldwide but our objectives and targets are still very distant. The talent of women, nearly half of the world's population, remains largely untapped. Provision of education and medical care facilities along with economic opportunities is fundamental for the empowerment and progress of women. Unleashing their dynamism is fundamental for the development not only of any democracy but also for inclusive and equitable socio-economic development of any nation state."[10] Though many countries especially the developing countries of the world have taken measures for the education vis-à-vis empowerment of women, we cannot have an equitable world order without the full and equal participation of women, and this is possible only when a country generates a strong educated female human resource.

Education is the prime contrivance for the empowerment of the marginalized sections of the society. The civil society organizations, media, NGOs etc. should help in the mission of educating the underprivileged. As she says, "efforts should be made to create awareness about literacy. All forms of media, both print and electronic should be harnessed for this purpose. Moreover, learners should be encouraged to continue with their literary aspirations, and undertake lifelong learning processes, by pursuing training and higher education options. It would also mean looking at developing an equivalency framework, in order to improve the pathways for the newly literate, to achieve equivalent qualifications to formal education and facilitating bridges to the formal system."[11]

In her Inaugural Speech at the International Conference on 'Women's Literacy for Inclusive and Sustainable Development' on the occasion of International Literacy Day, New Delhi, she brought about another significant dimension to education or literacy. She observed, "An approach to literacy that is both holistic and relevant for development, by linking it with the learning of other skills necessary for human and socio-economic development, can bring greater benefits. Linking literacy with broader skills, such as technical and vocational skills is important. Mahatma Gandhi once said, "The literacy campaign must not begin and end with knowledge of the alphabet, it must go hand in hand with the spread of useful knowledge." This is valuable advice for all literacy promotion approaches. I think education of both the head and the heart is necessary for building a civilized society. ... On this International Literacy Day, let us once again, reaffirm our resolve for the universalization of the literacy goal with a redoubled effort and commitment."[12] Vocational education indeed brings tremendous empowerment to women and other weaker sections of the society.

Since education has the enchanting powers of transforming the society, all the countries of the world should co-operate and collaborate with each other in the field of education. Sharing of expertise, techniques and policies on education among the countries of the world will certainly help to introduce new impetus to the education sector in their countries. The Government of India is keen on forming linkages with many countries in the field of higher education. Government of India always strives for creating linkages and collaborations of Indian universities or institutes of higher learning with leading academic institutions of the world as knowledge partners. Smt. Pratibha Patil strongly believes that it is the collaboration with the countries of the world in the sectors of education that will give new dimensions to our approach towards education. Education needs to cater to not only the diversity of a country but also the diversity of the world. In the present day globalized world we speak of globalized citizens, a human being not confined to a particular territorial boundary, and we can create world citizens only when the youth or the younger generation are exposed to the diversity of the world. This is possible through the collaborations in education. It is to be remembered that it is through the educational institutions, writings, textbooks etc. that the youth is introduced to the diversity.

Smt. Pratibha Patil believes that, "Education is an important dimension of our (India and Mauritius) bilateral relations and I would like to encourage greater cooperation in this field."[13] She was very happy to note that many students from Mauritius are enrolled in Indian universities and "over 100 scholarships are given annually to Mauritian students to pursue studies in various streams in India."[14] She expressed the optimism that in coming years many more students will be enrolled in Indian universities. Also many of the Indian educational institutions are opening up their institutions in Mauritius. These developments certainly help in providing a platform for the youth of both these countries to interact on many issues common to them, reiterating this view she said, "with management and business institutions also coming in, the circle of quality institutes of engineering, medicine and management, all working hand in hand with their Mauritian counterparts would auger well for the development of the educational linkages between our two countries. Youth are the pillars of future development and I believe that the youth of our two countries must interact with each other not only because of many commonalities that we have, but also because the bridges of friendship built by our forefathers and leaders, must continue into the future with vigour, especially when India is fast emerging as a land of opportunity. And, one more important thing which I always say is that along with education we must inculcate moral, social and human values in our youth because education without values is like a flower without fragrance."[15]

In a similar echelon in Santiago, Chile, she held that, "educational cooperation between India and Chile holds tremendous potential and would benefit the people of both our countries. I invite Chilean universities, think tanks and major academic centers to consider collaborations with their Indian counterparts. We need greater academic interaction in S&T, humanities, engineering, medicine, Ayurveda and the knowledge sectors such as Nano-technology, bio-technology and information technology. My visit to Chile, I hope, will serve to bring awareness and amplify the foundation of our mutual interest in each other's countries and release the latent potential for cooperation between India and Chile including in the fields of science and technology, culture and education."[16] Smt. Pratibha Patil strongly believes that the developing countries of the world should collaborate with a broader vision in the sector of education. The developing countries share the same kind of experiences in almost all the aspects. So, the spirit of mutual aid will help them in generating new techniques, methodologies and policies in framing forward looking dimensions of education. She also believes that the best practices of the advanced countries should be gauged to assess the applicability in educational technologies in India. The policy framework in education also needs to be internationalized. India has always been open to exchange of ideas from others, as she says, "… India has always been willing to share its experience with all other developing countries …. Developing countries have their unique problems and challenges. These have to be understood from their perspective. Hence, interaction between the academic institutions of the developing world is an important aspect of their partnership. Universities should study the socio-economic implications of an interconnected and a globalized world, the origin and impact of financial crises, and how our countries can work together for mutual benefits, as also areas of science and technology."[17]

Smt. Pratibha Patil strongly believes that education brings progress, enlightenment and real salvation in a human being. India's growth in economy, rise in political consciousness and socio-cultural awareness among people, and India's elevation as a key global player has been possible only due to the augmentation of education. After India's independence, the prime objective of the various governments in India has been to educate its people. Now, India prides on possessing one of the largest qualified professional human resources in the world. Indian doctors, researchers, engineers, academicians, software professionals etc. can be found in every corner of the world, a true testimony to India being an educational hub.

References

Note: If a reference number occurs twice or more in the chapter, it is another reference to the same source.

[1] Speech by the President of India, Shrimati Pratibha Devisingh Patil at the Inauguration of the International Conference on 'Women's Literacy for Inclusive and Sustainable Development' on the Occasion of International Literacy Day, New Delhi, 8th September 2011. [Online: web] Accessed 1 May 2012, URL: http://presidentofindia.nic.in.

[2] Acceptance Speech by the President at the Ceremony Conferring the Doctorate Honoris Causa on Her by the University of Chile, Santiago, Chile, 22nd April 2008. [Online: web] Accessed 1 May 2012, URL: http://presidentofindia.nic.in.

[3] Speech by the President of India, Shrimati Pratibha Devisingh Patil at the Ceremony Conferring Degree Doctor Honoris Causa on her by the University of Mauritius, Port Louis, Mauritius, 28th April 2011. [Online: web] Accessed 1 May 2012, URL: http://presidentofindia.nic.in.

[4] Speech by the President of India, Shrimati Pratibha Devisingh Patil at the Ceremony Conferring Degree Doctor Honoris Causa on her by the University of Mauritius, Port Louis, Mauritius, 28th April 2011. [Online: web] Accessed 1 May 2012, URL: http://presidentofindia.nic.in.

[5] Acceptance Speech by the President at the Ceremony Conferring the Doctorate Honoris Causa on Her by the University of Chile, Santiago, Chile, 22nd April 2008. [Online: web] Accessed 1 May 2012, URL: http://presidentofindia.nic.in.

[6] Speech by the President of India, Shrimati Pratibha Devisingh Patil at the Ceremony Conferring Degree Doctor Honoris Causa on her by the University of Mauritius, Port Louis, Mauritius, 28th April 2011. [Online: web] Accessed 1 May 2012, URL: http://presidentofindia.nic.in.

[7] Speech by the President of India, Shrimati Pratibha Devisingh Patil at the Inauguration of the International Conference on 'Women's Literacy for Inclusive and Sustainable Development' on the Occasion of International Literacy Day, New Delhi, 8th September 2011. [Online: web] Accessed 1 May 2012, URL: http://presidentofindia.nic.in.

[8] Speech by the President of India, Shrimati Pratibha Devisingh Patil at the Inauguration of the International Conference on 'Women's Literacy for Inclusive and Sustainable Development' on the Occasion of International Literacy

Day, New Delhi, 8th September 2011. [Online: web] Accessed 1 May 2012, URL: http://presidentofindia.nic.in.

[9] Speech by the President of India, Shrimati Pratibha Devisingh Patil at the Ceremony Conferring Degree Doctor Honoris Causa on her by the University of Mauritius, Port Louis, Mauritius, 28th April 2011. [Online: web] Accessed 1 May 2012, URL: http://presidentofindia.nic.in.

[10] Acceptance Speech by the President at the Ceremony Conferring the Doctorate Honoris Causa on her by the University of Chile, Santiago, Chile, 22nd April 2008. [Online: web] Accessed 1 May 2012, URL: http://presidentofindia.nic.in.

[11] Speech by the President of India, Shrimati Pratibha Devisingh Patil at the Inauguration of the International Conference on 'Women's Literacy for Inclusive and Sustainable Development' on the Occasion of International Literacy Day, New Delhi, 8th September 2011. [Online: web] Accessed 1 May 2012, URL: http://presidentofindia.nic.in.

[12] Speech by the President of India, Shrimati Pratibha Devisingh Patil at the Inauguration of the International Conference on 'Women's Literacy for Inclusive and Sustainable Development' on the Occasion of International Literacy Day, New Delhi, 8th September 2011. [Online: web] Accessed 1 May 2012, URL: http://presidentofindia.nic.in.

[13] Speech by the President of India, Shrimati Pratibha Devisingh Patil at the Ceremony Conferring Degree Doctor Honoris Causa on her by the University of Mauritius, Port Louis, Mauritius, 28th April 2011. [Online: web] Accessed 1 May 2012, URL: http://presidentofindia.nic.in.

[14] Speech by the President of India, Shrimati Pratibha Devisingh Patil at the Ceremony Conferring Degree Doctor Honoris Causa on her by the University of Mauritius, Port Louis, Mauritius, 28th April 2011. [Online: web] Accessed 1 May 2012, URL: http://presidentofindia.nic.in.

[15] Speech by the President of India, Shrimati Pratibha Devisingh Patil at the Ceremony Conferring Degree Doctor Honoris Causa on her by the University of Mauritius, Port Louis, Mauritius, 28th April 2011. [Online: web] Accessed 1 May 2012, URL: http://presidentofindia.nic.in.

[16] Acceptance Speech by the President at the Ceremony Conferring the Doctorate Honoris Causa on Her by the University of Chile, Santiago, Chile, 22nd April 2008. [Online: web] Accessed 1 May 2012, URL: http://presidentofindia.nic.in.

[17] Speech by the President of India, Shrimati Pratibha Devisingh Patil at the Ceremony Conferring Degree Doctor Honoris Causa on her by the University of Mauritius, Port Louis, Mauritius, 28th April 2011. [Online: web] Accessed 1 May 2012, URL: http://presidentofindia.nic.in.

Engaging the Pravasi Indian

"Sometimes we feel we straddle two cultures; at other times, that we fall between two stools."

—*Salman Rushdie**

"Every overseas Indian is a representative of India. I know that, as peaceful and law abiding citizens, you act as ambassadors of India, winning goodwill and respect. As an overseas community you have made a distinctive contribution by virtue of your dedication, hard work and success. It is also a matter of equal gratification to see amongst all of you, the cultural and scholarly effervescence which is characteristic of the Indian community."

—*Smt. Pratibha Patil***

India has been witness to the migration of its population to varied corners of the world from time immemorial. In older times, despite many hardships and the socio-cultural and religious taboo of crossing the sea, Indians have undertaken hazardous voyages to various parts of the globe as traders, religious preachers (Buddhist Bhikkhus) and gypsies during the ancient and medieval period. The mid of the nineteenth century saw a massive transportation of Indians as indentured labourers to British and European colonial plantations in the Caribbean, Fiji, Africa etc. The oppression and impoverishment germinating out of the imperialistic British colonial dispensation as well as the hierarchical socio-cultural structure of India forced impecunious Indians to leave the country only to stumble upon a more repressive life in the distant plantation estates. The Indians were also transported to replace the slave

---
*Salman Rushdie, *Imaginary Homelands: Essays and Criticism 1981–1991*.
**Speech by the President of India, Shrimati Pratibha Devisingh Patil at Reception for the Indian Community, Laos, 9th September 2010.
  [Online: web] Accessed 21 May 2012, URL: http://presidentofindindia.nic.in

labours who were reluctant to work as free labour in the plantations after the abolition of slavery in the 1830s. The tough lives led by the Indians made some critics label the indentured labourers as 'neo-slaves'. Mahatma Gandhi, Gopal Krishna Gokhale and other pioneers of Indian freedom struggle were deeply disturbed by the depraved lives led by these overseas Indians, and with their intervention the colonial government in India put an end to this system in the 1920. By the mid of twentieth century the younger generation of these indentured Indians by their sheer resistance, determination and diligence climbed the economic, socio-cultural and political ladder in the adopted countries and made their presence prominent in most walks of life.

Post-Independence, a different set of Indians migrated to various parts of the world in quest of new opportunities and prosperity. Businessmen from Gujarat and Punjab went to different parts of the globe to engage in trading activities. In the 1970s and 80s, many skilled and semi-skilled Indian labourers journeyed to the Gulf countries to work in the oil boom economies of these countries. During the 1980s and 90s, several Indians left for the developed countries of the west as software and technical professionals. By the end of the twentieth century roughly 20–30 million overseas Indians have added to the economic boom in the host countries apart from implanting our cultural ethos in diverse parts of the world as the global Indians.

After India's Independence Jawaharlal Nehru's advice to the overseas Indians to integrate into the host countries was marked by his policy of non-interference in the internal affairs of any country, and at the same time his apprehension that any kind of attachment with them may be perceived by the host countries as a threat to their sovereignty. Till the 1990s, India's attachment with its diaspora has therefore, mostly been marked by this Nehruvian approach of non-interference. However, this approach changed by the 1990s, with the economy opening up the Indian diaspora was beginning to be perceived as a soft power which can help India in crisis, generate social and intellectual capital, contribute to the economic development of India and at the same time become a facilitator of diplomatic relationship between the host and home country. In the present day scenario, we have moved from the brain drain scenario to brain gain position.

Smt. Pratibha Patil played a significant role in building the linkage between the Pravasi Indian and the country of the birth, India, she infused new blood in the bond. On one hand, she initiated business delegation to be part of her overseas state visits, thereby opening up a dialogue on business expansion, cultural exchanges and memoranda of understanding with not just the foreign country but the overseas Indians, on the other, she welcomed the diaspora to be inspirational models for India. The twenty first century emerging as the age of immigrants as global citizens it was time to address a new set opportunities. In her address at the Valedictory Session and Conferment of the Pravasi Bharatiya Samman Awards at the Sixth Pravasi Bharatiya Divas, Smt. Pratibha Patil appreciated the extensive contributions made by the overseas Indians to the host countries as well as to India. She said, "The overseas Indian community is impressive in terms of its size, spread and its growing influence. Estimated at about 25 million in 130 countries, the Indian Diaspora is a significant economic, social and cultural force in the world today. ... The divergent patterns of settlement, the varying degrees of integration with their new homelands and the emergence of new identities and ethos make the Indian Diaspora unique. It is difficult to speak of one great 'Indian Diaspora'. There are communities within communities whose bond with India and the manner and extent of engagement is marked by its own experiences as well as by time and distance. However, what binds you all with India is your origins, roots and links with India."[1]

She reflected on ways in which the Pravasi Indians can engage in the development of the nation "overseas Indians are representatives of India and its people, regions, religions, languages, values, culture and history. The general reputation of Indians living abroad is that they are hard working, as also loyal and committed to the country in which they live and work. This should be kept up. At the same time, overseas Indians should also look at ways in which they can be partners in the growth of India. ... I call on the Overseas Indian community to engage proactively in contributing to the growth of India."[2] She further emphasized that "there is an important role that each one of you can play in India's journey to becoming a strong, just and equitable society. The time has come for a strong and sustained partnership between India and its Diaspora."[3] While commending their interest and involvement she is vastly appreciative of their contribution in her speech at the 7th Pravasi Bharatiya Divas Convention, Chennai, 9th January 2009 "there are over five million overseas Indian workers who remit to India equivalent to between US $ 10 to 12 billion every year. They are at the lower end of the income scale; their remittances however, not only support household consumption back home but also provide resources for investment in the rural sector, particularly agriculture. The Ministry of Overseas Indian Affairs should consider whether it is possible to institute a separate set of awards from next year onwards to recognize the contribution of overseas Indian workers. This will serve as a morale booster to them who work tirelessly overseas in difficult conditions. The genuine grievances of the overseas Indians should be addressed expeditiously. The Government could also look at innovative approaches to channelize foreign remittances, especially of workers for productive investment."[4] In the postcolonial era diasporas have been both the products and the drivers of globalization process. Globalization has also brought worldwide disparities of incomes to the fore. The effort needs to be to reduce the disparity through capacity building and providing access to knowledge and resources needed for a meaningful life and equitable society. The knowledge, experience and expertise of the diaspora community can be helpful in this regard.

One also needs to reflect on the hardships and drudgeries that the overseas Indians have gone through in creating a space for themselves in the distant lands. In the midst of their present day success story is the untold history of their sweat and struggle. The indentured labourers of the mid-ninteenth century were for all practical purposes 'neo-slaves'. Satendra Nandan, the Fijian Indian poet and critic observes about the harsh lives of the Indian indentured workers in his *Lines Across Black Waters*:

> *Homeless I had come in search of paradise*
> *This house of hell was now all mine.*

They had to suffer tremendous hardships to pave the passage for their younger generations to sail through perhaps difficult days to fathom their journey from an imperialist world. Truly, the previous generation of Indians had to undergo incredible tribulations on one end to protect and propagate Indian civilizational heritage, and on the other by educating their children and preparing them for the white collared jobs occupied generally by the superior white colonials. Smt. Pratibha Patil encapsulates the struggle and success through the story of overseas Indians across the world which is best captured in the words of Vishwamitra Ganga Aashutosh, the renowned poet from Mauritius:

> *No gold did they find,*
> *Underneath any stone*
> *They touched and turned,*
> *Yet, every stone they touched,*
> *Into solid gold they turned.*[5]

She expresses her confidence that, "with your caliber, creativity and enterprise you will continue to contribute to the advancement of human civilization, particularly as your roots lie in this, one of the most ancient civilizations of the world, in which acquisition of knowledge and universal welfare have been laudable objectives…. There is immense capacity that you have both in talent and in financial terms, that can be invested in India. We hope to see your greater participation in the coming years in the development of India. Of course, India's remittances from overseas Indians, estimated at over US Dollars 50 billion last year, were the highest in the world. What is less known, though, is the fact that nearly forty percent of these remittances—about US Dollars 20 billion annually—come from overseas Indian workers in the Gulf consisting of temporary contractual skilled and semi-skilled workers. They often face harsh living and working conditions and are separated from their families for long periods of time. I take this opportunity to salute Indian workers in the Gulf…."[6] She lauded the Ministry of Overseas Indian Affairs for initiating many welfare measures for the overseas Indians.

In the present day world scenario, the diasporas is to be defined in the context of a world order which is marked by the celebration of multi-lateralism. It is the recognition and appreciation of the 'multi' that defines the world order. Diaspora is to be perceived from its responsibility towards its country of adoption, its country of origin and of course the globalized world of which it is a part. Elucidating the significant global role to be played by the diasporic community, Smt. Pratibha Patil claimed that "we are gathered here today not only because we share common bonds of ethnicity, language, culture and tradition, but also because we are part of a global village—a society and an economy in which, as it rapidly changes due to technological advances, we all have to constantly redefine our roles and positions, while at the same time retain our central values and rich heritage. There are indeed, very few conventions of the kind that we have here today, in which the delegates are so diverse, and yet have so much in common. Looking into the future, we must identify the interests that will continue to hold us together, and explore the common activities that will benefit all of us.... Our attempt is to engage with the Indian community overseas in a mutually beneficial manner, in all spheres of life and nation building."[7] She goes on to reassert, "... Last year, I had mentioned that Overseas Indians have come to be recognized as the "Knowledge Diaspora". Your expertise and skills will be a vital resource for India's efforts to forge inclusive growth for all its citizens. Your immense capacity in talent, skills, experience and finances are known to all. I hope that we will see a rapid increase in the number, size and scope of developmental activities in India by overseas Indians. I am sure that we will also see these initiatives evolving into more comprehensive and long-term projects that will have a significant positive impact on many lives. ... Therefore, I call upon each and every one of you to participate to the best of your ability, in at least one endeavour in India for building a better future for the disadvantaged sections of society. Your contribution in the health and education sectors, in efforts to make India slum-free, as well as your participation in infrastructure development projects would be most welcome."[8]

Her confidence that the diaspora will help India in its endeavor of nation building is well placed. India will certainly be aided and will benefit by the knowledge and expertise sharing by its diaspora in its expansion and improvement of higher education, health, infrastructure development, and environment. She informed the gathering that "for close interaction with Overseas Indians, we now have made it a practice to hold a regional Pravasi Bharatiya Divas every year in one of the countries which have a significant number of Indians. The last such regional convention was held at Durban, South Africa, on 1st and 2nd October 2010. It was attended by about 500 delegates from 12 countries in Africa and was graced by President Jacob Zuma of South Africa. The following meeting was held in Toronto in (2011)."[9] She also congratulated Shri Vayalar Ravi, Minister for Overseas Indian Affairs, "for initiatives that have benefited our Indian Diaspora overseas and especially the workers. Just couple of months ago, I had the occasion to inaugurate the first Indian Workers Resource Centre at Dubai. The Ministry of Overseas Indian Affairs has also piloted the efforts of the Government of India to provide voting rights for Non Resident Indians. It has taken steps to set up a Memorial for Indentured Workers at Kolkata Port. This memorial marks the indomitable spirit of Indian emigrants, reminding me of a quotation by Rabindranath Tagore, 'Let us not pray to be sheltered from dangers but to be fearless when facing them'."[10]

Overseas Indians have been the ambassadors of India's diverse cultures in the foreign countries. Recognizing this Smt. Pratibha Patil observes that "numerous languages and a variety of customs and traditions have together created a vibrant Indian culture. Its impact is evident in many countries across the world and, in this the Overseas Indian community has played an important role. The cultural vitality of the global Indian is so powerful, that some Indian scholars have even begun to redefine their own identity in terms of your cultural achievements. Take the example of the great Indo-Trini culture of Trinidad and Tobago, which has been created and nurtured over the years. It impresses all with its strength and beauty. Its impact has also been felt in India.[11]

She focuses on their globally well appreciated calibrated attainments, "Overseas Indians, who number over 27 million, are symbols of India in their adopted countries. They have done extremely well in their chosen fields and have done us proud. We always look forward to meeting with them and learning from their rich experiences. The theme of this year's Conference, 'Global Indian: Inclusive Growth' is very apt in terms of co-operation of our overseas Indian community that we need, to bring about great inclusiveness to India's growth story. I am given to understand that over the last two days, you have deliberated in detail on how you can contribute to the development of your ancestral homeland. You have discussed several ideas regarding partnerships in health, social entrepreneurship in water, investment and Research and Development in solar energy, and issues of youth connectivity."[12] Further she posits on the role of Indian Government to extend possible assistance to overseas Indians, "We deeply cherish our relationship with the Indian Diaspora. The Government of India is keenly interested in the well-being of the people of Indian origin living overseas. The year gone by saw major development in West Asia and North Africa. This is a region of great importance to India, because of our traditional warm ties with these nations, and also because a large number of Indian nationals live there. The Government of India had to evacuate about 19,000 Indian nationals from Libya and Yemen. The Government sent special aircraft and ships to these countries to bring back Indian citizens free of cost. Similarly, special flights were flown out of Egypt for more than 700 Indian tourists and Indian nationals working with various companies there."[13] Smt. Pratibha Patil strongly believes that undoubtedly the overseas Indians have tremendous capabilities to become a very significant partner in the development and transformation of India's growth.

References

Note: If a reference number occurs twice or more in the chapter, it is another reference to the same source.

[1] Speech by President of India, Smt. Pratibha Devisingh Patil, at the Valedictory Session and Conferment of the Pravasi Bharatiya Samman Awards at the Sixth Pravasi Bharatiya Divas, New Delhi, 9th January 2008. [Online: web] Accessed 21 May 2012, URL: http://presidentofindia.nic.in.

[2] Speech by President of India, Smt. Pratibha Devisingh Patil, at the Valedictory Session and Conferment of the Pravasi Bharatiya Samman Awards at the Sixth Pravasi Bharatiya Divas, New Delhi, 9th January 2008. [Online: web] Accessed 21 May 2012, URL: http://presidentofindia.nic.in.

[3] Speech by President of India, Smt. Pratibha Devisingh Patil, at the Valedictory Session and Conferment of the Pravasi Bharatiya Samman Awards at the Sixth Pravasi Bharatiya Divas, New Delhi, 9th January 2008. [Online: web] Accessed 21 May 2012, URL: http://presidentofindia.nic.in.

[4] Speech by the President of India, Shrimati Pratibha Devisingh Patil, at the 7th Pravasi Bharatiya Divas Convention, Chennai, Tamil Nadu, 9th January, 2009. [Online: web] Accessed 21 May 2012, URL: http://presidentofindia.nic.in.

[5] Speech by the President of India, Shrimati Pratibha Devisingh Patil, at the Valedictory Function of the 8th Pravasi Bharatiya Divas Convention and Conferment of the Pravasi Bharatiya Samman Awards, New Delhi, 9th January, 2010. [Online: web] Accessed 21 May 2012, URL: http://presidentofindia.nic.in.

[6] Speech by the President of India, Shrimati Pratibha Devisingh Patil, at the Valedictory Function of the 8th Pravasi Bharatiya Divas Convention and Conferment of the Pravasi Bharatiya Samman Awards, New Delhi, 9th January, 2010. [Online: web] Accessed 21 May 2012, URL: http://presidentofindia.nic.in.

[7] Speech by the President of India Shrimati Pratibha Devisingh Patil at the Valedictory of the 9th Pravasi Bharatiya Divas Convention and Conferment of the Pravasi Bharatiya Samman Awards, Vigyan Bhavan, New Delhi, 9th January, 2011. [Online: web] Accessed 21 May 2012, URL: http://presidentofindia.nic.in.

[8] Speech by the President of India Shrimati Pratibha Devisingh Patil at the Valedictory of the 9th Pravasi Bharatiya Divas Convention and Conferment of the Pravasi Bharatiya Samman Awards, Vigyan Bhavan, New Delhi, 9th January, 2011. [Online: web] Accessed 21 May 2012, URL: http://presidentofindia.nic.in.

[9] Speech by the President of India Shrimati Pratibha Devisingh Patil at the Valedictory of the 9th Pravasi Bharatiya Divas Convention and Conferment of the Pravasi Bharatiya Samman Awards, Vigyan Bhavan, New Delhi, 9th January, 2011. [Online: web] Accessed 21 May 2012, URL: http://presidentofindia.nic.in.

[10] Speech by the President of India Shrimati Pratibha Devisingh Patil at the Valedictory of the 9th Pravasi Bharatiya Divas Convention and Conferment of the Pravasi Bharatiya Samman Awards, Vigyan Bhavan, New Delhi, 9th January, 2011. [Online: web] Accessed 21 May 2012, URL: http://presidentofindia.nic.in.

[11] Speech by the President of India, Shrimati Pratibha Devisingh Patil at the Valedictory Function of the 10th Pravasi Bharatiya Divas Convention and Conferment of Pravasi Samman Awards, Jaipur, Rajasthan, 9th January 2012. [Online: web] Accessed 21 May 2012, URL: http://presidentofindia.nic.in.

[12] Speech by the President of India, Shrimati Pratibha Devisingh Patil at the Valedictory Function of the 10th Pravasi Bharatiya Divas Convention and Conferment of Pravasi Samman Awards, Jaipur, Rajasthan, 9th January 2012. [Online: web] Accessed 21 May 2012, URL: http://presidentofindia.nic.in.

[13] Speech by the President of India, Shrimati Pratibha Devisingh Patil at the Valedictory Function of the 10th Pravasi Bharatiya Divas Convention and Conferment of Pravasi Samman Awards, Jaipur, Rajasthan, 9th January 2012. [Online: web] Accessed 21 May 2012, URL: http://presidentofindia.nic.in.

Section–IV
Conclusion

Conclusion

A leader is best when people barely know he exists, when his work is done, his aim fulfilled, they will say: we did it ourselves.

—*Lao Tzu*

Smt. Pratibha Devisingh Patil's journey from a small sleepy town of Jalgaon, in Maharashtra to the Rashtrapati Bhavan at Raisina Hills, New Delhi is a voyage of triumph of a quiet and determined woman, who made a pledge to herself at the age of 27, to serve the nation. When she was elected with a pulsating majority vote as the President of India, for her it was yet another prospect of dedicating herself to the service of the nation. After sixty years of sovereignty, India was finally willing to be piloted by a woman as the President of India. Her long and enduring work for the Congress Party, her ability to take up challenges and turn them into opportunities, her success at the grass root level in Maharashtra, and also not hankering after self promotion and media hype, all added to her accomplishments. There has to be some merit to be credited with this premier position, if this has intrigued the critics, Smt. Pratibha Patil in her quiet manner has chosen to respond with her works. Her tenure of five years has not been free of controversy, something I do not wish to dwell on, I rather choose to focus on the modest but resilient plan she set for herself. It is imperative for me to learn and present what a woman can achieve given the colossal responsibility of leading the nation, and not get involved with the political debate of the veracity of her choice. This book, therefore, has a limited focus; I have not dwelled on her personal journey or her emotional trajectory during the tenure, rather I have sought to study the objectives she set for herself, given the added strain of being studied as a woman and therefore judged not being up to the mark and the pressure of coming immediately after Dr. Abdul Kalam. I found, and this book will tell you, that nothing unnerved her. She was in a happy and confident space; the opportunity to serve in the position of the President of India was bigger than any condemnation the critics can come up with. And so, she deliberated and designed her route for herself, her landmark initiatives of women empowerment with a practical and achievable goal; 'Roshni', an ingenious and resourceful process of disseminating awareness and maintaining ecological balance, beginning with Rashtrapati Bhavan and moving to several Raj Bhavans leading the way to be emulated by organizations and the common man; buttressing overseas business collaborations; as primarily an agrarian country we need to innovate and augment research on dry and wet land farming, several discussions and debates were called in by the President Smt. Pratibha Patil; and measures for social concerns. The book also focuses on her reflections on education as well on the role the 'Pravasi', overseas Indians can play in the development of the nation. The book ends with one of her final interviews as the President of India. It has been an enriching experience for me and also a matter of satisfaction that the first woman President has not let her country down, she has brought more to the table to be reflected upon and the innumerable that can be achieved for the country if self-driven and motivated.

There was this national angst that, can the new President fill the vacuum created with the end of term of one of the most prominent Presidents of India, Dr. A.P.J. Abdul Kalam, can the new President help in building and maintaining the coalition ethos at this critical juncture of Indian politics? And can the new President help and steer India in its economic growth and drive India in its rising stature at global level? When India was grappling with these issues and speculations, marched in the quiet champion, the first woman President of India. To be at the pinnacle is not an easy job as the post represents the diversified ethos of a country of vast multiplicity, so naturally integrated. In this political structure, the President has to maintain impartiality, integrity and dignity of the position. And the President has also to ensure that the government is working properly for a just and equitable society, representing the diversity of people.

Smt. Pratibha Patil as the twelfth and first woman President of India pursued her goals and initiatives in the five years with a missionary zeal turning them into accomplishments, she indeed has reinvented her leadership role. What distinguishes Smt. Pratibha Patil is her commitment and engagement with the common man. It was her belief that in the growth process of India all the sections of the society need to be partners, particularly the weaker sections as they are the indicators of our success. Her humble background and her political activism at the grass root level have made her understand the harsh realities of the marginalized sections of the society. On her assumption of office, she had committed to serve in the best interests of the people of India, her journey as the President has been to fulfil this commitment.

The ethoses of diversity and plurality were kept in view when the Constitution of India was adopted in 1950. The Constitution of India demonstrates the intrinsic vigour of the working of the Indian federalism fulfilling the varied aspirations of this diverse population. Smt. Pratibha Patil has been a true believer and champion of the representation of diversity in India. Moving into all the corners of India, she has spoken of the respect for the natural diversity of societies, cultures and religions in India, and it is from this diversity that India derives its strength. India is a case study to the world, as she reiterates, of people from many cultures, religions, languages etc. speaking in a single vibrant voice. India moreover has believed in a world order based on mutual trust, co-operation and acceptance of each other's existence. Certainly in the present day, we lead a world based on multi-lateralism. No country can grow without its engagement with other countries. In this phase of interdependence and multi-lateral engagements, it is the mutual trust and benefits that determine the relationship at the international level. No country can stand at the apex and regulate the world order. Smt. Pratibha Patil speaks about the world order based on reciprocal respectability, trust and benefits, and where the developed countries help the developing and less developed countries to grow. Jawaharlal Nehru, the first Prime Minister of India, on the eve of the most precious moment of Indian history, spoke about the building of India as a vibrant, democratic, tolerant and progressive nation, and he also pledged that India will cooperate with people of the world in furthering peace, harmony, freedom and democracy. It is the practice of justice, liberty and the democratic imperatives that brings India closer to many countries of the world. Respect for the human rights and a harmonious world without any kind of threat of environmental or ecological disaster constitute the hallmark of

Smt. Pratibha Patil's world view. Smt. Pratibha Patil has shown lot of courage and commitment and has steered India with distinction. She has upheld the dignity of the position through her integrity and impartiality. Being a great believer in Gandhian and Nehruvian ideals, she has been a big practitioner and promoter of non-violence and simple living, and at the same time she has appealed to the people to develop scientific temper which will help in the progress of our country. She has relentlessly advised the government that fruits of India's development must reach the marginalized sections of the society. The book sets out to illuminate the dynamics the first Pioneering Woman President of India, a woman of quiet distinction, of manifold unsung accomplishments and poised grit and determination, silently marching towards shaping an emerging new India. If the biographical book 'An Inspirational Journey' focused on her personal and political journey culminating into the Rashtrapati Bhavan as the first woman President, this book is aimed to look at Smt. Pratibha Patilji, who through her diverse initiatives and accomplishments transcends even the gender bracket of 'Woman President'.

The main focus of the book has been to cover the entire spectrum of her sojourn as the President of India, covering the period of her presidency, from aspirations for the nation to achievements and realization of the goals. As we know, no professional achievement is possible without the calibre, determination and a strong will-power at the personal level, a flexible and dynamic balance of both aspiration and achievement, this redefines her full-spectrum leadership.

The attempt in this book has been to place the first woman President's world view and her modest endeavour to bring improvement and development into the country through her initiatives and vision. It is for the readers to evaluate her contribution.

Postscript-Interview with Praveen Swami
'The Quiet Legacy...'

Photo Courtesy: Rashtrapati Bhavan

A conversation with India's first woman head of state, towards the end of her term:

> "My image of a President before I came here," President K.R. Narayanan said in a rare televised interview with N. Ram in 1998, "was that of a rubber-stamp President, to be frank". "But having come here", he went on, "I find that the image is not quite correct. My image of a President is of a working President, not an executive President, but a working President, and working within the four corners of the Constitution".

> "I have to agree with my esteemed predecessor," says President Smt. Pratibha Patil, whose five-year term will end on July 25.

> "Five years ago, when I was elected, I had the feeling that the President doesn't have much to do. I've realised, though, that this is not a rubber-stamp position."

In a conversation with *The Hindu*'s former Editor-in-Chief N. Ram and me, President Patil offered some rare insight into her vision of India's highest constitutional office, and how she has used it to advance causes of profound concern to her—critically, the rights of women and alleviating the crisis in the country's agrarian economy.

President Patil's term in office has been remarkably free of the kinds of friction that erupted during the tenures of some past Presidents—controversies that, on occasion, led Rashtrapati Bhavan towards collision with the political executive.

In the United Kingdom, the social scientist and essayist Walter Bagehot famously wrote in the nineteenth century that the monarch "has the right to be consulted, the right to encourage, and the right to warn". In the quietest possible way, President Smt. Pratibha Patil has sought to exercise all three of these rights, while avoiding public controversy of any kind. Parliament, she points out, consists of both its Houses and the President—though the President has no executive authority.

How then, over the last five years, has a textbook President influenced the course of the nation?

On Women's Rights

Long before she entered Rashtrapati Bhavan, the rights of women had been an important political concern for President Smt. Pratibha Patil. In a 2009 conversation with N. Ram, she flagged child marriage, addiction, and social suppression, all of which contribute to their low social status, as her key concerns.

In our conversation, it is clear the issues she dealt with as an activist continue to be of great importance to her. "Women are 50 per cent of our population," she says, "and there is simply no way our nation can progress if its population is left behind."

In 2008, the President summoned the first of the two Governors' conferences that are normally held during her five year term in office. The conference led to the setting up of a new committee of Governors which consulted State governments, legislators and non-governmental organisations before calling for a new high-level initiative to push forward reform.

Their report—a report which the President feels represents decades of on-ground experience of the interstices between government and societies sometimes hesitant to embrace change—was discussed with the Prime Minister. "I impressed on him that this was of the greatest importance," the President recalls, "and I have to say he was extremely supportive."

The gains, the President says, have been slow—but are nonetheless evident. Last February, former Supreme Court Judge Ruma Pal was appointed to chair a high-level committee to study the status of women. There is now a National Mission for Empowerment of Women that coordinates and monitors system wide implementation of women related programmes.

President Patil is particularly optimistic about the Rashtriya Mahila Kosh, which will provide finance to women-owned enterprises nationwide.

"I'm very worried," President Patil says, "by the latest census figures, which show an alarming drop in the gender ratio. This is a matter of real concern." In meeting after meeting, the President has been speaking out in public on the issue—in one case, taking the unusual step of addressing a rally of thousands in Punjab.

"Things move slowly," President Patil concludes, "but I think you can see they are moving in the right direction. People are realising what the issues are, and coming to understand the need for us to act. You will see the results—perhaps not as fast as we would all like, but surely."

On the Agrarian Crisis

President Patil has also quietly used her office to focus attention on the crisis in India's countryside—a crisis that has claimed thousands of lives in Maharashtra, a State that she has decades-old ties of kinship and social engagement with. In her time in office, she has often spoken publicly on the need for change in India's agrarian policies; on one occasion, she addressed a farmers' rally at Nagpur. Key thinkers on agrarian issues, among them the eminent agricultural scientist and food policy expert, M.S. Swaminathan, have been regularly consulted by the President.

For millions of farmers, the President notes, "every monsoon is a gamble". In her view, there is an urgent need for a second green revolution, focusing on rainfed regions. It seems apparent that the President does not believe government-driven policy reform alone, though, will be adequate to bring about this change. She underlines the need to "think out of the box" to ensure that technology and knowledge can be used to revolutionise the agrarian economy, particularly in rainfed areas.

President Patil has worked to build a coalition involving the Planning Commission, chambers of commerce, public sector undertakings, and experts to see what measures might be taken. She believes that the foundations for this economy can only be laid by a partnership between industry and agriculture.

"Everything else in India can wait," she says, "but agriculture cannot. Agriculture holds the key to creating foundations for our future growth and prosperity."

On India's Future

In the President's view, one key reason for this happily controversy-free tenure has been the excellent relationship she has enjoyed with Prime Minister Manmohan Singh. The Prime Minister and President have, she recalls, met on average once every month over the last five years. The President has also been fortunate in not facing the kinds of divided electoral verdicts that led some of her predecessors into controversy, though in 2009 constitutional experts were consulted well in advance in case the 15th Lok Sabha election produced a hung Parliament. The President also appears to have a clear sense of the mood in India's cities and villages: more than 150,000 visitors have been to Rashtrapati Bhavan during her tenure, and she has met with thousands more during her tours through the country.

In spite of the growing frustration with corruption in India's national life, which has engendered growing bitterness directed at organised politics and frustration with the country's institutions, President Patil says she remains an optimist. She strongly believes that corruption is like a cancer and we have to fight against it.

"The Constitution," she reflects, "has been a compass that has guided this nation of 1.2 billion people, the world's largest democracy, through very difficult times. Yes, some situations have developed that are challenges, but these are temporary. The Constitution's core values, like secularism, have helped us negotiate the pulls and strains that are imposed by our great diversity."

Source: Swami, Praveen, "The quiet legacy of President Pratibha Patil", *The Hindu,* May 25, 2012.

URL: http://thehindu.com/opinion/interview/articles3453077.ece.

www.ingramcontent.com/pod-product-compliance
Lightning Source LLC
Chambersburg PA
CBHW071158160426
43196CB00011B/2115